FAITH AT WAR

FAITH AT WAR

A JOURNEY ON THE
FRONTLINES OF ISLAM,
FROM BAGHDAD
TO TIMBUKTU

YAROSLAV TROFIMOV

HENRY HOLT AND COMPANY   ◆   NEW YORK

Henry Holt and Company, LLC
Publishers since 1866
175 Fifth Avenue
New York, New York 10010
www.henryholt.com

Henry Holt® is a registered trademark
of Henry Holt and Company, LLC.

Library of Congress Cataloging-in-Publication Data
Trofimov, Yaroslav.
    Faith at war : a journey on the frontlines of Islam,
from Baghdad to Timbuktu / Yaroslav Trofimov.—1st ed.
        p. cm.
    ISBN-10: 0-8050-7754-5
    ISBN-13: 978-0-8050-7754-4
    1. Islamic countries—Description and travel. 2. Trofimov,
Yaroslav—Travel—Islamic countries. 3.   United States—Foreign
public opinion, Muslim. 4.   Public opinion—Islamic countries.
5. Muslims—Attitudes. I. Title.
    DS49.7.T76 2005
    909'.09767'083—dc22   2004060616

Henry Holt books are available for special promotions
and premiums. For details contact: Director, Special Markets.

First Edition 2005

Designed by Victoria Hartman

Printed in the United States of America

3   5   7   9   10   8   6   4   2

To Susi, Jonathan, and Nicole

Contents

✦ ✦ ✦

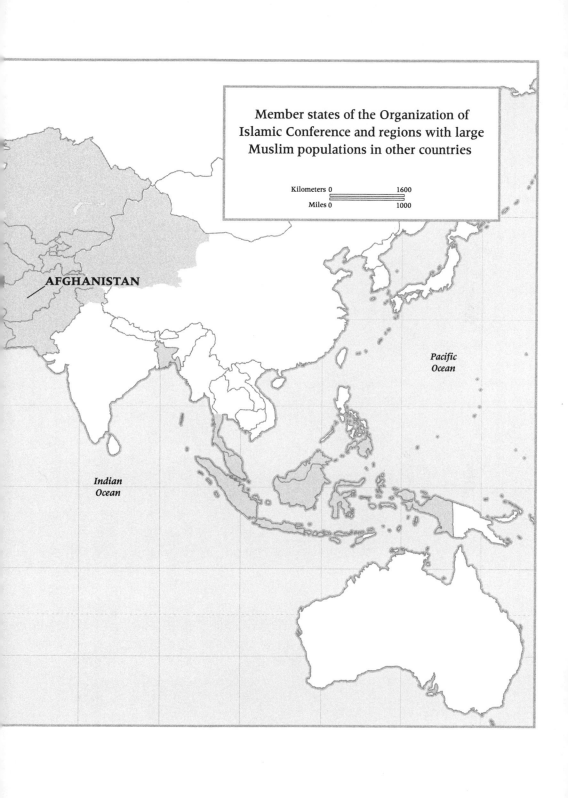

Member states of the Organization of Islamic Conference and regions with large Muslim populations in other countries

Kilometers 0   1600

Miles 0   1000

AFGHANISTAN

Pacific Ocean

Indian Ocean

Introduction

✦ ✦ ✦

The week of September 11, 2001, when airliners were still grounded in the United States, I found myself staring into a plate of cold pasta aboard a nearly empty Alitalia jet. The previous night, my *Wall Street Journal* editor—whose home and office were both rendered uninhabitable by the Twin Towers' ashes—had asked me to explore the Muslim world's reaction to America's tragedy.

Over the next three years, I crisscrossed the Islamic universe—a community of over a billion people who, although linked by a common religion, speak dozens of languages and lead vastly dissimilar lives across three continents. From Arab capitals like Baghdad to ramshackle African villages, from the snow-covered mountains of Bosnia to the Afghan deserts of Kandahar, I chronicled two major wars and a worldwide proliferation of carnage that shows no sign of abating. In all those places, a common thread ran through my conversations: a nagging suspicion among some Muslims, a firm belief among others, that what started as a war against terrorism in 2001 is mutating into an intractable, almost apocalyptic conflict between the West and Islam.

While the Twin Towers still smoldered, my first destination was Cairo—the hot, sweaty Egyptian capital I visited often in a more comforting age, when Middle East peace seemed tantalizingly close. The

FBI hadn't yet released the September 11 hijackers' identities, and the world didn't know the name of Mohammed Atta, an Egyptian graduate student in Germany. But I had little doubt that some Egyptians must have participated in the plot: Egypt's Islamic Jihad, a militant group that until recently had battled it out with security forces on Cairo streets, was Qaeda's cofounder. An Egyptian doctor, Ayman Zawahiri, was Bin Laden's second in command.

At the exit from Cairo's airport, a sentry took down my name and my taxi's license plate—a security procedure established after Islamic militants started massacring Western tourists. I headed straight to Embaba, a poor Cairo neighborhood that was at times a no-go area for Egyptian police because of local support for the jihadis.

It's on these streets, among the Boolean movement of men wearing galabia gowns, donkeys carrying rotting bananas, and dented cars belching out black fumes, that Islamist radicals had recruited their foot soldiers for murder in Afghanistan and beyond. Yet, amid the stench of Embaba's gutters, I found surprisingly little joy at the American tragedy. In a corner tea shop, that quintessential Egyptian institution, sullen men sipped their tea, waving off flies and listening intently to the latest 9/11 news blaring from an ancient TV set.

"How can we be happy? These are people who died there, human just like us," one of them said. Down the road, a father sat on the porch outside a dilapidated house and cradled his newborn son. "Why kill?" he repeated sadly, rocking the baby. "Why?" So much for the cauldron of fundamentalism, I thought after a couple of hours in Embaba. Maybe things aren't so bad after all, maybe the clash-of-civilizations Cassandras are wrong. I moved on to the ritziest part of the city, the nouveau riche Mohandeseen neighborhood, where I expected to hear even more articulate sympathy for America's plight. There, sandwiched between a Rolex outlet and a BMW dealership, glowed a McDonald's restaurant, as potent a symbol as any of the pervasive American influence around the world—and an island of luxury in a country where a Big Mac costs more than most people earn in a day. Customers inside this sanitized bit of America in a rambunctious Third World megalopolis seemed to have little in common with the bearded hermits who plotted mass murder from the caves of Afghanistan. Neat haircuts—occasionally obscured by an Islamic headscarf—were complemented by Levi's jeans and Nike sneakers. The whiff was of Marlboros, not cheap Egyptian cigarettes. This was Egypt's young, cosmopolitan elite—the people who should be the West's natural allies against an Islamic obscurantism that seeks to drag the world back to the Middle Ages.

But they weren't. Sitting under a poster advertising CRISPY AND DELICIOUS MCWINGS, Radwa Abdallah, an eighteen-year-old university student, volunteered that she called up all her friends to share her joy after learning that thousands of Americans had died in Washington and New York. "Everyone celebrated," she said, dipping her french fries into ketchup, as her girlfriends giggled. "People honked in the streets, cheering that finally America got what it truly deserved."

Across the formica table, Raghda Mahroughi also wanted to talk about her delight at watching the World Trade Center crumble and collapse into a cloud of death. "I just hope there were a lot of Jews in that building," she said, folding a napkin. "Yeah, America was just too full of itself," agreed Sherihan Ammar, an aspiring doctor in elaborate makeup and a skimpy T-shirt.

As I walked from table to table, I heard chillingly similar views—from middle-class Egyptians, from visiting Palestinians and Saudis—until a restaurant manager unceremoniously kicked me out. In the following months, most of those who had celebrated on September 11 learned to disguise such feelings in public. But in talk after talk, and in one Muslim city after another, a pattern emerged. Often those with the most bloodthirsty ideas were the well-to-do and the privileged who have had some experience with the West—and not the downtrodden and ignorant "masses" that are usually depicted as the font of anti-Western fury.

That's perhaps not surprising, considering that one of the founders of modern political Islam, the Egyptian writer Sayyid Qutb, got his anti-American zeal during a miserable sojourn as a graduate student in Greeley, Colorado, in 1949—seventeen years before being executed in Cairo. Khalid Sheikh Mohammed, the mastermind of Qaeda's September 11 project and a graduate of North Carolina State University, class of 1986, followed the same path. In Cairo that week, I was troubled by a thought that called for introspection: Sometimes those who know us best hate us most.

✦ ✦ ✦

The conflict that destroyed part of the Pentagon and altered the New York skyline didn't start on September 11, 2001. Ever since the bulk of Muslim lands fell under infidel rule in the nineteenth and early twentieth centuries, Islamic thinkers, from Egypt to Turkey to India, have grappled with the reasons for the precipitous, humiliating decline of their civilization—which, for most of its history, was stronger and wealthier than Christian Europe.

For most Muslim nations, political independence has brought no reprieve. A glaring exception in the global embrace of democracy, the Islamic world—outside a few happy enclaves—remains a frustrated swath of the planet where citizens chafe under brutal regimes, often propped up by the West, and where mineral wealth developed by foreigners is the main source of prosperity.

Two verses of the Quran encapsulate the debate over how Muslims should emerge from this existential crisis—a debate that's often waged with bullets and bombs, and whose outcome will affect us all. One of these verses (2: 256) proclaims: "There is no compulsion in religion." It's often quoted by those who see the way forward in re-creating, on Muslim soil, the ingredients of the West's own success: individual freedom, separation of religion and state, and life under man-made laws adopted by the people. Turkey moved this way, and so did, to a lesser extent, countries from Tunisia to Mali to Indonesia.

But the Quran has another verse (5: 51): "O you who believe, take not Jews and Christians as friends. They are only friends to each other, and who befriends them becomes one of them." That's the argument of those who see the solution in rejecting wholesale Western ideas and concepts that infiltrated the Muslim *ummah*, and in returning to the kind of pure, total Islam that allowed Prophet Mohammed and his companions to conquer much of the known world fourteen centuries ago. In recent decades, Saudi Arabia's petrodollars have been generously spent to promote such a vision across the planet.

This dream of a resurgent Islamic civilization destined to clash with and eventually triumph over the West was articulated in the late 1920s by Hassan al Banna, the Egyptian founder of the Muslim Brotherhood, a fraternity that in the following decades spawned a global web of Islamist movements, parties, and terrorist groups. According to Banna, even the most innocuous Westernizing influence constitutes an act of violence against Islam. "Doomed be the Western civilization, which follows us at every step," he wrote. "It is constantly at war with us. It has started an awful battle, and this battle it is fighting with such bewitching and enchanting objects as knowledge, wealth, civilization, culture, plans and politics, luxury goods and articles of enjoyment and pleasure, with which we have not thus far been familiar."

Like its early twentieth-century contemporaries Nazism and Communism, political Islam is grounded in a totalitarian idea of purity, in this case of religion rather than of race or class. It has taken a world war and decades on the brink of nuclear holocaust to discredit and discard the other two ideologies. But the twinkling lights of Islamist utopia still hold sway over millions of Muslims across the planet. "Islam is the answer," goes Banna's slogan, picked up by a galaxy of political groups that thrive on poverty and resentment across the lands of Islam. This political idea of Islam as a magic cure for all economic and social ills, more than the religion itself, unifies the disparate parts of the Islamic world in a way that's hard to imagine for Christian nations. Not all Islamists espouse violence, of course. But the very existence of a global political culture that defines Islam's identity by its opposition to the West, and that rejects the notion of universal civilization, keeps breeding recruits for Qaeda's death cult in virtually every Muslim community, from Morocco to Indonesia. Sometimes the pool of potential murderers is tiny; often, outsiders don't realize how frighteningly large it has become until it is too late.

After September 11, 2001, the West—realizing how much is at stake for its own survival—forcefully claimed a place at the table of this debate about Islam's future. Barely a month after the attacks on Washington and New York, the United States and its Western allies unleashed an intrusion of Muslim lands without precedent since colonial times a century ago—and, for some European participants, since the Crusades. Since 2003, hundreds of thousands of mostly Christian soldiers from the United States, Europe, and Australia have found themselves administering the daily lives of 25 million Muslims in Iraq.

Western countries that didn't send troops to Iraq, such as Germany, Canada, and France, still saw battle as part of the force that controls another 28 million Muslims in Afghanistan and that patrols the chaotic shores of Islamic East Africa. In Europe itself, the mainly Muslim Kosovo and Bosnia-Herzegovina had already become de facto protectorates in the 1990s, living under a benevolent foreign administration propped up by Western soldiers. On a smaller scale, the United States has engaged, since 2001, in military missions against Muslim radicals from the southern Philippines to Yemen to the deserts of the Sahara.

Even those Muslim countries that weren't subjected to Western military onslaught after 2001 couldn't resist the pressure to give up chemical weapons, as happened in Libya, or to revamp hate-preaching school curricula, as Saudi Arabia grudgingly did. An escalating test of wills over Iran's nuclear ambitions may yet slide into outright war.

Alongside Western bullets and bombs come the "bewitching and enchanting objects" of culture and knowledge, as America tries to spread its ideas about democracy and the proper place of religion via a slick Arabic-language satellite TV channel and a U.S.-run FM radio network that now beams the latest pop tunes, Arab and American, to listeners from Marrakech to Dubai.

The reasons for Western involvement seemed obvious early on. The September 11 outrage made it painfully clear that the Islamic world was sick with the infection of homicidal radicalism and that the disease was now mortally dangerous to the West's survival. The intervention in Afghanistan was meant to be an emergency procedure that targeted the greatest concentration of jihadis, depriving the movement of its safe rear base. For many of its proponents, the Iraq war was supposed to be a systemic treatment designed to change the entire Muslim world by nurturing a model Western-friendly democracy.

A shining, prosperous postwar Iraq, the thinking went, would puncture the Islamist idea by offering, for the first time, an appealing pro-Western alternative. In a way, the endeavor was meant to be a rerun of Western Europe's success in discrediting Communism in the Soviet bloc. "A liberated Iraq can show the power of freedom to transform that vital region, by bringing hope and progress into the lives of millions," President George W. Bush declared optimistically weeks before ordering the invasion in March 2003. "Stable and free nations do not breed the ideologies of murder. They encourage the peaceful pursuit of a better life."

But every treatment requires a qualified, cautious doctor—bound by the rule "First, do no harm." All too often, however, ideologues blind to the facts and oblivious of the risks are in charge. While getting many things right, this Western assault frequently aggravated rather than healed the disease it was meant to cure, and the result of the 2004 U.S. presidential election means that the course won't be changed. Far from an example of freedom and prosperity in the region, Iraq has become probably the most dangerous place on earth; barely a year after cheering their "liberation," many Iraqis were growing nostalgic for Saddam Hussein's sadistic dictatorship. Afghanistan, too, remained a war zone, with the Taliban once again controlling large parts of the country. By 2005, tens of thousands of people—most of them Muslim, but including some two thousand Americans and Europeans—paid with their lives for this experiment in changing the world of Islam. Senseless Islamist violence against civilians has spread to previously unscarred places, from Madrid to Bali to Casablanca, causing perilous rifts inside the Western alliance. Too many Muslims, including those who sided with America on September 11, have concluded that they themselves are now in Western crosshairs. An end to this spiral is nowhere in sight.

For any Muslim liberal eyeing the pictures of American-inflicted torture at Abu Ghraib prison in Iraq, or the "collateral damage" of American bombs falling on villages in Afghanistan, it is increasingly hard to argue that emulating the West—the source of such outrages—is something Muslims should pursue. For the Islamist peddlers of hatred, by contrast, this has been a great ride. Once the issue is defined as Muslim versus Christian or Jew, it's natural that the jihadis take charge and that the voices of reason go mum. And it's usually innocents, on both sides, who end up paying the price.

This book is not an attempt to find a solution or to critique specific policies, decisions, and concepts. Based on three years of travels in Muslim countries that the West is trying to revamp by persuasion or force, it is a personal account of what's happening on the ground and of the way Muslims themselves are reacting to changes imposed on them. The stories contained in this book point to some bright spots and to some reasons not to lose hope. But they also show numerous signs that the battle isn't going as planned, and that—in this part of the world—the law of unforeseen consequences is, once again, proving to be the law of the land.

FAITH AT WAR

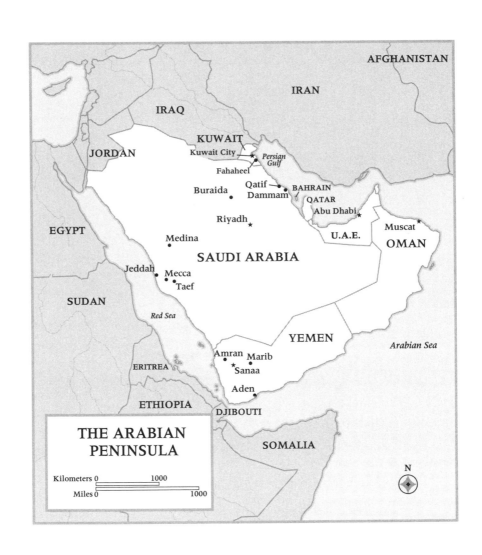

AFGHANISTAN

IRAN

IRAQ

KUWAIT

JORDAN

Kuwait City

Persian Gulf

Fahaheel

Buraida

Qatif

Dammam

BAHRAIN

QATAR

Abu Dhabi

EGYPT

Riyadh

Medina

SAUDI ARABIA

U.A.E.

Muscat

OMAN

Jeddah

Mecca

Taef

SUDAN

Red Sea

YEMEN

Arabian Sea

Amran

Marib

ERITREA

Sanaa

Aden

ETHIOPIA

DJIBOUTI

SOMALIA

THE ARABIAN PENINSULA

Kilometers 0   1000

Miles 0   1000

N

· 1 ·

SAUDI ARABIA

Abdel Wahhab's Sons

The palatial antechamber impressed me at first. An oversize carpet graced the floor. Tribal sheikhs in gilded shawls, bearded scholars in pristine white robes, and government clerks in bad shoes dozed on faux rococo chairs that lined the walls, waiting to be ushered in. Once every few minutes, subcontinental manservants, silent and fearful lest they look into our eyes, appeared with trays of tiny tea glasses. The frazzled gatekeeper's old-fashioned phone buzzed nonstop.

Like me, all these men waited to be seen by the minister, one of the Saudi kingdom's more powerful men. After a half hour of fidgeting, I began to notice that the once luxuriant carpet was stained and dirty. The whole room badly needed fresh paint, and parts of the kitsch plasterwork on the ceiling had fallen off; one piece hung precariously by the wire. My tea glass was chipped, too.

I wasn't surprised. The Saudi state, with all its petroleum, no longer had enough cash even to maintain top ministers' offices. By the time of my first trip, in 2002, this was no longer the Saudi Arabia of Western imagination, a magic kingdom brimming with ostentatious wealth because, by God's special dispensation, it happened to own one-quarter of the world's oil. There was still dazzling excess in some royal palaces, of course. But the rest of the country was visibly sinking back into the Third World morass from which Saudi Arabia had briefly escaped thanks to the 1970s oil boom. Saudi international airports—unlike the separate royal terminals used by fleets of princely jets and hidden from public scrutiny—had become so dreary and drab that they wouldn't be out of place in the poorest parts of Africa. In the dusty back streets of Riyadh, and under the decayed lattice windows of the Old City of Jeddah, the stench of open sewage gave off the unmistakable sign of an economy in a tailspin.

✦ ✦ ✦

I learned this firsthand while on a different trip to the kingdom, walking through a slum that had been inspected by Saudi Arabia's de facto ruler, Crown Prince Abdullah. In a rare public admission of Saudi decline, the prince had visited the kingdom's poor with a message that charity money should be funneled to help the needy at home, rather than Islamic causes abroad. Saudi newspapers heralded that visit as an example of Saudi-style *glasnost*. My government-supplied minder, embarrassed by what I might see, required plenty of persuasion to show me the maze of crumbling mud houses just a few blocks from a thoroughfare of glittering shops. While the residents were Saudi citizens, most of those who lived here were black. That's simple, the minder explained: these are former slaves. Slavery, the existence of which the Saudi government had denied for years, was formally abolished in 1962. Freed slaves and their progeny had then been told to settle in this part of Riyadh, without much government help in obtaining education and jobs.

As soon as I stepped out of the car, a crowd gathered around me: men with wrinkled, weary faces and pus-filled eyes, toothless women wrapped in black cloth. Several immediately started shoving laminated petitions into my hands. "They are illiterate, but they think you are from the government and can give them money," the minder said, amused by such an improbable idea. Salem al Qahtani, a sixty-one-year-old in a soiled gown, pushed to the front of the crowd. His humble house was the one visited by the crown prince months earlier, he said. "When the prince came, I told him about all of our problems, about how we have no jobs and no money, and he said we should be optimistic and everything will be okay for us," said Qahtani, who couldn't read but insisted he could write his name. "But then the prince went away and nothing happened. I'm still waiting for improvements to happen."

I had barely finished jotting down his words in my notebook when a patrol car of the Saudi security services raced into the alley, its lights flashing red and blue. As the driver hit the brakes, a puff of dust rose up around us, making me choke. Someone, seeing a troublesome stranger in the neighborhood, had tipped off the police. Leaving a submachine gun inside the car, an officer walked out and sternly demanded identification from everyone present. He read the riot act to my minder. The last thing he wanted was to see foreign journalists in such an unflattering area. Saudi Arabia, after all, is a happy, prosperous land, thanks to the boundless wisdom of His Majesty, and of Their Royal Highnesses, by the grace of God. "Make sure that he takes no pictures," the police officer barked at the minder; he stayed put to listen to our conversations. Intimidated, the men and women around me quickly shrank and withered away.

✦   ✦   ✦

Although Saudi authorities tried hard to hide such spots of abject misery, they couldn't fool their own people. By the time fifteen Saudi men packed their box cutters and boarded American planes the morning of September 11, 2001, the average Saudi's income had shrunk by as much as three-quarters in one generation. Every family—except for the royal one—felt the pinch. The reason for things going from bad to worse, Saudis were told in newspapers and mosques, was crystal clear: an American conspiracy to control the Middle East and keep oil prices low.

"If my children can't find a place in school or a job, it's all your fault," an otherwise soft-spoken Saudi professor blurted out with surprising anger as we munched dates, the kingdom's main product in the preoil era, in the fading lobby of a Jeddah hotel. "We are being robbed. Why is it that a barrel of oil costs $20, like in the 1970s, while a car that we buy from the Americans costs $10,000, not $1,000 like back then?"

The professor's calculation, I realized later, wasn't altogether accurate. A typical Detroit-made subcompact sold for over $4,000 in

1979, the year when Saudi crude nearly doubled in price to $24 a barrel. But such resentment remained undiminished even after oil prices surged past $50 in late 2004.

The professor was a liberal American-educated intellectual. He didn't subscribe to the harsh worldview of Saudi Arabia's clerics who divide the universe into the true believers and the infidels—the latter a source of corruption who should be shunned and eventually converted or destroyed. The very fact that he agreed to share food with me marked him as unusually open-minded. Some Saudis I had tried to meet wouldn't socialize with a Westerner out of principle. One Saudi cleric agreed to be interviewed only through a fellow Muslim, who relayed my questions and answers by telephone—lest the holy man be defiled by direct contact with me.

As long as Saudi Arabia was getting wealthier, from the 1970s hike in oil prices and until the 1990–1991 Gulf War, the kingdom's tradition of religious bigotry and violent zeal was contained. As the economic safety valve broke, a resentment that is natural in any society undergoing hard times melded with radical religion into a lethal combination. The result was Saudi militants increasingly acting out their frustrations with the West. In 2002 and 2003, the years I visited Saudi Arabia, infidels and "apostate" Muslims tainted by fraternization with unbelievers were being killed by Saudis in bombings around the world and inside the deceptively quiet kingdom itself. The U.S. embassy in Riyadh, and many residential compounds around the country, built glass-free rooms to which people should run at the first sound of danger. (These rooms would avoid the most common cause of death and injury—piercing by flying shards—in the frequent blasts.) Saudi newspapers ran pictures of young, unremarkable-looking militants sought by police who themselves were infiltrated by the terrorists. Every week, a shootout was reported. And every day, Saudi money trickled beyond its borders and throughout Islamic lands to pay for what many here—as in Washington—saw as the unfolding battle of Good and Evil.

✦　✦　✦

Since September 2001, I have been fixated on understanding Saudi Arabia. Despite all its problems, it is still the richest Arab country, a place where irate men have the means to make themselves heard, with a bang, continents away. Saudi Arabia is also the homeland of the Islamic faith, and of Osama Bin Laden. No other nation is more important to the Muslim world than Saudi Arabia, and no other nation has done more to change the Islamic religion's nature in modern days, essentially using its oil cash to take over international Islamic institutions. While Saudi Arabia has long been counted as part of the pro-Western camp in the Middle East, no other country in the region is as defiantly different from the West in its core.

I first watched Saudi Arabia, then forbidden to me, from an empty restaurant atop a tower in the middle of the Persian Gulf, just days after September 11. The tower marks the international border on the causeway that links the kingdom and the independent island of Bahrain. Underneath, hungover Saudi men sped through the customs checkpoint after a weekend of binge-drinking whiskey and ogling long-legged girls in Bahraini fleshpots. "This is great here," one of these Saudis had told me in a particularly seedy Bahraini bar the previous day. Before ordering another cherry-topped cocktail and turning to the beauties from Belarus, he straightened his crisp white robe and added matter-of-factly: "But I would never want this allowed in my own country. We Saudis want to stay pure."

Always reluctant to expose itself to outside scrutiny, Saudi Arabia rarely grants visas to foreign writers. By the time I finally got mine, six months later, I had visited almost all of the kingdom's eight neighboring countries and spent hours and hours writing letters into the black hole of Saudi officialdom, cultivating well-connected Saudis abroad and hassling Saudi embassies on three continents. At that point, even getting to the stage of filling out visa forms under a life-size portrait of King Fahd seemed like a dream come true.

The Saudi application form, as these things often do, revealed a lot about the country. One of the first questions on the form was my religion. The question after that was about my "sect."

For an answer, I followed an idea unwittingly suggested to me in late 2001 by the Lebanese prime minister, Rafik Hariri, an affable billionaire who had made his fortune in Saudi Arabia. The downside to having a name like mine when representing an American newspaper is that, however I meet people in the religion-obsessed Middle East, I am often required to start the conversation with an explanation of my personal history.

Here it is, again. I was born in Kiev, Ukraine, in a family as mixed as they come: my paternal grandfather hailed from Russian Orthodox polar fishermen and explorers on Russia's Far North, while his Catholic wife traced her lineage to petty Polish aristocracy. My maternal grandmother came from a family of Jewish sugar industrialists in the Ukrainian shtetl of Uman and was briefly married to an officer of Cossack descent. She used to joke that we could organize a three-way pogrom without leaving the family apartment.

Things got more exotic after my birth. I spent part of my childhood living a happy colonial life on the African island of Madagascar, where my father taught statistics at the local university and where I fed freshly captured grasshoppers to my pet lemur monkey as I learned from French textbooks that my ancestors were the Gauls. Having left Ukraine before it reemerged as a separate country, I lived virtually my entire adult life first as a student and journalist in New York City and then as a foreign correspondent based in France, Israel, and Italy—my new home country in whose elections I vote and whose language has become the father tongue that I speak with my pizza-addicted children and Roman wife.

I have always refused to pigeonhole myself into a particular group, "religion," or "sect," as the Saudi visa form now asked me to do. If anything, years of chronicling life in Jerusalem had made me wary of priests, rabbis, and mullahs of all denominations.

But Prime Minister Hariri, coming from a country where an individual's prospects in life are closely correlated with his or her membership in one of Lebanon's seventeen officially recognized religious subgroups, left me no choice as I met him for an interview. After issuing compliments about his lavish palace ("This is extremely impressive, Mr. Prime Minister"—"Ha ha, you haven't seen my home yet"), I launched into my usual introduction: "I'm a reporter for the *Wall Street Journal,* and if you're wondering about my name, I am an Italian of Ukrainian origin." Before I had a chance to ask my first question, the prime minister paused for a minute of puzzled silence, calculating, and then came up with my proper place: "So, so you must be Orthodox, right?"

"Well, I'm not really religious," I started mumbling, but then it hit me. If my father ever went to church, or my mother to a synagogue (occurrences that I have not yet witnessed), I figured they'd probably go to the Orthodox ones. "Yes, Mr. Prime Minister," I replied, "You can say I'm Orthodox." He was satisfied with his erudition. I was "Orthodox" from now on, on the Saudi form and on multitudes of other Middle Eastern visa applications thereafter.

When I finally picked up my Saudi visa, a sticker embossed with a hologram of a palm tree and two crossed swords, the religion entry marked me as an obvious unbeliever; the consul didn't mistake me for an orthodox Muslim. Having been branded an infidel ruled out any thought of entering the holy city of Mecca. Set among volcanic black hills a short drive east of Jeddah, Mecca is the birthplace of Islam and its prophet, Mohammed. It was the seizing of this city in 1924 that gave Saudi Arabia's ruling family, al Saud, that hails from the Nejd highlands hundreds of miles to the east, such authority and prestige across the Muslim world. Mecca, which every able-bodied Muslim is supposed to visit at least once in a lifetime, is off-limits to infidels. The four-lane expressway between Jeddah and Riyadh, Saudi Arabia's two main urban areas, passes through Mecca's hallowed grounds. Well before the holy city begins, there is a huge control post, strikingly similar to the U.S.–Mexico border gate between San Diego and Tijuana. "For Muslims Only" announce the freeway signs pointing ahead, to the booths where officers carefully check papers—the ID cards that, for Saudi residents, are color-coded to distinguish between Muslims and unbelievers. In late 2001 a European ambassador obsessed with Mecca dressed up in Bedouin garb and sneaked in; when he was caught on the way out, he had no choice but to convert on the spot. The occasion was trumpeted by Saudi newspapers as an important victory for the true faith just as America started bombing the Taliban.

✦　✦　✦

Just before the Mecca checkpoint, a narrow bypass road branches out from the highway, snaking through the mountains. On maps it is officially called the Non-Muslims' Road. The name itself is probably the most poignant reminder of the staggering culture gap between Saudi

Arabia and the West. While the kingdom is crammed with American cars, American fast-food outlets, and American retailers, and while its diplomats and top princes often speak accentless English acquired after years of study in America's most expensive private schools, the ideas that made the West what it is are rejected without appeal. In the Saudi system, not even lip service is paid to the humanistic ideals that have shaped the modern world since, say, the eighteenth century.

Freedom of religion, in the concise words of the U.S. State Department's annual human rights report, "does not exist" in Saudi Arabia. Only Muslims can be Saudi citizens, and any public expression of other religions—even by the six million or more foreign workers who make the Saudi economy run—is a crime. Saudi authorities have been known to bar companies from using the letter X in their names, on the grounds that X looks too much like a Christian cross. Unrelated women and men cannot socialize—even McDonald's restaurants keep isolated male and female sections, with separate entrances. Crimes like sorcery, adultery, apostasy, blasphemy, and witchcraft are still punished by death—often by stoning or beheading on a Riyadh plaza, ringed by cafés and toy stores, and popularly known as "chop-chop square." Nor is there freedom of the press, speech, or assembly. In fact, the name of the country itself denotes personal ownership by al Saud, whose chief Abdelaziz, the father of the current king, seized the land through bloody tribal conquest in 1902–1932. Not even sham elections of the kind held elsewhere in the region legitimize al Saud's rule. And, at every step, the Muslims and the infidels must take different paths.

✦ ✦ ✦

In Riyadh, as I waited for my turn in the minister's antechamber, I flipped through a book I had bought on that trip—a memoir of Wilfred Thesiger, a British explorer who crossed the Arabian peninsula in 1947. Thesiger much preferred Bedouin company to that of the English, and his books—republished by the United Arab Emirates—grace the lobby stores of most Middle Eastern luxury hotels frequented by business executives on expense accounts. I was struck by the pages that described his passage through Saudi Arabia. In the town of Laila, Thesiger was taunted by street urchins "who explained at length that I was unclean" and "reviled me for being an infidel and not praying." The shopkeepers accepted Thesiger's money only "after it had been publicly washed." And as he tried to get a guide, local Bedouins asked his Arab companions, from the gentler lands of Oman farther south, "why they had not murdered me in the desert and gone off with my possessions."

The more time I spent in Saudi Arabia in the following months, the more I felt that—beneath a modernized veneer—attitudes toward non-Muslims hadn't changed that much since Thesiger's days. In its long history, the Islamic civilization often shone as a beacon of humanity in a brutal, nasty world. Unlike Christian Europe in medieval times, Muslim lands rarely attempted forced conversions and allowed extensive self-rule to Christian and Jewish communities in their midst. A lot of what we know about Europe's ancient thinkers was preserved thanks to Arabic translations. Few societies at the time were as tolerant as the Ottoman Empire, which welcomed hundreds of thousands of Jews who had been expelled in the name of racial and religious purity by fifteenth-century Catholic Spain. (Spain, of course, expelled its Muslims, too.) But this heritage had little to do with the kind of Islam that emerged in the Saudi desert in the late 1700s. People here took a path toward uncompromising zeal at about the same time as the French Revolution championed religious freedom in Europe and the founders of the United States drafted the Bill of Rights.

The roots of Saudi Arabia's religious establishment—which spends billions of dollars in oil money a year to propagate itself, quite successfully, as an example to follow across the Muslim world—were laid down when al Saud were living in the obscure village of Dirriya, near Riyadh, struck an alliance with a cleric by the name of Mohammed bin Abdel Wahhab. Eager to bring the Arabian Peninsula's Bedouins back to the pure, harsh faith practiced by Prophet Mohammed twelve and a half centuries earlier, the cleric rejected most of the vast culture amassed by the Islamic world in the preceding millennium as *bidaa*—a heretic innovation. He reserved particular wrath for the Sufis, mystical religious brotherhoods that often venerated tombs of revered scholars, and the Shiite sect of Islam. Together with al Saud's tribal warriors, Abdel Wahhab spread his beliefs at the tip of the sword. Raiders destroyed ancient mosques, cemeteries, and shrines, calling them places of idol worship. They invaded Iraq and burned down the libraries of Karbala, the ancient center of Islamic learning and a holy place for Shiite Islam, preaching that there was nothing to learn from the infidels. Frightened neighbors, their towns pillaged and gutted by desert warriors acting in the name of God, dubbed this strange new sect the Wahhabis.

Today, the same al Saud family runs the twenty-first-century state. And the progeny of Mohammed bin Abdel Wahhab, the house of al Sheikh, still dominate the religious and judicial establishment that shapes Saudi society. Without their religious backing, al Saud's rule would probably collapse.

Saudi Arabia's top religious authority, the grand mufti and head of the Supreme Council of Ulemas, or Islamic scholars, is an al Sheikh. The minister of Islamic affairs is Abdel Wahhab's descendant, too, as is the powerful man in whose antechamber I waited, Justice Minister Abdullah Mohammed al Sheikh. The kingdom is run under Islam's Sharia law, and so the justice ministry is a body as much religious as governmental. Judges or lawyers in Saudi Arabia are usually clerics with curly beards rather than dapper graduates of Western law schools. All this, I figured, meant one thing. If anyone could explain the puzzle of Wahhabism and Wahhabi society to me, Abdel Wahhab's direct descendant and His Excellence the Minister Abdullah al Sheikh was the one.

✦   ✦   ✦

I landed in Saudi Arabia a few days before my appointment with the minister, and customs officials waved me in after X-raying my luggage and inspecting it for contraband alcohol, ham, or books. I started out in Jeddah the following day by taking a drive to the Non-Muslims' Road, where I experienced my first visceral bout of utter alienation in Saudi Arabia—something, I'm told, that happens often to foreigners here. On that desolate stretch of the Mecca bypass, where even cell phones stopped working, I chatted with my Indian driver, a man in a well-pressed shirt whose formal English testified to years of assiduous study. He was making only $200 a month—the kind of money I paid the Saudi-owned limousine company every two days—and was sour on the kingdom and desperate to return home.

As we talked, the road rejoined the highway past Mecca and climbed into the mountains on the way to the city of Taef, once the summer capital of the kingdom. The featureless landscape suddenly gave way to breathtaking vistas. At the mountain pass, several cars were parked by the curb. I told the driver to park, too, and we saw why others had stopped. Hundreds of baboons, in a display of chaotic, unbridled vitality, were jumping on the rocks by the road-side. Under a gentle afternoon sun, mother baboons nurtured their infants—reminding me of the pet lemur that I owned as a child—and males fought each other for scraps of bananas and for female attention. In a nation of ugly concrete and fast-food outlets where most ancient landmarks had been deliberately bulldozed, this was a moment of rare beauty.

Until a minivan with a half dozen young Saudis pulled up. These young men, wearing white gowns and sandals on bare feet, burned with excitement. Making guttural cries, they raced toward the baboons, pelting the animals with a shower of rocks. Bloodied, the animals scurried away, amid the helpless pitched noise of pain and sheer terror. One of the baby apes, hit in the head, wriggled in the con-vulsions of death. I looked at a handful of other Saudis—families with small children—who were also watching. I expected them, at the very least, to chide the intruders. Instead, they burst out in hearty, plain laughter, clearly amused by the spectacle. My vegetarian Indian driver couldn't watch it anymore. He turned his back and walked toward the car, muttering quietly: "The savages, the savages."

✦ ✦ ✦

Back in Jeddah, I braved the sweltering heat to walk the two blocks from my hotel to the consulate of India—a nation with some 1.4 mil-lion citizens in Saudi Arabia. Third World expatriates from India, Pakistan, the Philippines, and elsewhere came to Saudi Arabia after the 1970s oil boom, lured by relatively high salaries to take up jobs that ranged from street sweeper to corporate CEO. Three decades later, these foreigners—mostly male and barred from bringing in children and spouses—still make up the bulk of the country's work force. A Western pedestrian was a rarity in these parts, and every few minutes a taxi driver pulled up near me, honking insistently and clearly amazed by my preference for walking.

The Indian consul, Syed Akbaruddin, was a Muslim himself—hailing from the world's largest Muslim community, which, despite the creation of Pakistan, preferred to remain in a majority-Hindu but secular Indian state. Unlike the usually sheltered Westerners, Indians—Muslim, Hindu, or Christian—are allowed no immunity from harsh Saudi rules; they experience Saudi Arabia as it is. Although slavery no longer officially exists in the kingdom, the condition of Indians and other Third World workers isn't far removed from medieval serfdom: newspapers all over the Persian Gulf are full of "absconder notices" that feature mug shots of runaway help and offer compensation for their capture.

Akbaruddin began with the tale of an Indian male nurse whose troubles had provided Indian diplomats with plenty of work. The nurse, Prabhu Isaac, had finished his long stint at a Saudi hospital and, just before returning to India, threw a farewell party in a rented hall. A Christian, he invited mostly Christian friends from India, the Philippines, and Eritrea. Apparently, at some point in the party, there was a prayer for Isaac's safe return. The next day, Saudi religious police—the ubiquitous Committee to Promote Virtue and Prevent Vice—swooped down on Isaac's residential compound. They arrested Isaac and, after watching the farewell party's videotape, rounded up dozens of other participants. The detainees' crime: holding non-Muslim religious ceremonies. The Indian nurse spent more than six months behind bars in baking-hot Saudi jails.

In Akbaruddin's consulate, I also picked up a "death compensation" schedule. A table in this document outlined how much money families of victims should receive from the perpetrators of deadly accidents and crimes. The very concept of such "blood money" is rooted in Islamic religious law. Insofar as similar payments exist in American civil law, the amount is based on many variables used in calculating the victim's lost potential earnings. In Saudi Arabia, only two things mattered, in death as in life: religion and sex.

A male Muslim's life, the table explained, was worth 100,000 riyals (about $27,000); a male Christian or Jew, 50,000 riyals; a male "Hindu, Buddhist, Jain, etc.," merely 6,666.66 riyals. And a heathen woman was worth only half that—or less than her plane ticket home. Death was foremost on Akbaruddin's mind—and not only because fatal accidents happened with frightening frequency to Indian workers in a country where safety rules are rarely enforced and where insurance is considered ungodly. Apart from exceptional circumstances— say, when a man was beheaded by government executioners—dead non-Muslims must be flown out of the kingdom lest their unclean remains defile Saudi Arabia's soil. Since cremation, preferred by the Hindus, is specifically barred by the Sharia, the Indian embassy must employ an entire department dedicated to shipping non-Muslim cadavers home. A private industry has already developed to transport what was listed on cargo manifests as "human remains."

Indian diplomats were hard at work making sure that Saudi employers pay for that last passage and securing the exit visas that all foreign workers, dead or alive, need in order to be released from Saudi Arabia. "We're very keen on dead bodies," Akbaruddin said softly. "At least in death they should get the respect they didn't have when alive."

✦ ✦ ✦

Dressed in a gray European suit, another Indian, M. N. Jayaprakash, the Jeddah regional manager for the shipping conglomerate Kanoo Cargo, ran an important part of this cadaver transportation industry from his air-conditioned office in the north of the city. At first, the executive was surprised by my questions but then quickly warmed to the topic. "Saudi [Arabia] does not have much to send abroad apart from oil in the way of exports," he confided. As oil is shipped by tankers, cargo planes often leave the kingdom half empty, after unloading imported foods, electronics, and clothes. "So, on the export side, for us it's mostly personal belongings. . . . And we do a lot of human remains business, unfortunately."

For details, Jayaprakash sent me downstairs, to an aide who dealt almost exclusively with cadaver shipping. M. R. Hari, also from India, let me sit at his cluttered desk and look over the case he was processing.

It was of a twenty-nine-year-old laborer from Nepal, named Sunil Tamrakar. "You can live in Saudi Arabia, but you can't die in Saudi Arabia," Hari sighed as he fingered the wafer-thin papers. The Nepalese man had been riding in the passenger seat of a Honda Civic in central Jeddah when the car crashed into a tractor; he suffered cerebral bleeding and, the file said, died on the spot.

Tamrakar, a Buddhist, could not be buried locally. The dairy company that had employed him assembled all the right paperwork and booked him on the final flight to Kathmandu. After asking to see the cargo manifest, I noticed that Tamrakar himself was coded as "HUM," for human, in the cargo description box. Next followed the short list of his personal belongings, collected in three years of work in the kingdom: "Blanket (one); bag (one); Personal clothes; Photo album (one); 3,700 Saudi Riyals (about $990 at the time) found in the wallet; Pocket diary (one)."

✦ ✦ ✦

Later that day, on the Indian consul's advice, I went to explore one of Jeddah's secrets: a hidden cemetery for non-Muslims, the only one still functioning in the country. The cemetery was established in the nineteenth century, before al Saud and their Wahhabi warriors seized the city, ousted the Hashemite ruling family that now governs Jordan, and swept away the Red Sea port's traditionally tolerant society. Created in those distant times to bury European merchants who hadn't survived hazardous travels in Arabia, the cemetery was now run by a committee of foreign consuls in Jeddah.

I had a hard time finding the place. Stuck in the middle of Jeddah's electronics bazaar, the cemetery had no sign at the gate. People I asked in the neighborhood were mostly shocked that such an infidel enclave could remain in the kingdom at all. "Formally, the non-Muslim cemetery does not exist, for obvious reasons," Italian consul Antimo Campanile, who chaired the consuls' committee, cautioned me. "Nothing non-Muslim can exist in Saudi Arabia."

When I finally found the compound, I discovered a reminder of a more relaxed era inside. An elaborate carved tombstone marked the grave of a nineteenth-century Dutch consul with a large cross. Next towered the tombs of two Jewish merchants, from Germany and from

Smyrna in Turkey, who died here in 1912. I was amazed by the fact that the Jewish tombstones had retained the Stars of David and Hebrew lettering—in a country that now zealously prohibited such symbols. In fact, the Saudi religious authorities had just banned the Japanese Poké-mon game, after allegations that it was a Jewish conspiracy to corrupt Arab children, because the name of one of the characters, Pikachu, allegedly meant "become a Jew" in Japanese. (It didn't.)

These days, the Jeddah cemetery no longer accepts adults. Small children are the only exception to Saudi Arabia's rules that require dead infidels to be shipped abroad. As a result, bereaved Filipino, Indian, and Sri Lankan families keep bringing dead babies, to be buried atop each other in tiny graves. "Here, it's nothing—just baby, baby, baby," the cemetery's Chadian guardian, Mohammed Younis, told me dismissively as he pointed to the rows of tiny marble plaques. Prayer on the site was prohibited, and few of the recent tombs are adorned with a cross or other religious symbols. "The marble masters are too afraid to carve crosses," the guardian explained. "And when they do it, it's very, very small."

✦ ✦ ✦

With a day still to go before the justice minister's interview in Riyadh, I wanted to get an introduction to Wahhabi thought—and so I went to see another descendant of Abdel Wahhab, seven generations down the line. My host, Abdulmuhsen al Sheikh, taught Islamic law to future judges at the Umm Qura University in Mecca, ground zero of the Saudi religious orthodoxy. As a Westerner, of course, I couldn't visit his Mecca home, he reminded me with a giggle. Instead, he would see me in Jeddah—in the opulent residence of his brother, who cemented the alliance between Abdel Wahhab's progeny and al Saud by serving as one of the top officials in the Saudi intelligence services.

As befits a wealthy Saudi's residence, a black servant stood at the ready with a brass coffee pot, filling up tiny cups with a bitter, herb-spiked liquid. I was expecting to meet a stern, fiery man, a repository of Wahhabi scorn for the corrupt outside world. Instead, the professor was jolly, round-faced, and bent on explaining that Wahhabi rules are not nearly as strict as people imagine.

We started with fornication, a natural topic of conversation between two men in a country as sex-obsessed as Saudi Arabia. It's true that illicit sex is punishable by death, he said. But in Saudi Arabia, the act must be proven by at least four eyewitnesses—and, the professor said as his eyes twinkled, "believe me, that's not something that happens that often." The famed Committee to Promote Virtue and Prevent Vice wasn't all that bad, either, he went on. I'd already heard many Saudis express dismay with the committee's thuggish enforcers, who beat up passersby with canes for not being inside the mosques at the five daily prayer times, and who wouldn't let women students leave a burning school in Mecca in March 2002 because they had not been properly covered when the fire erupted. (More than a dozen students burned alive at the time.)

Such criticism of the committee, the gentle professor said, was a result of a misunderstanding of what the organization was all about. He knew: he taught the committee's officers, too. "First of all, it is to promote virtue, and only then to suppress vice," he said, in a tone laden with gravity. All in all, the committee wasn't so different from normal police forces in other lands. Take, for example, its attempts to crack down on alcohol, a substance that is strictly prohibited in Saudi Arabia, to Muslims and non-Muslims alike. "In the kingdom, no doubt, there are people who drink alcohol in their houses, and nobody cares. The problem occurs when neighbors complain that such activities are going on, and the committee intervenes," he said. "It's just like in the U.S., where there is a law that bans smoking in public spaces, but nobody minds when you do it at home."

Grinning after this exposition, the professor stood up and led the way to a huge dinner table that displayed the delights of Arabian cuisine, from steaming rice-and-lamb dishes to fried Red Sea fish to hummus and spicy pickles. I had the place of honor, at the head of the table. A half dozen male relatives and aides joined us for the meal. "This one is very good, it makes you stronger in bed with a woman," the professor advised with a knowing smile as he heaped a brownish paste on my plate.

From there, it was natural that our conversation turned again to women. I hadn't seen many during my stay. The rare ones on the streets could be easily classified by nationality: Saudis had to hide their faces under the *niqab,* or full veil; Muslim foreigners could get away with covering only their hair under a regular veil; and the Western ones went bareheaded. All had to wear a stifling black *abaya* gown, and couldn't be seen talking to male nonrelatives when unsupervised. In some conservative parts of the kingdom, I'd read in a local newspaper, the insistence on hiding women behind a veil extended even to immediate family—so that children grew up without ever seeing their mother's face, and husbands had no idea how their wives looked, at least not above the waist.

A walk on Jeddah's beachfront corniche just before my dinner with the professor showed the throbbing frustration caused by one of Saudi Arabia's more peculiar restrictions on women—the ban on driving cars. The beach—where no one of either sex entered the water because taking off clothes was illegal—buzzed with activity as dune buggies raced back and forth, whipping up clouds of sand and zooming between illuminated camel carts. The camel carts, which carried loud generators to power the Christmas-tree-like garlands of lamps that adorned them, were mostly idle, but I had to jump aside to avoid a collision with one of the roaring buggies. These infernal machines were piloted by small children—and their Saudi mothers. Eyes glowing through the veil slits, black *abayas* fluttering in the wind, dozens of women raced the beach at breakneck speed. Frightened children moaned silently, holding on tightly, as their moms enjoyed with abandon the only motoring freedom available to women in the kingdom. Some women had tried to drive actual cars. The last such attempt happened in 1990; amid male outrage, women drivers were arrested and later kicked out of their jobs. I tried to take a snapshot of the buggies, but my nervous driver hurried me away. "If the committee people see you photographing women, we'll be in big trouble," he said.

Professor al Sheikh, surprisingly, told me that he had taught his wife how to handle the steering wheel—in case something happened to him during a long desert trip. He also readily accepted that the ban on driving had nothing to do with Islam—Prophet Mohammed's widow, after all, had personally driven a camel to battle. The prohibition followed Bedouin tribal customs—which, the professor added, should stay in place to maintain proper mores. "By keeping a woman away from driving, we're keeping her away from trouble," he chortled. "It's best for her this way."

Such taboos have a social toll. Since women can't drive, the kingdom spends vast resources on hundreds of thousands of drivers, imported from India, Pakistan, and elsewhere. In 2002, government efforts to give these jobs to local Saudis collapsed because of the same conservative prejudice that bars Saudi women from driving. Saudi fathers and husbands simply refused to let their womenfolk be chauffeured by sex-obsessed compatriots. "As a father, I won't let my teenage daughter go with a Saudi driver to school or university. A Saudi would turn back to look at her face, or even talk to her. A Pakistani driver is too scared to do that," explained Mohammed Aljadayel, a Jeddah business executive and a spokesman for the Jeddah Chamber of Commerce, which lobbied hard against the new rules.

Barely ten minutes later, when I asked him about entertainment options in the city, Aljadayel made a conspiratorial wink and urged me to go to the walled Obhur beach, a resort enclave for Westerners located some forty minutes' driving north of the city. "That's where you can see girls in bikinis," he said, putting his fingers together and blowing a kiss. I can report that after a brief visit, the most curious thing about the beach—apart from the stunning coral reef—wasn't the pasty expatriate ladies but the stern notices, at every turn, warning, as if the bathing spot were a top-secret military facility: PHOTOGRAPHY IS FORBIDDEN. Not without reason: by Saudi standards, a snapshot of these beachcombers would be considered porn.

✦   ✦   ✦

I flew to Riyadh the following morning to see Professor al Sheikh's distant cousin, Justice Minister al Sheikh, in whose antechamber I continued to wait, sparking envious stares from Saudi favor seekers. The minister's flunkies appeared without a warning at about the time I began to doze off and ushered me into the big man's office, staying behind to take notes. I couldn't stop thinking how, once again, a jovial appearance contradicted everything I knew about the harshness of Wahhabi orthodoxy. The justice minister, a man of oily eyes, meaty fingers, and patchy beard, apologized profusely for keeping me waiting and offered tea. Then, a broad smile permanently glued to his lips, he held out a gift—a velvet-covered green box that contained a plastic shingle with the ministry's coat of arms. The coat of arms consisted, unsurprisingly, of the scales of justice. But instead of being held by a blindfolded goddess of justice (no women; we're Saudis, after all), the scales were suspended from the tips of curved swords, the same kind that are used on the "chop-chop square."

Endlessly patient and polite, the minister began to explain the kingdom's rules to me. First, the basics. Democracy or political debate was simply un-Islamic and therefore not an option: "Publicly opposing the government is not an Islamic way of raising one's cause, because doing so will bring chaos and anarchy." Freedom of religion was a nonstarter, too. The minister was unapologetic about the ban on non-Muslim prayer, or the fact that Saudi customs officers routinely confiscated crucifixes, Bibles, or Hindu religious books as illicit contraband. "This is simply not authorized," he said curtly. "The Arabian peninsula is the heart of Islam, just like the Vatican is the heart of Christianity. Nobody can go to the Vatican to practice their religion there, and we follow the same line here. This is not just what our scholars decided; this is what our scriptures say." I told the minister that I happen to live right next to the Vatican's walls and that his own country had financed, in Rome, the building of one of Europe's biggest mosques. It was hard to imagine the pope's Swiss guards, in their red, blue, and yellow knickerbockers, confiscating Qurans or Jewish prayer books on Saint Peter's Square.

The minister kept smiling. "There is a difference between Christianity and Islam, you know," he accepted. "With Christian religion, what you have is just advice. In Islam, most major issues come from the Quran or the sayings of the Prophet—including the prohibition on practicing any other faith on the Arabian Peninsula." He left unsaid the fact that anything other than a literal interpretation of the Quran or Prophet Mohammed's sayings and actions, which together comprise the Sunna, would be considered open blasphemy in Saudi Arabia and likely a ticket to Riyadh's chop-chop square.

I replied that the other six countries on the Arabian Peninsula didn't quite see it this way. From Kuwait to Yemen, each interpreted

Prophet Mohammed's injunction only as meaning that Islam should be the peninsula's preponderant faith; therefore, freedom of religion was extended to Christians, Hindus, and, in countries like Bahrain, even Jews. To the Saudi minister, those neighbors were unacceptably lax. "From the religious viewpoint, it's forbidden," he said without appeal. The ban on burying foreign workers in Saudi Arabia boiled down to the same issue, he said. "The funerals for Muslims and non-Muslims alike involve religious practices—so if we allow non-Muslims to be buried here, this will lead to non-Muslim prayers."

Changing the subject from such a horrifying prospect, I asked the minister about his famous ancestor Mohammed bin Abdel Wahhab. That was a delicate issue, and the flunkies' eyes quickly turned toward the boss. Wahhabism is a label invented by the enemies of the true faith, the minister exclaimed. Wahhabis usually refer to their sect as Muwahiddun, or Unitarians, although the minister personally preferred to be seen as just Muslim. "Sheikh Mohammed [bin Abdel Wahhab] always insisted in his letters that he is not deviating from the main-stream religion, not inventing a new sect," the minister said. "His coherent following of the Quran and the Sunna upset many Islamic communities that are not in favor of such strict adherence, which will take away some of the advantages and benefits that they enjoy."

The perception outside Saudi Arabia that the kingdom's ways are somehow repressive or extreme is downright wrong, the minister added. "Many consider Saudi Arabia to be a country that practices moderate Islam," he said. "Look, we even accept six million foreign-ers to live among us—and they are not feeling any discrimination, none at all."

Aware of the Wahhabis' dismal reputation in the West, the minister was determined to make me understand that the teachings of Abdel Wahhab are in tune with modern sensibilities. So he picked an example. In the four main traditions of Sunni Islamic jurisprudence, the minis-ter said, a man convicted of murder during a robbery should be cruci-fied. Saudi Arabia, of course, followed Islamic law to the letter. But look at the details!, the minister exclaimed. Under a different school of Islamic law, "the man should be crucified while still alive, as a punish-ment," he said, grimacing disapproval at such barbarous brutality.

Yet, in following Abdel Wahhab's teachings, Saudi Arabia showed much greater kindness. Saudi executioners killed the prisoner first, and only then nailed a dead body to the cross. "We think crucifixion is merely an example for the public," he assured me, radiating compassion.

Saudi Arabia has shown that it will spare no effort to ensure that its progressive, enlightened ways are adopted by the world's more than one billion Muslims, and eventually by non-Muslims too, the minister added. "The duty of the kingdom is to spread real Islam—not by fire, not by money—but first of all by setting an example as a country that strictly adheres to the Sunna and the Quran."

2

SAUDI ARABIA

Chuck E. Cheese and
Richard the Lion Heart

Just weeks before the 2003 invasion of Iraq, I drove south from Riyadh to see war preparations at the enormous Prince Sultan Air Force Base, the epicenter of the oft-resented American military presence in the kingdom.

American troops streamed in here during the 1990–1991 Gulf War and ended up staying in the kingdom for well over a decade. It was easy to see why their arrival caused so much frustration: after wasting billions and billions of dollars on American weapons, Saudi Arabia had to concede that it was humiliatingly unable to defend itself against Saddam Hussein's threats. More important, the appearance of armed Christians and Jews on Saudi soil, with the purpose of offering ungodly help against fellow Muslims, went against everything that Wahhabi thought considered right.

Official clerics and the royal family, of course, declared the American presence to be compatible with Wahhabi Islam. To the religious establishment, maintaining the monarchy—and, with it, curbs on women and on non-Muslim minorities inside Saudi Arabia—was a priority; jihadi causes abroad or Saudi Arabia's emancipation from the United States came second. In Jeddah, Professor al Sheikh told me that even a Saudi recognition of Israel, a state viewed as an illegitimate "cancerous growth" by the most moderate of Islamists, would be acceptable if al Saud decided to take such a step for national security reasons. "From the standpoint of Islam, the public must obey the ruler," the professor explained. "No one in the public has a say in matters of war and peace, except the ruler." Such views suited the house of Saud just fine. The West had accepted them, too, at least until September 11.

But the American deployment and the 1990–1991 war had the side effect of unshackling a large part of the Wahhabi religious world from blind obedience to al Saud. The public now wanted to have a say. Bin Laden was one of those prominent Saudis who broke with the royal family over the 1990 arrival of U.S. troops; he and fellow critics blasted al Saud and the official clerics as "hypocrites," a serious charge under Islamic law. In the early 1990s, when Bin Laden called the U.S. military presence on Saudi soil a Crusader "occupation" of the Land of Holy Places, he again struck a chord with many. It took me only a short trip to the Prince Sultan Base to understand why.

As we traveled from an ultraconservative Saudi town directly outside the base to what can only be described as an imitation of small-town America inside the facility, my Saudi government escorts gaped with shock. They couldn't keep their eyes off female U.S. soldiers driving trucks on the tarmac or jogging in tight T-shirts and shorts.

After deadly suicide bombings of American barracks elsewhere in the kingdom, this isolated desert facility housed almost all of the American forces in Saudi Arabia at the time, including the main unit, the 363rd U.S. Air Force Expeditionary Wing. In January 2003, the last weeks of large-scale American presence in the kingdom, most Saudi-based troops were preparing to relocate to Iraq, Qatar, and other Gulf states.

As we came up the stairs to the Expeditionary Wing chaplain's office, my Saudi minders were visibly rattled by a leaflet decorated with a Star of David and entitled *About Judaism* on display. The Christian chaplain, who, in defiance of Saudi Arabia's alcohol ban, kept stocks of wine for sacrament, chuckled when I told him he ran the only legal church on Saudi soil. "It's a lot like Phoenix here," one of the pilots told me. "But we never get to go off base. Having flown with Saudi pilots is the closest I've come to culturally experiencing Saudi Arabia." Next came the command room. Walls and bookcases were adorned with commemorative banners and plaques of American units deployed here before. My Saudi minders' worst conspiracy theories were confirmed as they stared agape at the most visible one. It screamed in red letters that the 532nd Expeditionary Squadron is also known as "The CRUSADERS."

✦　✦　✦

As protests against the American presence grew in the mid-1990s, the Saudi government dispatched to prison at least four hundred dissident clerics, academics, and professionals. Most of these Islamists, including the two fiery preachers often cited by Bin Laden as his spiritual guides, Salman al Awda and Safr al Hawali, were freed four or five years later, after signing letters of allegiance to the royal family; they retain wide audiences across the Islamic world.

Awda, once dubbed by Westerners as "Saudi Khomeini," hails from the Buraida oasis north of Riyadh, the most conservative area of Saudi Arabia and the stronghold of Wahhabi zeal. In the 1990s, his *fatwas* against America circulated widely in the Muslim world, as did cassettes with his sermons against the corrupt West and the Saudi royals. Like Hawali, Awda studied Islam with prominent members of the Muslim Brotherhood who had been exiled in Saudi Arabia after fleeing repression in more secular Arab lands such as Egypt and Syria. When mixed with traditional Saudi fundamentalism, the Brotherhood's ideology of political activism, violent if necessary, produced an explosive cocktail. Awda's and Hawali's preachings marked a turning point on the ideological path from the ultrarigorous but status quo Wahhabi sect to Bin Laden's expansionist death cult. The confluence of Brotherhood and Wahhabi ideas led to practical alliances. In forming Qaeda, Bin Laden relied on his deputy Ayman Zawahiri, the Egyptian chieftain of a radical Brotherhood offshoot.

Having heard so much about Awda, I wanted to meet him, and spent days calling his aides and planning a trip to Buraida—an idea that my minders, no matter how easily shaken off, wouldn't approve.

When I finally got my appointment with Awda, it wasn't in the desert oasis; instead, we met in a wealthy follower's home on the same cosmopolitan Jeddah corniche where Professor al Sheikh had plied me with dinner.

The follower, who remained nameless to me, lived in a palatial home filled to the brim with luscious Persian carpets and silver vases and trays. It stood just behind a giant Chuck E. Cheese pizza parlor, a piece of gaudy Americana facing the sea. In perfect English, the host asked point-blank whether I was a spy. He explained that someone had recently presented himself as a Dutch reporter to Awda and then began asking strange questions. To make matters worse, the home's owner had just returned from a business trip to Florida. "The other day, a woman came up to me in a mall in Florida and asked where I'm from," he said. "When I answered I was from Saudi Arabia, she was so happy. She smiled and went: Ah, great, my brother works there for the CIA."

No matter, I still got to meet the sheikh. Nursing a cold, the barefooted cleric, scrawny and surprisingly young, sat on propped cushions. The freedom accorded him by al Saud was still conditional—he was barred, for example, from making TV appearances—and so he was careful not to say anything too controversial about the royal family. Ours was an exasperating conversation that showed the cleric's mastery of the art of not being pinned down. Every time I tried to provoke him—asking about September 11, about Bin Laden, about the looming war on Iraq—he replied with a loaded counterquestion. By the end of an hour, I realized that it was I who was doing almost all the talking, explaining the rationales behind U.S. foreign policies and the actions of Israel. While tepidly condemning the September 11 attacks, the sheikh made it clear that he was no fan of America, which was guilty of "terrorism" in his eyes. His bottom line was that Muslims are facing annihilation from massive attacks by the immoral and greedy West. It was, once again, the familiar discourse of the battle of Good and Evil.

After several guests had joined us to pay their respects, the sheikh opened up. This was the cream of Jeddah's beau monde—businessmen, lawyers, and university professors. Because of Arabian politeness, I was allowed to sit in, even though my scheduled interview time had run out. The guests' conversation quickly turned to the question of Awda's students, many of whom were now held as terrorist suspects at the U.S. detention camp in Guantánamo Bay, Cuba. The sheikh, who wanted help in organizing their defense, was clearly uncomfortable discussing the issue in my presence. "The Americans, they simply hate Muslims and Islam," he said.

Interrupting, I explained that it's not as if Saudi Arabia was without its own prejudices. In fact, I had just read a long article written by a prominent professor in the official *Al Riyadh* newspaper that explained how Jews use the blood of gentile children to prepare pastries for the Purim holiday. (In breathlessly repeating the blood libel that had long been used to inspire pogroms in medieval Europe, the learned professor had gotten her festivals mixed up; she confused Purim with Passover.) Wasn't that an example of the Saudis' intolerance?

"Why?" the cleric asked. "The professor is right. This is a scientifically proven fact. All the world knows about it."

The house's owner hissed with anger. "You Westerners, you always care for the Jews. You always talk about the Holocaust," he said. "What about us Muslims? We suffered much worse. When you entered our Jerusalem, your Crusaders marched up to their knees in our blood! Why aren't you feeling guilty about that?" I was taken aback by his raw emotion. But that—that was a long time ago, I blurted out. A whole nine centuries. My words were met with cold stares, and a long unwelcoming silence. "I guess no matter how much we speak, we'll never understand each other," the host said. It was time to go.

I gathered my things and said good-bye. On the hot Jeddah seafront, lined with abstract sculptures, I couldn't help thinking about the invisible wall that separated me from these otherwise polite men. Here I was, expecting to discuss modern life just a stone's throw from Chuck E. Cheese, and instead I was cornered into justifying the exploits of Richard the Lion Heart. Somehow, it is only the depredations suffered by Muslims that are still remembered, both in the Arab world and the West, and only Muslim victimhood retains a vivid political urgency in the political discourse. How many Westerners, by contrast, know that, in August 846, an Arab expeditionary force showed up in the Roman neighborhood where I live today, sacking the Vatican's Saint Peter's Basilica, hauling off its relics and vandalizing St. Peter's grave after failing to capture the rest of the holy city? Nobody in the Western mainstream dwells on how Muslim armies, before and after the Crusades, burned and pillaged Christian towns all the way from Budapest to Bordeaux, or how lands from Tunisia to Turkey used to be Christian. Yet virtually every Arab capital has a street or a neighborhood named Andalus, as a memorial to a Muslim Spain wiped out by Christian reconquest in 1492.

On the other hand, after rolling back Islam from their continent and then colonizing the Muslim heartland, Europeans of recent generations must have found it less difficult to forgive and forget millennium-old slights.

◆ ◆ ◆

Compared to Awda, the next Islamist, also formerly jailed, I met in the kingdom was positively pleasant. Mohsen al Awaji—another native of the Buraida area—had not always been a cleric. He studied agriculture in Birmingham, England, and taught in Riyadh's King Saud University before the royal family got fed up with his political activism and threw him behind bars. Now prohibited from teaching, he was an "Islamic scholar," a "lawyer," and editor in chief for a political Web site, Wasatiya, a word meaning centrism or moderation. This was, of course, centrism Saudi-style, in the Wahhabi continuum between the official establishment and open Bin Ladenism.

When Awaji walked into the lobby of my Riyadh hotel, he looked around with obvious discomfort, scanning the area for government spies. He then stroked his long beard and proposed to have tea in an outdoor coffee shop. We settled under the neon lights of the futuristic Faysali skyscraper, one of Riyadh's two main landmarks. (The second landmark is a skyscraper with the top scooped out like a giant U; the span, the local post–September 11 joke goes, was made wide enough for a Boeing 747 to fly through.)

Awaji's robe was pitched to midcalf, revealing bare feet in the fashion practiced by rigid *salafi* Islamists, who emulate the prophet's seventh-century companions, the *salaf*. On his head he wore an unwrapped white scarf, its ends hanging down along the sides of the face. Awaji was famous, having just appeared on Al Jazeera, the Qatar-based satellite TV network, to air his mild criticism of the royal family. The repressive regimes in the Middle East, he said on TV, are to blame for the emergence of terrorism. As we sipped our tea, young passersby stopped at the table, paused as they recognized Awaji, and then enthusiastically embraced him. "You are so brave," some said. "It was great."

Awaji was a little embarrassed. "The people are thirsty for heroes. But I am no hero," he said with a dull smile. As I talked to him, that evening and several times afterward, I fought mixed emotions. His discourse was refreshingly modern when compared to official Saudi Islam, but I couldn't figure out whether he actually meant what he said or was simply trying to charm me. Would the West, and Saudi Arabia, be necessarily worse off if people like him were allowed to seize power one day?

Politically, like many Islamist activists of his generation, Awaji was far more confrontational than official Wahhabi scholars. Even as he delivered his views to a Westerner with the smoothness of a public relations guru, he didn't hide his belief that America is a clear threat to Islam and Muslims worldwide, nor his faint admiration for Bin Laden. Awaji thought that the Taliban in Afghanistan and the guerrillas in Iraq are fighting a justified jihad against American colonialism, and he yearned for the day when America and the West are defeated and expelled from the Persian Gulf. And, like every Islamist, he was aghast at the very idea of reconciling with the "Zionist entity."

"We believe our rights were taken from us by those who invaded our lands," Awaji said. The only solution to such violence, he added, was counterviolence: "Might is right. Palestinians, for example, have developed a special weapon—the suicide bomber. And they have been very successful."

But unlike the guardians of establishment Islam, such as Justice Minister al Sheikh, Awaji has mastered the politically correct language of the modern world. He said he wanted to improve women's rights and eventually extend freedom of religion to the kingdom. He campaigned for freedom of the press and Western-style democratic elections. "People who are ignoring the facts and trying to show to others that we have no problems are the same ones responsible for the explosive problems that threaten to destroy our society," he scoffed. Every few minutes he mentioned human rights: "We want a reasonable relationship with the royal family, not the one of masters and slaves." He even had kind words to say about Majlis al Shura, the toothless Saudi legislature whose members are appointed by the king and can't adopt binding decisions.

"It's good that we learn how to sit down at a table, how to raise our hand for permission to speak, and how to ask questions," he said. "In the future there will be the same chairs and the same microphones. The only difference will be that the deputies will be elected." It occurred to me that this idea of democracy wasn't necessarily comforting—surely the reason why the United States never actually pushed the Saudis toward democratic reform. "If I wanted to be elected in Saudi Arabia, I would not campaign on the issue of coexistence," Awaji explained with frankness. "If you want to be elected here, you have to raise the issue of jihad against the Crusaders."

✦   ✦   ✦

Like the Soviet Politburo in the 1980s, the top rungs of the Saudi ruling family are hard for outsiders to scrutinize. "The ones who know what's going on in the family don't talk, and the ones who talk don't know," goes a frequent refrain.

To the house of Saud, Awaji and even more radical clerics directly involved with the terrorist underground are not without use—if only to scare away post–September 11 Western pressure, limited as it is, to uphold human rights and introduce democracy. "If you want to imagine Saudi Arabia without al Saud, look no further than Afghanistan under the Taliban," one slick Saudi spook told me earnestly as we talked over $10 espressos in a five-star London hotel. But, I wondered, can the royal family really keep its kingdom under control now that the genie of Wahhabi fanaticism has increasingly turned against it? And how exactly does this desert dynasty function?

Even among the world's royal families, usually not the most harmonious of households, al Saud are a peculiarly dysfunctional bunch—

tragically so, considering that a crisis in the kingdom is capable of generating shock waves thousands of miles away.

The family lives in a state of suspended quarrel largely because of the rules of succession established by the modern Saudi Arabia's founder, King Abdelaziz, who died in 1953. Unlike European royals, the Saudi kings do not pass the crown from father to son or—unthinkable—daughter. Instead, power is transferred among Abdelaziz's sons, going to the younger ones as the oldest brothers die off, a system of succession that's not uncommon in Muslim monarchies. Four of Abdelaziz's sons have already served as kings. But Abdelaziz, who kept divorcing one or another of his four wives and remarrying every few weeks, fathered over forty boys, so there is still a large pool of aging monarchs-in-waiting.

The princes' order of seniority isn't strictly dependent on age. Merely being the oldest of Abdelaziz's surviving sons doesn't directly lead to the throne. For example, one of the most senior sons disqualified himself by an unfortunate camping accident. When the prince's retinue arrived at his favorite desert camping spot, the area was already occupied by a commoner. When he refused to budge, the prince slapped the commoner, who slapped the prince back. The prince, naturally, killed the offender. In an unpleasant complication, the dead man hailed from a powerful tribe, which yearned for revenge. So, as penance, the prince forfeited his claim to the throne and went into business.

As they wait their turn, the most senior princes, all of them now in their seventies or eighties, have presided for decades over Saudi Arabia's top national institutions, such as the ministries of defense, foreign affairs, and interior, the army and the National Guard. These bodies have become personal fiefdoms, with little central control over the purse strings and with minister-princes' sons often serving as deputy ministers to their fathers. And as top princes weave intrigues against each other, the parts of the government machinery that they supervise have become parties in this silent power struggle.

Every evening, Saudi TV newscasts open with the details of the top princes' comings and goings. Subdued classical music provides a background to the footage, organized strictly by the pecking order. First we see His Majesty the Custodian of Two Holy Places, Prime Minister and King Fahd bin Abdelaziz, paralyzed and by all accounts senile since the mid-1990s, as he's ferried out in a wheelchair to stare with blank eyes at visiting dignitaries. We never hear him speak, although he does occasionally manage a faint wave.

We then see the daily meetings of Crown Prince, First Deputy Prime Minister, Commander of the National Guard, Abdullah bin Abdelaziz—the kingdom's de facto ruler because of Fahd's malady. Tall and rough, he has a guttural voice that betrays his Bedouin upbringing in the barren wasteland that central Saudi Arabia was before the oil boom. Petitioners kiss him on the shoulder, bow, and gently hand him their letters. Briefly glancing at the requests, the octogenarian prince passes them to the aides standing behind. When a more formal meeting is called, we are shown the greetings and the farewells, and are told the full list of those present, down to the lowliest bureaucrat. But viewers rarely learn what was actually discussed or the outcome of the talks, even though, the next morning, pictures of the silent encounters take up entire pages of Saudi newspapers. On one unusual occasion, Prince Abdullah received a group of liberal activists petitioning him for gradual reforms; they told me about it hours later. The newspapers the following morning printed a picture of the petitioners' backs, with the crown prince looking into the camera, and the caption: "His Royal Highness received a group of citizens yesterday." Not a mention of the petition or its contents, or the petitioners' identity. The crown prince enjoys the reputation of a tepid reformer. But he isn't a full ruler, and he cannot do much because he can't give orders to the next men we see in the newscasts.

Following protocol, the TV news footage of Prince Abdullah is followed by a video of his main rival, His Royal Highness, Second Deputy Prime Minister, Minister of Defense and Aviation, Prince Sultan bin Abdelaziz. Probably the richest man on earth thanks to his oversight of lucrative defense contracts, Prince Sultan is counting on King Fahd's outliving Prince Abdullah, making him the next king.

After Prince Sultan comes another brother and rival, Interior Minister and Head of the Supreme Media Council, Prince Nayef bin Abdelaziz. He controls the security services and the police, and can hire and fire

Saudi newspaper editors at will. It took him two years after September 11 to admit that participation by Saudi citizens in the attack on America was not, as he put it initially, "malicious lies spread by the Zionist press." After Prince Nayef, who, like Prince Sultan, is a full brother of the king, we are shown a slew of lesser royalty. It isn't until the half-hour newscast's final minutes, if at all, that the real news begins. (In 1990, it took Saudi TV days to bother informing the citizenry that neighboring Kuwait had been captured by Iraq and that Saudi Arabia itself was in danger.)

✦ ✦ ✦

After meeting Wahhabi clerics among the establishment and the dissident fringe, I had to talk to Saudi Arabia's owners—the royal family. They were the people whose political skills would determine whether Saudi Arabia blows up one day in a revolution that may offer the kingdom's giant oil wealth to clerics bent on destroying the West, or instead manages a transition into the modern world. In a country unburdened by democratic institutions, it's the royal family who decides the speed of the political and economic reforms that are obviously needed to prevent just such a meltdown.

My wish came true well after midnight, when I was ushered into the seaside Jeddah palace of Prince Nawaf bin Abdelaziz, the head of the Saudi intelligence services and, as his name made clear, one of Abdelaziz's sons. The time wasn't all that unusual: many senior princes like him, well in their seventies, suffer from insomnia and prefer the relatively cool nights to the searing days. Working hours for many bureaucrats in the Saudi gerontocracy were rearranged accordingly.

His stern, lean face creased by the sun, Prince Nawaf began to seize the moral high ground by lecturing me on the behavior of America and Israel. He wasn't used to being interrupted, so it took a good hour of nodding to switch him to the topic of Saudi Arabia. Your Royal Highness, what about this country's crisis? What about the formerly jailed citizens, like Mohsen al Awaji, who are now openly pushing for reforms? What about your Islamist critics? "Well, we know that there are some people who have some ideas," he grunted. "We are trying to bring them back. We are discussing it with them. They must understand that we are part of this world." He thought for a moment. "If these people don't understand, we won't follow this path. But"—he looked at me—"we are not a regime that touches any person just because of political reasons." Although I knew otherwise, I didn't contradict.

Prince Nawaf, an ally of Prince Abdullah, was determined to uphold the kingdom's orthodox ways—to out-Islam the dissident Islamists. There will be no relaxation of Wahhabi traditions, he said. "Saudi Arabia is governed by Islam, we are in Islam, we have the law of Islam, and we are the heart of Islam around the world," the prince enunciated, waving his index finger. "Spreading Islam is our duty. This is what makes Saudi Arabia what it is. King Abdelaziz used Islam to make this country united, and Islam is the basis of everything here."

✦ ✦ ✦

Most of the nearly dozen other Saudi princes I met sounded just like Prince Nawaf. Sure, they would admit, as if letting me in on a state secret, there are some malcontents in the kingdom. But in the same breath they would assert that the royal family is basking in popular love and that there is little need for change. One of the more articulate princes I met, Prince Faisal bin Salman, a political scientist, nephew of the king, and son of the powerful governor of Riyadh, put it this way: "Many Saudis do not necessarily like our government, but they do recognize that it is necessary to maintain the stability and the coherence of the state." The dissidents, he assured me, "didn't have much support among the ordinary people. They were marginalized not just by the state but also by society."

Such soothing consistency from the princes didn't prepare me for the shock of meeting Prince Talal bin Abdelaziz. I knew that he was something of an oddball, one of the modernizing "Red Princes" who was briefly exiled in Egypt in the 1960s. A brother of King Fahd and Prince Abdullah, and the father of the jet-setting billionaire Alwaleed bin Talal, one of the largest investors in Citicorp, Prince Talal is a potential king and part of the royal family's eighteen-member council. In a visibly bad mood, he sat behind a desk in the large headquarters of a development fund that he chairs, addressing me in clipped, angry English.

"The family is divided—we used to come together, but now we see each other only on rare occasions," he said. "The family council—it doesn't meet anymore." Wow, I thought, that's the kind of frankness that only a king's brother, or the most foolhardy dissident, could afford in Saudi Arabia. But what about reforms, I wondered. Isn't Prince Abdullah trying to make things work? "Reforms? It's only words, unfortunately," Prince Talal shot back. "We live under one-man rule, and that man thinks he's God and a brilliant man, which is not true. Initiatives are made haphazardly, on a whim. We should sit down, all of us. We should know what is going on, know the background of all decisions. Right now, we are like in a cave—if you stand up, you bump your head against the ceiling."

Every Saudi king, he reminded me, promised moves toward democracy but stopped short of acting on these promises. Not such a bad thing, Prince Talal said after a pause. Elections without modernizing the country's Wahhabi society—a long, arduous process—would, he thought, make matters worse. Only real, rapid reforms will allow al Saud to survive.

He chafed at the restrictions on religious minorities. "The UN will ask us one day, Why are you not giving minorities their rights? Why do we always have to wait for pressure from the outside?" He also railed against Saudi education, which is dominated by the Wahhabi establishment and focuses on teaching Islam rather than sciences, foreign languages, and practical skills—yet more reasons why the kingdom must rely on foreign workers. "Our curriculums are known to be backward. So, when a child joins our education system, he often comes out half-illiterate," the prince said. "The accumulation of all these traditions has made a Saudi a lazy man."

In his final invective, Prince Talal called for sweeping away the conservative norms that are so close to the heart of Wahhabi clergy. "Is it plausible that Saudi Arabia is the only country in the world where there are no cinemas and the women can't drive?" he bellowed. I pondered these words for a few minutes. Then I understood why I couldn't find a single Saudi who believed that Prince Talal will ever be king.

✦　✦　✦

The United States has had to indulge the Saudi royalty for decades, abstaining from pressure for democratic reform and turning a blind eye to the proliferation of Wahhabi zeal around the world, for one simple reason. Saudi Arabia is the world's biggest oil power, and the United States, not to mention the global, economy would collapse if the kingdom turned off the tap one day. The result is a vicious circle: as we use Saudi petroleum to power our economies, some of the monies paid in exchange end up indirectly financing Islamic zealots who—in addition to committing terrorist acts that kill and injure thousands—blow up oil tankers off Yemen and pipelines in Iraq; the destruction makes our oil even more expensive. Reforming Wahhabi society or cutting the West's addiction to Saudi oil, if at all possible, will take a lot of time and effort. But what about simply decoupling the oil from Wahhabis?

My interest in this question was piqued in 2003, on a freezing January day in northern Virginia. I met there for coffee with a Saudi Shiite exile by the name Ali al-Ahmed. While the Shiite Muslim minority accounts for only about 10 percent of the kingdom's citizenry, it's a narrow majority in the Eastern Province—home to all of Saudi Arabia's oil. The Saudi Shiites derive little advantage from their land's mineral wealth and are usually excluded from prominent jobs. No Shiite has ever served as a Saudi government minister, and official religious tracts refer to Shiite Islam as a "heresy" invented by the Jews to undermine the true faith. The Wahhabi cleric from Riyadh who would talk to me only via an intermediary, Abdullah Saadun, put it this way: "The Shiites? They are enemy number one. And the victory will be ours, because God is with us."

From his exile in America, Ali al-Ahmed runs a Web site dedicated to exposing Wahhabi abuses and a think tank called the Saudi Institute; his activities have already prompted Saudi authorities to jail his brother as punishment. As we talked about Shiite suffering in the kingdom, Ahmed casually mentioned attending a conference on the Eastern Province sponsored by the Hudson Institute, a conservative U.S. think tank. There the institute's Max Singer had proposed splitting the Eastern Province, and its oil, into a separate, Shiite-run Muslim Republic of East Arabia. This proposal, allegedly backed by some Pentagon officials, was supposed to solve, very neatly, all of America's problems with the kingdom: Western economies would get cheap oil

from a new puppet state, while the Wahhabis in the rest of the kingdom would slide back into oil-less poverty and irrelevance. "If there is
such a republic, I would probably be one of the leaders," Ahmed said
dreamily, cradling his Styrofoam cup as snow fell outside. He already
had a name for the new country: the Republic of Hajjar.

Intrigued, I wanted to explore whether the Saudi Shiites really
wanted out of Saudi Arabia. Stranger things have happened. Many
similarly obscure dissident exiles, after all, ran newly independent
republics of the former Soviet Union—lands colonized by Moscow
centuries before Saudi Arabia coalesced in its present form in 1932.
Eastern Province separatist talk, I learned quickly, was taken with
extreme seriousness inside Saudi Arabia itself, enjoying a dual starring
role in the Islamist Web sites and the nightmares of Saudis of Wahhabi
stock. "Without Eastern Province oil, we'd be another Somalia,"
summed up Mohsen al Awaji, my dissident acquaintance in Riyadh.

✦ ✦ ✦

To explain the roots of this Shiite–Sunni divide, the source of often
violent tension from Pakistan to Lebanon to Iraq, one must reach back
to the dawn of Islam. The losers of a seventh-century contest for
power over the Muslim world, the Shiites practice an aggrieved,
mournful religion that is the product of a history that can only be
described as tragic. Shiites are a minority in all Arab states except Iraq
and Bahrain—and even there have always lived under the rule of the
Sunni elite. They are a plurality in Lebanon, where the president,
according to the constitution, must be a Christian and the prime minister a Sunni Muslim. Sunnis predominate in the wider Muslim world,
from West Africa to Indonesia. Among non-Arab Muslim countries,
only Persian-speaking Iran and Turkic-speaking Azerbaijan are firmly
in Shiite hands.

Iran's attempts to export its Islamic revolution after Ayatollah
Khomeini's takeover in 1979 have made Americans and Arab regimes
deeply suspicious of Shiites everywhere. One of the first major attacks
on Americans in Saudi Arabia, the 1996 bombing that killed nineteen
servicemen in the Al Khobar Towers compound in the Eastern Province, was blamed by Saudi authorities and the FBI on Saudi Shiites

affiliated with Iran; later, some U.S. officials concluded that Bin Laden may have been involved instead.

The initial schism between Shiite and Sunni sects of Islam erupted over the critical issue of who should succeed Prophet Mohammed as the caliph, or ruler and spiritual guide, of the entire Muslim community. The bloody events that led to the seventh-century divide are still alive in the Shiite popular imagination—and, just like Nativity and Passion plays in some Christian countries, are reenacted every year at Shiite festivals, at least in places where such productions are permitted by Sunni authorities.

The Shiites—a name that comes from Shiat Ali, or Party of Ali—thought that Ali ibn Abi Talib, the cousin and son-in-law of Prophet Mohammed, and the prophet's grandsons down the line, should be caliphs. Most Muslims at the time didn't believe in nepotism; in fact, the first three caliphs weren't related to the prophet by blood. The practice changed after the third caliph, Othman, was murdered under mysterious circumstances in Medina, in today's northwestern Saudi Arabia. Ali, who was married to the daughter of Prophet Mohammed's younger wife, was chosen by the faithful as the fourth caliph. Mohammed's jealous older widow, Aisha, didn't like the decision—and she famously rode a camel to battle against Ali, who by then had moved the Muslim capital from Medina to the Iraqi city of Kufa. Muawiya, the powerful governor of Damascus, also refused to recognize Ali, accusing him of harboring Othman's assassins. After Ali accepted independent arbitration, an extremist sect of his own supporters cried treason and sent an assassin to strike him with a poisoned sword in the year 661. Muawiya became the caliph.

Sunni domination over most of the Muslim world was sealed with the Shiite rout and the killing of Ali's son Hussain in the Iraqi city of Karbala, in 680—a commemoration of which, known as the Ashura, marks the central event of the Shiite calendar. (Saudi Shiites, unlike the ones in Iran, Lebanon, and now Iraq, aren't permitted to stage the self-flagellating marches to weep for Hussain that occur during Ashura.) The martyrdom of Hussain in the Shiite imagination parallels the sacrifice of Jesus in Christianity—and the cheap Iranian-made woven pictures of Hussain that are ubiquitous in Shiite lands, depicting his serene eyes and flowing long hair, could easily be mistaken for Christian imagery. In recent centuries, Sunni Ottoman sultans held the title of caliphs, until Turkey's secular ruler Ataturk wiped out the caliphate system altogether in 1924.

Since the age of Abdel Wahhab, Shiite "heresy" has been an enemy of the Saudi state. In 1801, Wahhabi raiders gutted the golden-domed mosque around Hussain's shrine in Karbala. Over a century later, in 1913, many Shiites were massacred and expropriated along the western shore of the Persian Gulf when al Saud's warriors seized what is now the Eastern Province from the Ottoman state.

This history meant that I wasn't going to tell the Saudi authorities—who, after much begging, granted me only a seven-day visa for a second trip to the country—what exactly I planned to do when I got to the kingdom's Shiite heartland.

✦ ✦ ✦

First I had to resolve a problem. The usual way to enter Saudi Arabia is to fly into Jeddah or Riyadh, where, as a foreign journalist, I was required to be met in the airport by a government minder. Once I was under his control, it would be hard to sneak away to the Eastern Province, because any trip there would automatically alert the authorities. A few months earlier, a colleague of mine from the *Wall Street Journal* traveled to oil-less southern Saudi Arabia to talk to tribal leaders of the Ismaili sect, an offshoot of Shiite Islam. The Ismailis—far less of a threat to the Saudi state than Eastern Province Shiites—complained about systematic discrimination at the hands of the kingdom's rulers. The government's reaction was to arrest almost all the Ismaili leaders who had dared to speak to my colleague. These men, who spent more than a year in jail, were freed only thanks to public pressure by Amnesty International and other human rights groups. Just weeks before the war on Iraq, the Shiite issue was even touchier. Long-oppressed Shiites make up the majority of Iraqis, and it was clear across the region that the looming war would open the prospect of a major Arab state run by Shiites for the first time in centuries. As it happened, Iraq's first postwar head of government, Eyad Allawi, was a Shiite, albeit of a secular kind.

So I devised a plan to tell the Saudi government that I would enter the kingdom from neighboring Bahrain. From there, I explained, I would take an internal flight from Dammam to Riyadh right away. In Riyadh, a minder would welcome me in the airport on the first morning of the work week. I made sure not to call, from overseas, the Shiite contacts given to me by dissidents, in case the Saudi authorities, who no doubt tap some of these activists' phones, would have time to preempt me.

It all worked. I flew a circuitous route via Germany and Qatar to Saudi Arabia's eastern back door, and, bleary-eyed, crossed the frontier early on Thursday morning—the beginning of the Islamic weekend. After dropping my bags at the hotel, I made the first call to Jaffar al Shayeb, a Shiite businessman and former Washington-based dissident who negotiated a truce with King Fahd in the 1990s that led to the removal of some of the harshest restrictions against the Shiites. Shayeb was only too eager to talk, and he quickly took me from Dammam, the provincial capital mostly populated now by Sunni migrants from the rest of Saudi Arabia, to the town of Qatif, once a bustling port, a center of the Gulf pearl trade and of Shiite religious life.

The town's depressing main square showed everything that is wrong with the eastern part of the country. It is in Qatif that repressed Shiites revolted in the wake of Iran's revolution, in a bloody uprising they call their first intifada. The Saudi government didn't just crush the revolt and machine-gun the protesters; it also sent an army of bulldozers to raze all of old Qatif, including its medieval alleys and narrow streets that had offered protection to rebels. Twenty years later, the former old town remains a vast expanse of rubble and rubbish, a reminder of the price that was paid for rising up against Riyadh. In one corner towers a huge new mosque. It is, of course, of the Sunni Wahhabi kind and attended only by Pakistani guest workers. Local Shiites go to the tiny *husseynia,* or community center and prayer hall, on the square's edge.

Shayeb invited a dozen Shiite notables into his home, and we all sat along the walls in his salad-green reception room. Like many Shiites, some of the guests wore Western-style clothes, dispensing with the white Bedouin robes and desert headdress that make up the virtual uniform of Saudi citizens in other parts of the country. For many, this was the first time they got to talk to a Western reporter, and they all wanted to make sure I understood how bad things were. Since many of these men were also shunned by American diplomats—careful not to offend Saudi officialdom—the atmosphere of pent-up anger and dizzying expectations was electric. At times I felt like a new age Lawrence of Arabia in the middle of a Bedouin plot to redraw the map of the Middle East. Some of my interlocutors clearly assumed that I must have represented official Washington and brushed off my earnest protestations to the contrary with a knowing smile.

Asking these men about their feelings for the Saudi state, I was well aware of the risks of frank speech in the kingdom and expected loaded allusions rather than explicit complaints. But, to my surprise, these Shiites didn't hold back. "Al Saud ruled over our resources for eighty years, and in all this time we got nothing. It is very difficult to achieve changes here unless we are supported by an outside power," intoned Syed Hassan Alawami, the community leader who ran the *husseynia* of old Qatif. The syed, a descendant of Ali, made sure I understood him fully. "The Shiites are not in direct conflict with the United States and are under oppression from others—so they would be the right group to coordinate with the United States."

Because Saudi officialdom banned Shiite books, he complained, all religious literature had to be smuggled, at great cost, from Bahrain, a neighboring country where violent opposition by the disenfranchised Shiite majority had recently prompted the Sunni ruling family to open up jails, allow free newspapers, and invite former Shiite dissidents to the top rungs of government. Other men in the room chimed in. One's son learned at school that Shiites are infidels. Another cited an official memorandum that forbade sharing food or charity with the Shiites. A third reminisced about how Shiites were treated fairly when Saudi Arabia's oil giant Aramco was under American management; now all desirable jobs went to Wahhabis from outside the Eastern Province. Wahhabi activists recently patrolled the streets of Dammam, distributing leaflets that urged fellow Sunnis to boycott Shiite-owned businesses. "If change doesn't come from above, it will come from below. If I stay nonviolent, my son won't," one man said.

Talk naturally veered to the great conspiracy theory: after Iraq, the United States will turn its attention to Saudi Arabia and carve out a Shiite petrostate in the Eastern Province. The Hudson Institute conference notwithstanding, I knew that virtually nobody in official Washington approved of the idea—at least not aloud. I had just been to Washington, I told my hosts, and I think only a very small part of the U.S. establishment actually advocates splitting up Saudi Arabia. There was a moment of silence. Then one of the men waved his hand at me and shouted at the top of his lungs: "A small part? Make it bigger, make it bigger." Others erupted in nervous giggling.

✦　✦　✦

Later that day, Shayeb took me from house to house to meet similar groups of prominent Shiites in neighboring towns. Together we sat cross-legged on the floor and shared grilled chicken in the house of Mohammed Mahfudh, the editor of a local literary magazine published in Lebanon and clandestinely brought into the kingdom. The man surveyed his guests—many of whom had been jailed for Shiite activism—and said quietly: "We've had enough of discrimination. National unity is not a goal in itself. If separation means that we'll get our rights, then of course we'd want it." Seconds later, just as bitterly, he accused America of always standing on the side of the tyrants in this part of the world. It was hard to decide whether these Shiites sought a real alliance with America, as dreamed by some people in Washington, or simply used a momentary confluence of interest in Iraq to further their own goals.

From Mahfudh's home we continued to the village of Awamiya, where I heard the story of another dispute stoking local, and historical, grievances. Some 125 years earlier, a local sheikh bought a beachfront piece of land, known as Ramiz, from the Ottomans. The land was bequeathed as a *waqf,* or communal property, to the entire village, which defended it against Wahhabi Bedouin raiders from farther inland. Awamiya men, famed for being fierce and sturdy, usually managed to repel the intruders. Shrimp and fish nested in the mangroves along the property's shore, providing jobs to local fishermen. The inner part of Ramiz produced succulent tomatoes, for which Awamiya is known across the area. Zaki Ali al Saleh, a member of the village committee and my escort, made sure we stopped by a cart full of these tomatoes on one of Awamiya's rundown streets so I could taste how sweet and juicy they are.

Then, in 1996, Prince Sultan, the minister of defense and second in line to the throne, simply decided he wanted to take the land, measuring some 8.4 million square meters and worth hundreds of millions of dollars. Unlike Wahhabi tribes in other parts of the kingdom, the Shiites here had no political connections or clout to oppose such expropriation. So the prince just seized the property, saying the villagers never held legal title, and quickly resold it to a private developer. Six years later, that developer—aided by Saudi security services—moved in with bulldozers to raze farms and crops. The villagers tried to resist, and a violent clash with the police ensued; scores ended up behind bars. Saleh wanted me to see the land; at sunset, we drove in his old car through the sands surrounding Ramiz. I became alarmed as the car almost got stuck twice and as occasional police patrols gave us dirty looks. But Saleh just kept talking.

"Our grandfathers shed blood for this land, and we are ready to do the same," he said as we passed a desolate landscape of bulldozed farm sheds, uprooted mangrove trees, and massive land reclamation works, all located behind a wall that ringed much of the beach. "See these birds? Soon they won't be here," he said as we drove near the shoreline. "This sea belongs to us, not al Saud. The government took our land simply because we are Shiite."

Later in the week, back in Riyadh, I described my trip to another prominent Saudi Shiite, university professor Alabdul Hai. "This problem is not in Awamiya and not in Qatif. This is a problem across the country," he replied, as his wife joined us for a cake—the first time that a Saudi man introduced me to his wife. Remarkably liberal for this country, the two believed the rot in the kingdom to be systemic. "The problem with the fanatical and narrow-minded interpretation of Islam does not concern the Shiites alone," the professor told me. "Everyone, except for the special elites, is suffering here."

3

TUNISIA

Teaching Freud to the Mullahs

Dressed in the best Saville Row fashion, Oussama Romdhani winced with disgust as he looked at the flat plasma screen suspended in his office. Below, on a Tunis avenue named after a French Socialist, women in jeans and short skirts—none of them veiled—congregated near fashion boutiques and chatted in sidewalk cafés. On TV, a fully veiled housewife touted the advantages of Ariel detergent to the pan-Arab audiences of the Abu Dhabi satellite channel.

"Satellite TV is a problem. They're bringing all this religious nonsense here, all those things that are alien to us," Romdhani sighed in flawless English as he examined the black *abayas* of the women in the next TV spot. Sophisticated Tunisia, he went on, had little in common with the primitive Bedouins of the Persian Gulf. "We're only a few dozen kilometers from Europe, after all," he said. "We're much closer to the Italians and the French."

I could appreciate the difference. I came to see Romdhani, the supremely efficient director of Tunisia's government information office, just a couple of weeks after leaving the country of another Oussama—or, as the name is more frequently spelled in English, Osama—Saudi Arabia.

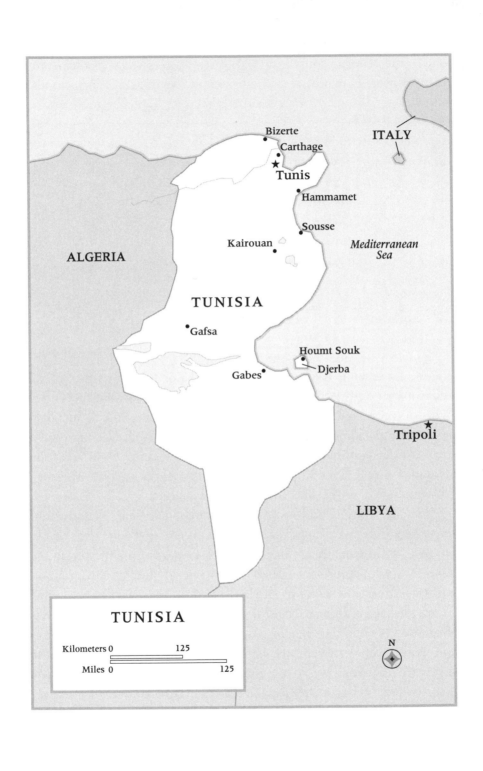

Bizerte

Carthage

★ Tunis

Hammamet

Sousse

Kairouan

ALGERIA

*Mediterranean
Sea*

TUNISIA

•Gafsa

Houmt Souk

•Djerba

Gabes•

ITALY

Tripoli ★

LIBYA

TUNISIA

Kilometers 0   125

Miles 0   125

N

A sunny nation of beachfront budget hotels just an hour's flight from Rome, Tunisia touts itself as a rare success story in the Arab world, especially when compared with its two neighbors, blood-soaked Algeria and international pariah Libya. In recent decades, a well-managed free-market economy, powered by tourism and labor-intensive industries like textiles, has transformed oil-less Tunisia into one of the most prosperous Arab states. Romdhani was right, in a way. Tunisia was very different from the rest of the Arab world. The land of ancient Carthage—whose ruins abut the presidential palace—Tunisia is the most secular Arab country and the only one that guarantees equal rights for women and men, bans polygamy, and even allows no-questions-asked abortions. Since independence from France in 1956 and until his demise three decades later, Tunisia's first president, Habib Bourguiba, himself married to a Frenchwoman, attempted a rerun of Ataturk's 1920s success in Westernizing another Muslim country, Turkey.

As nearby Algeria was scrapping French-language education and bringing in Muslim Brotherhood teachers from Egypt in the 1960s, Bourguiba took his country in the opposite direction, making sure that most Tunisians could converse in a European tongue. He disbanded the famous Zeitouna University, the oldest school of Islamic learning in the Muslim world and a hotbed of clerical opposition to his reforms. In 1964, Bourguiba caused considerable scandal by drinking a glass of orange juice on TV during the Islamic fasting month of Ramadan, and arguing that the fast was an unnecessary distraction from developing the country. Even Tunisia's flag is uncannily similar to Turkey's—a heritage of Tunisia's past as a dominion of the Ottoman Empire.

When Bourguiba reached the age of eighty in 1983, he proudly bore the title of president for life and could gaze upon statues of himself that towered above city squares across the country. At the same time, however, he started losing his grip. Energized by Bourguiba's haphazard governance and an economic downturn, Islamist politicians, led by the charismatic philosopher Rached Ghannouchi, pressed for power and for re-Islamizing the land. Tunisia's closest neighbors increasingly fretted that Bourguiba was too old and too sick to prevent the emergence of a militant Islamic state a mere hundred miles from Western European shores. Thus in November 1987, Tunisia's just-appointed prime minister, General Zine el Abidine Ben Ali, launched what would be known as the medical coup. Armed with a medical certificate proclaiming Bourguiba to be senile and therefore unfit to rule, and without firing a single shot, Ben Ali seized the presidency for himself. Italy's chief of intelligence claimed later that the Italian prime minister until 1987, Bettino Craxi, orchestrated the takeover. In a twist of history, Craxi himself died in self-imposed exile in Tunisia in 2000, convicted of fraud by an Italian court but sheltered by Ben Ali, who kept turning down Italy's extradition requests. Bourguiba died the same year, after a comfortable, if closely monitored, retirement.

✦ ✦ ✦

Since 1987, Ben Ali has unleashed an all-out campaign to smash Islamists—exiling Ghannouchi, imprisoning hundreds of dissidents, and reinvigorating the secularist drive. At the same time, even the limited political liberties enjoyed under Bourguiba were whittled away. As I arrived in Tunis in mid-2002, the nation's newspapers—even more controlled than Saudi Arabia's—brimmed with paeans to Ben Ali. His smug face smiled omnisciently from the numerous posters, billboards, and portraits that hung, it seemed, in every restaurant, office, or store. The government had just claimed that 99.5 percent of Tunisians voted to amend the constitution in a way that allowed Ben Ali, regularly reelected with over 99 percent of ballots cast, to serve as president indefinitely. A month earlier, in a worrying sign of suppressed resentment, a young Tunisian man smashed a truck filled with a daisy chain of cooking-gas canisters into a synagogue on the island of Djerba. In a twin blow against the country's Jewish minority and the Tunisian tourist industry, the government's key source of income, he managed to kill nineteen people, most of them European tourists. This side of Tunisia was depressingly familiar.

How lasting could Tunisia's secular experiment be? Ataturk, after all, had dragged the rump of the defeated Ottoman Empire into modernity in the distant 1920s—playing on Turkish nationalism at a time when human rights groups barely existed, democracies were on the defensive, and government foes couldn't whip up passions via satellite TV channels and the Internet. Yet even in Turkey, jihadi feelings still rumbled behind the surface, and Turkish Islamist radicals, like their Tunisian brethren, delighted in blowing up synagogues. In more recent times, a secularist effort by the shah of Iran ended up producing a religious backlash, turning over that country to the ayatollahs' theocracy. Isn't the Tunisian regime, probably more autocratic than the shah's had been, doomed to the same fate? The explosion in Djerba, and the prominent role of exiled Tunisian Islamists in terror attacks around the world, including the March 11, 2004, devastation in Madrid, certainly gave reason to worry.

On my first night in Tunis, I picked up a bottle of cold beer from my hotel minibar and recalled Ghannouchi's often-cited dictum. "Secularism came to us on the back of a tank," the exiled philosopher had written, "and it has remained under its protection ever since." Then I switched on the TV. In a demonstration of where true sympathies might lie in this secular state, someone among the hotel's staff preprogrammed the satellite TV to start with Al Manar, the channel of Lebanon's fundamentalist Hezbollah militia, which is considered by the United States to be a terrorist organization. Hezbollah's veiled announcer was crowing about the latest heroic attacks on Zionist bus passengers in Tel Aviv and about the American enemy's evil designs on the Middle East.

✦   ✦   ✦

To understand the changes in Tunisian Islam, I was told again and again, from day one in the country, I had to learn about Zeitouna—now, and in the past. The name of the famed academy popped up in nearly all conversations, a symbol claimed by government secularizers and Islamist dissidents alike.

For most of its history, the university was part of a mosque, just like its younger Egyptian counterpart, Al Azhar. Founded around 734, on the ruins of once-Christian North Africa, Zeitouna flourished after Mongol invaders sacked the two older academies of Muslim learning, in Baghdad and Damascus. Unscathed by wars, Zeitouna still dominates the lively old city of Tunis. A compound of arched walls and cobbled plazas ringed by ancient columns stripped from Carthage, Zeitouna is topped by a carved stone cupola—and is locked up except for the short prayer times. That's official policy for all Tunisian mosques, lest they become breeding grounds of dissent. The empty courtyards, once bustling with students, provide a sleepy abode for hundreds of pigeons. Infidel tourists are bused in every day to peer through the mosque's fence.

For more than a millennium before President Bourguiba evicted Zeitouna's bearded scholars and students, in 1956, this university spread Islamic knowledge across North and West Africa as far away as Nigeria and Senegal, educating generations of scholars and politicians. The curriculum went beyond pure theology, inculcating Muslim-colored versions of science, history, and math. The university itself was at the peak of a Zeitouna system of Islamic education that began with elementary school and, before 1956, taught 27,000 students a year. Zeitouna was where Ghannouchi and many other prominent dissidents of the older generation learned to embrace political Islam.

Sensing my interest, Romdhani instantly set me up with a man who had studied in the old Zeitouna—and who has become a most uncompromising enemy of religious education. Abdallah Amami, who introduced himself as a writer and former Tunisian diplomat, sat on a cushy leather chair in a room next to Romdhani's office and didn't mince words.

The old Zeitouna was nothing to wax nostalgic about, he thought. "This was an archaic, medieval place. Back in 1956, we were still studying an Islamic law course on how to treat slaves and on how to punish a slave who escapes from a master—and this in Tunisia, which abolished slavery in 1846!"

The three thousand male-only university students—Tunisians, Algerians, Libyans, and Africans from farther south—used to lounge on the mosque's mats, learning by rote. "They didn't teach us to think but to memorize," Amami told me. "The goal was to perpetuate the tradition, so that the present resembles the past, and the year 2000 looks like the year 1000."

After leaving Zeitouna and tasting secular education, Amami was shocked by the disparity. At the Islamic academy, he had been told that Vasco da Gama was following the real explorer, Arab navigator

Ibn Majid. Descartes, he had thought, copied from the Moghul Muslim emperor Shah Jahan, who built the Taj Mahal. And Dante plagiarized from the blind Arab poet Abu al Alaa al Maari. "For fourteen centuries the Muslims have been falsifying their history. They never learned it as it was. The truth was always adapted to improve the image of Islam," Amami said.

After my weeks-long stay in Saudi Arabia, these words sounded refreshingly bold—and I told Amami, half joking, that he'd probably be considered a blasphemer and put to death in the Saudi kingdom. This mention of Saudi Arabia, and of Persian Gulf charities funding Islamic causes around the world, made him cringe. Tunisia, of course, was interested in developing Gulf markets and maintaining friendly ties with the oil-rich monarchies, he said. "But," he added, "we must take our precautions. The cultural products, and especially the books from the Gulf, don't enter here." In the twilight of the Bourguiba era, Saudi Arabia's Wahhabi religious establishment flooded libraries in Tunisia—as in the rest of the Muslim world—with Qurans and books propagating its particular brand of Islam. When I learned this, I nodded in recognition—on a visit to Pakistan, I had a hard time finding a non-Saudi book on Islam in Islamabad's English-language bookstores.

When Ben Ali's regime cracked down on Islamists in the late 1980s, it quickly understood the perils of such proselytism. Legions of censors have been dispatched to comb bookstores and libraries for Wahhabi propaganda. "We noticed that a huge percentage of books in the libraries had been sent by Saudi Arabia, and so we took them all out and turned them into pulp," Amami recalled with a self-satisfied smile.

But wasn't this an exaggerated response? I asked. After all, Tunisian Islamists such as Ghannouchi, Amami's former classmate at Zeitouna, were viewed as remarkably moderate by the region's standards. Unlike their brethren in Algeria, who responded to government repression in 1991 by launching a civil war that killed some 200,000 people and still continues, the Tunisian movement was, by and large, nonviolent—at least until the synagogue bombing in Djerba.

But to Amami, all political Islam was inherently evil and bound to become violent if circumstances permit. Referring to "moderate Islamists" was an oxymoron, like "moderate Nazis." "Islamism is a totalitarian way of thinking. It negates the existence of an individual, dividing the world into a Muslim *ummah* and the infidel rest. The Islamists do not share with us the minimal set of values that makes coexistence possible," he said. I wasn't surprised to learn later that Amami was better known to Tunisian dissidents as a former senior censor.

As I bade my farewell, Romdhani caught up with me in the hallway and handed over a dossier of clippings on Ghannouchi and other Tunisian Islamists. Among other things, the folder included a fiery speech Ghannouchi had given at a convention of Islamic revolutionaries in Khomeini's Tehran. "Make no mistake. They are all dangerous," Romdhani assured me.

◆　◆　◆

Zeitouna itself, I learned from Amami, wasn't quite dead. Ben Ali reopened the university, now strictly a theological school, after coming to power in 1987. Unlike Bourguiba, who rejected Islamic institutions wholesale, Ben Ali sought to create an official theology, a sort of Islam-lite that would give a religious blessing to the secular reforms. But even though it was no longer housed in the hallowed Zeitouna mosque, the school quickly resumed its role as a focus of Islamic unrest. The government felt that it had to reinvent Zeitouna from scratch—and so it brought in a secularist intellectual, Mohamed Mahjoub, to revamp the curriculum in 1995.

Mahjoub, too, was ready to meet me—again in the same leather chair adjoining Romdhani's office. Just like Amami and Romdhani, he wore an elegant European-cut suit. Mahjoub, a philosopher who still edited Zeitouna's academic journal, told me he thought that the entire way of teaching Islam had to be revolutionized. "We need to reinvent Islam. It's necessary to be receptive to the spirit of other religions, to foster tolerance," he explained. "We need to inject skepticism, to teach people that what they think is a truth isn't necessarily so."

The challenge of reconciling Islam with modernity could be met, he believed. "If we marginalize the religion, it will breed fanaticism and extremism. But what we can do is to reunderstand our religion, to bring it alive." As I listened to him, I couldn't help noticing how well Tunisian officialdom mastered the politically correct language of the West, preaching the gospel of tolerance, while at the same time showing old-fashioned cruelty when it came to crushing potential opponents—religious or secular.

The next day, stirred up by all this talk of a new, tolerant Islam seeking to build bridges to the West, I went to see the new Zeitouna for myself. The nondescript building that now housed the Islamic academy—miles away from the Zeitouna mosque—was virtually empty. I had an appointment with the rector, Mohammed Toumi, and was half expecting a bearded, turbaned scholar in a traditional tunic. Instead, I was greeted by a short, clean-shaven man wearing a by-now-familiar bureaucrat's suit.

Toumi had been a professor of Islam in Qatar University, the base of probably the most influential Muslim cleric these days, the Egyptian-born Al Jazeera telepreacher affiliated with the Muslim Brotherhood, Yousuf Qaradawi. Toumi told me he had been fired from the job in Qatar for being insufficiently anti-Semitic, preaching respect for the Jews. When I asked him whether he had been on a pilgrimage to Mecca, he frowned and answered that he won't set foot in "unfree" Saudi Arabia. Once again, I listened to Tunisia's credo of force-feeding religious tolerance. "The Quran has 125 verses that insist on religious freedom and that ask Muslims to respect others," Toumi explained, as I mentally counted the number of times he used the word *tolerance* and its variations.

To open up students' minds and vaccinate future graduates against narrow-minded fundamentalism, he told me, Zeitouna taught such unconventional subjects as Darwin's theory of evolution and Freudian psychoanalysis. It also provided exhaustive lectures on non-Muslim religions and placed a special emphasis on foreign languages— including a course in Hebrew, taught by a female Muslim professor. Women, I was told, outnumber Zeitouna's male students—and, *mais bien sûr*, are forbidden to wear veils.

Enrollment for Tunisian students was highly restricted. During the weeks when I was in the country, Toumi said, all the local students were away on vacation, even though other Tunisian universities still had classes. But Toumi offered to introduce me to Zeitouna's foreign students. Although lacking the means of Saudi Arabia's Wahhabi missionaries, the Tunisian government, too, was eager to spread its rival version of Islam around the world. Ben Ali's regime picked up the bill for Zeitouna's foreign students, mostly from sub-Saharan Africa but also from as far away as Macedonia and Indonesia, and paid them a $50 monthly stipend. As far as I could tell, these students, who made up half the school, seemed thoroughly convinced by Zeitouna's—and Ben Ali's—brand of Islam-lite.

Diomande Soumaila, a twenty-two-year-old student from a Muslim region in the northern Ivory Coast, volunteered that Zeitouna's classes set his thinking apart from countrymen who had picked up generous fellowships to study in Saudi Arabia. "These people think that one must grow a big beard and don a Bedouin gown to be a good Muslim," he said. "Here in Tunis, they teach us to use our own heads, instead of simply following the Quran and the Sunna."

Zeitouna was only part of the government's apparatus of controlling Islam. At the head of the pyramid sat yet another bureaucrat in a suit, Religious Affairs Minister Jalloul Jeribi. He told me that all of the nation's thirteen thousand imams, or prayer leaders, had to be appointed by his ministry, after passing tests of religious and general knowledge—and of political correctness. Ministry supervisors, trained at Zeitouna, regularly visited mosques, making sure no untoward ideas were disseminated.

Another group of Zeitouna graduates—schoolteachers of Islam—protected young minds from the perils of religious zeal. "That's a very delicate task—after all, teachers can create fundamentalists at these lessons," the minister exclaimed.

I asked him whether that was how the suicide bomber in Djerba received his ideas. Taken aback, Jeribi hastened to point out that the bomber had spent several years in the West. "No, no, here in Tunisia, the entire society completely rejects fundamentalism. What happened in Djerba, this was a Western import," he said.

I pressed the minister on what was different about Tunisia's official Islam. He reflected and then beamed at me, outstretching his hands. "Here we interpret all the texts with a rational reflection. So, for example, we do not consider that for women to wear a veil is fundamental. In Islam, we should only follow the big headlines, not the small print."

The veil policy—as in Turkey—was the cornerstone of Tunisia's

Islam-lite doctrine and an inspiration for a later veil ban in France's public schools. The government's chief veil specialist at the time was Chedlia Boukchina, a senior bureaucrat in Ben Ali's party and the head of Tunisia's official women's association. An obligatory presidential portrait on her office wall was complemented by a flattering photograph of the veil-less first lady. A former schoolteacher of Arabic, Boukchina herself wore an elegant green suit and a scarf, wrapped around the neck rather than covering the head. Women had it better in Tunisia than anywhere else in the Arab world, she said. Laws ensured access to jobs and education, and a family code enshrined equal rights denied to Arab women elsewhere. "We are Muslims who live in harmony with modernity, just like the Christians do in Europe and America," she said. "Generations have now been raised on the idea of women's emancipation. No parent can think of keeping his daughter at home instead of sending her to school. No Tunisian these days can imagine living with two wives."

But what about the veils? Wasn't it unfair that the government—taking an example from Turkey—barred women who chose to wear a veil from schools, jobs, and government offices? What about personal freedom?

Boukchina smiled and organized a little fashion show for me. "When I was a teenager, I also wore one," she confided. The government, she explained, had no problem with traditional Tunisian women's headdress, such as the white *sefseri*—a contraption that old women hold in place by clutching the two ends of the cloth with their teeth.

Removing her scarf from the neck, Boukchina threw it atop her head in a loose wrap, leaving much of the hair exposed. "We also have no problem with this—a Benazir Bhutto–style modern veil," she said.

Then she spread out the scarf, covering all of her neck and all of her hair and ears, leaving open just the oval of her face. "And this, this is a political, Saudi-style veil. This we won't accept," she said. "Never."

✦ ✦ ✦

There was a grimmer side to Tunisia's Islam-lite, which I saw later that evening in the lobby of my hotel. My guest was Lassaad Jaouhari, an Islamist activist who coordinated the nation's committee for supporting the hundreds of Tunisia's political prisoners. In the 1980s, Ben

Ali started out by jailing Islamists, but in later years he increasingly imprisoned secular dissidents, too. Jaouhari himself spent seven years behind bars for supporting Ghannouchi's outlawed party, Nahdha. As Jaouhari walked in, scanning the lobby for the ever-present informers, he limped and balanced his body with a walking stick.

The disability, he explained right away as I watched him maneuver into a chair and order tea, was a result of long torture in Ben Ali's prisons. Jaouhari, who still preached nonviolent resistance to the regime, was alarmed by the bombing in Djerba and other bloodshed he saw on the horizon. "We're telling our young people that this is not the way, but many are so angry with what's going on in this country that they no longer listen to us," he said. "It's very dangerous."

Over tea, Jaouhari took out photocopies of government instructions that ordered police to detain women wearing veils and to forcibly remove them in public places. "That's their tolerance," he sneered.

I asked him about the experiment with reinventing Islam at Zeitouna. Wasn't there some merit in these attempts to bridge Islam with modernity? "Zeitouna? But there is no Zeitouna in Tunisia anymore," he replied. The only real Zeitouna nowadays, Jaouhari said, was on the satellite dial, in the form of a TV channel beamed by Ghannouchi's supporters from London. Only on this Zeitouna TV, he thought, was true wisdom taught—between images of Islamic "martyrs" tortured to death in Tunisian jails.

◆　◆　◆

Back when the anti-Islamist repression was in full swing, in the early 1990s, many secular Tunisians supported the crackdown—seeing political Islam as a greater evil than Ben Ali's dictatorship. One of them, magistrate Mokhtar Yahyaoui, personally prosecuted many Islamists, like Jaouhari, at the time. Then he demanded a more impartial justice system, and was promptly fired from his job and blacklisted as a dangerous dissident. When I met him, unemployed and harassed by police, in his apartment near the souk in Tunis, he openly regretted this past.

"The other political currents didn't want to help the Islamists, viewing them as more dangerous than the regime. So the regime followed up by destroying everyone else and confiscating all power," he lamented.

Now secular dissidents like Yahyaoui had no choice but to strike an alliance with the Islamists, the only opposition force with significant organization and financial muscle. I found this especially depressing. The West—by encouraging Ben Ali's repression in the name of combating Islamic radicalism—was pushing its natural allies, the secular and educated elite, into a deadly embrace with political Islam. This looked distressingly similar to the shah's Iran, where the ayatollahs used an alliance with secular left-wingers to overthrow the regime, only to eliminate erstwhile allies and erect an Islamic republic.

Another Tunis dissident, human rights campaigner Sihem Bensedrine, explained that secular pro-democracy activists like her were caught in a no-win situation. The previous year she had been arrested in the Tunis airport and jailed for six weeks, for criticizing Ben Ali on a London-based satellite TV channel, Al-Mustaqilla. Since then, Al-Mustaqilla had yielded to Tunisian government complaints and stopped its regular shows dedicated to Tunisian affairs. With Tunisia's own media ignoring the dissidents—or condemning them as traitors and Zionist spies—Bensedrine had only one other option: Ghannouchi's Zeitouna TV.

"I'm against fundamentalism, but I have no choice," she said, explaining that her phone and Internet access are cut off so often that she mostly works out of Internet cafés. "If I want to express myself, I've got to go on Zeitouna."

Bensedrine was a small, fragile-looking woman with unkempt hair, her messy apartment crammed with pro-democracy manifestos and copies of a samizdat magazine she was publishing. She reminded me of the Soviet dissidents who, in the 1970s and 1980s, composed similar newsletters in equally messy Moscow apartments. Except, of course, that in Tunisia's case the democratic West firmly backed Ben Ali's regime, not the dissidents. Hailed as a model moderate Muslim, the Tunisian president was a frequent guest to the White House and European capitals. To qualify as a moderate, he had only to use familiar language, employing catchwords like *democracy, tolerance,* and *human rights*— while emptying these concepts of any substance at home.

In the late 1990s, Europe and the United States seriously tried to push Tunisia to respect human rights. Now, in the name of the war on terror, all such pressure has been abandoned. "Everything is set back right to the beginning, and since September 11, Ben Ali has a free hand again," Bensedrine complained. The Islamists, of course, were the ultimate winners, with painful long-term consequences for the West, now seen by many Tunisians as betraying the ideals of democracy and backing oppression. "Wearing a veil has become a symbol of resistance for all," Bensedrine told me. "It's really a pity that resistance to the regime has become identified with Islam."

✦   ✦   ✦

The island of Djerba, where a suicide bomber had struck the previous month, has always been a refuge of persecuted minorities in the region. One of these groups that inhabited Djerba's flat, palm-tree-lined expanse of white stucco houses for centuries was the Jews. Another minority was made up of the Kharijites, adepts of a Muslim sect that almost vanished from the rest of the Middle East and was a byword for uncompromising radicalism at the dawn of Islam. It is the Kharijites who murdered Prophet Mohammed's son-in-law Ali and pioneered the practice of *takfir*—labeling as infidels fellow Muslims accused of insufficient observance. In recent times, this practice has been resurrected by Bin Laden and fellow jihadi ideologues to justify attacking Muslim governments in Egypt, Saudi Arabia, or Tunisia itself. Djerba's suicide bomber was not a Kharijite. But I found a certain historic irony in the fact that Qaeda-affiliated militants, denounced as "neo-Kharijites" by moderate Muslims, chose to strike in a rare spot where the original, and nowadays peaceful, Kharijite community still existed.

The blast's target was Djerba's Ghriba synagogue, the site of an annual international pilgrimage and, by most accounts, the oldest Jewish temple in Africa. By the time I arrived, the Tunisian authorities, who insisted for several days that the explosion had been accidental, had already repaired the synagogue's damaged courtyard wall. The striking white-and-blue building, its interior lined with jewelry donated by the faithful from all over the Mediterranean shores, was intact. I asked a guard where exactly the bomb detonated.

Showing the perfect reflexes of someone living in a totalitarian state, he looked straight into my eyes and asked, nonplussed: "What bomb?" A tourist season was starting, and nobody wanted to talk about bombs.

✦　✦　✦

Ghriba was one of fourteen still-active synagogues in Djerba—an island that long attracted the most pious and traditionalist families. Before the Zionist plan to create a Jewish national home in Palestine threw the region into turmoil, millions of Jews lived in the Arab world, often sharing their Muslim compatriots' nationalist feelings. The two most important Arab nations, Egypt and Iraq, both had Jewish government ministers in the 1920s. After the creation of Israel, the wave of pogroms and restrictions persuaded most of the Arab world's Jews to pick up stakes and leave, for the new Jewish state or the West. Almost all those remaining fled after a new round of anti-Jewish violence followed the Arab defeat in the 1967 war. My wife, then a wide-eyed two-year-old, was among those refugees, uprooted from the burning Jewish ghetto of Tripoli, Libya, and transplanted to Rome. Her parents, who still speak an Arabic dialect to each other and reminisce every day about a homeland lost, have never been allowed to return, even for a visit; they left most of their belongings behind. In the global scheme of things, they were, of course, lucky. While an independent Libya denied citizenship to Tripoli's Jews, Libya's former colonial power, Italy, recognized them as its own citizens and offered refuge. This gave my wife a chance to grow up a free person in a free country, accepted as an Italian and unburdened by ghetto walls. That's much better than the fate of all those Palestinians who trekked into exile before and after the same 1967 war, who ended up in squalid refugee camps, and who have been prohibited to this day from integrating into surrounding societies by the deliberate policy of most Arab states.

The Jews of Djerba were one of a handful of Jewish communities that survived in the lands of Islam after 1967. In part, their good fortune resulted from Bourguiba's relative tolerance. But more important, for the rabbis of Djerba, Israel and France—which now housed most of Tunisia's former Jewish community—were countries that seemed godless and corrupt. The only home for the truly faithful, they thought, was in the Hara Kbira, the ghetto of whitewashed homes with intense blue windows a few miles away from the island's capital city, Houmt Souk. This community saw hard times in the final years of Bourguiba's rule, when the Islamist movement was at its zenith and some government officials openly encouraged anti-Semitism. In 1985 a Tunisian police officer whose brother had been killed in an Israeli air raid on Yasser Arafat's PLO headquarters near Tunis went berserk and gunned down three people in the district of Djerba's Jewish-run shops.

But the bad times were, for now, gone. President Ben Ali was well aware that moderation on the issue of Israeli–Palestinian conflict and magnanimity with Tunisia's tiny Jewish community served him as valuable currency in Washington—and probably mattered much more than his overall human rights record. So in the 1990s, Ben Ali established a Tunisian mission in Tel Aviv, allowed Israelis to visit, and granted the Jews of Djerba a religious freedom that was denied to Tunisia's Muslim majority. Under Ben Ali's protection, Hara Kbira became the only oasis of tolerated fundamentalism in an otherwise assertively secular nation.

✦ ✦ ✦

Ben Ali's portraits now lined the Djerba ghetto's walls, welcoming passersby from every corner, sometimes in clusters of dozens—an intensity of adulation well outstripping the rest of Tunisia. Youssef Ouazan, the president of the Hara Kbira Jewish Committee and my minder while in the ghetto, flowed with gratitude. "The president of the republic loves the Jews and takes good care of us, so nobody dares to touch us anymore," he said.

Unlike ordinary Tunisians, who are required to attend state-run coed schools, the Djerba Jews run their own strictly religious, gender-segregated education system. Ouazan took me to the yeshiva for boys, its walls decorated with portraits of bearded rabbis provided by Shas, the Israeli party that represents ultra-Orthodox Jews from the Muslim world. The teacher, Mikhael Yaich, was busy drumming in a new prayer. Unlike virtually all the Tunisians I had met so far, he spoke no French. On my urging, Yaich asked the boys to raise a hand if they'd ever studied secular subjects like physics or math. Only a few hands went up—students whose parents had decided to supplement the yeshiva with a few courses in the state system.

"I personally never set foot in a secular school, and I won't let my daughter do it, either," Yaich puffed in a local Arabic dialect mixed with Hebrew words. "It's against our religion." Learning foreign languages such as French was undesirable because such knowledge would pollute the pure local minds, he said.

At a girls' school nearby, the ambience was a bit more relaxed. Israeli-trained instructors were teaching new songs, and the wall was covered with a huge fresco of Pikachu, the Japanese cartoon hero's name written below in steady Hebrew letters. I couldn't help wondering whether this affection for Pikachu was in any way connected with recent Saudi *fatwas* that banned Pokémon characters as a Zionist poison. At a local grocery, run by a Muslim, a sign warned in Arabic written with Hebrew script that the ice cream contained nonkosher ingredients. I tried to speak to a local woman, enveloped in a dress that would pass muster with Saudi Arabia's Committee to Promote Virtue and Prevent Vice. Ouazan quickly stepped in to stop me. "The rabbis have told our women not to speak with outsiders," he explained.

After a day in Hara Kbira, I met for dinner the only Djerba Jew living outside the ghetto. Annie Kabla, a buoyant restaurant and Internet café owner, decided to remain in Tunisia even though much of her family had emigrated. "I'm 100 percent Jewish, 100 percent Arab, and 100 percent Tunisian," she proudly said over spicy Tunisian sandwiches made of tuna and red-pepper paste. "I firmly intend to stay put. Here is our home."

Kabla was grateful for Ben Ali's protection of the Jews but was uneasy with the special treatment—sensing that allowing Jews what's prohibited to Muslims can only encourage lethal resentment. "All the world's eyes are on Tunisia, and on the Tunisian Jews, these days," she mused. "So if the police start bothering the Jews because they refuse to send children to secular school, it will be seen as an act of racism, unfortunately."

Tunisia's Islamists were already exploiting the Jewish card against Ben Ali's regime. Ghannouchi had loudly complained about the "discrimination against the majority" and even authored an article entitled

"If I Were a Jew, I Wouldn't Have Faced All the Difficulties I Face." As I looked up dissident Web sites following the synagogue bombing in Djerba, I was struck by the virulence of the attacks on Tunisian Jews—not, as one would expect, for supporting Israel but for their backing of Ben Ali's regime. This was, of course, a millennial conundrum faced by precarious minorities living under dictatorial rule. Seeking the dictators' protection was usually the only salvation—but, in the long term, such a policy turned the minority into a natural scapegoat once the dictatorship collapsed. And, one day, all dictatorships collapse.

✦ ✦ ✦

Thanks to Zeitouna—the satellite TV station rather than his former alma mater—Ghannouchi could still spread the Islamist message to Tunisia, bypassing Ben Ali's censors. The exiled philosopher lived in a small, northern London house in a mostly Pakistani neighborhood that radiated wrong-side-of-the-tracks desolation. I traveled there a couple of days after returning from a Tunisia that Ghannouchi himself hadn't seen since 1989.

An aide met me at a trash-strewn subway station exit and we walked several blocks under a drizzle. Ghannouchi's reception room was a sheer jolt of color amid all this drabness. Painted in an intense, almost painful, blue, the room doubled as a TV studio—Zeitouna TV technicians needed the blue background to superimpose other imagery, such as pictures of "martyrs" and verses of the Quran. From this living room, Ghannouchi continued waging war on Ben Ali and secularism back home.

Tunisia's Islamists—just like the Saudi, Algerian, or Egyptian dissidents who are often sympathetic to Qaeda—long used Britain's liberal laws to campaign against their countries' rulers. In a way, London—or, as some quipped, Londonistan—became in the 1990s an intellectual capital of the Arab world, a city where exiled revolutionaries put out dozens of newspapers and plotted political upheaval in run-down tea shops, makeshift mosques, and crowded Arab bookstores.

Ghannouchi, renowned around the Arab world for his books that expound the philosophy of political Islam, is a prominent figure on the Londonistan scene, with a stature far exceeding that of a mere dissident from a small place like Tunisia. Like many North African

Islamists, he shuns French—the language of the former colonizers and of the secular elite—and pointedly talked to me in the more neutral English. A calm, gathered man, he spoke in the soft voice of conviction, the voice of someone secure in the knowledge that history is on his side.

I asked Ghannouchi about the present incarnation of the famous university he had once attended and about Tunisia's efforts to reinvent the Islamic faith. "It's all only a facade. They want to convince people that Zeitouna still exists so that they would convince people in the Islamic world that Tunisia is still a Muslim country," Ghannouchi frowned. "Zeitouna today in Tunisia is like the elections they hold—all for show, just for export."

After years of wandering, Ghannouchi now thought in terms of the entire Muslim world, shunning Tunisian parochialism. Ben Ali's Islam-lite experiment was a hopeless endeavor, considering that Tunisia, with its ten million people, was a tiny sliver of the vast Arab and Muslim world. "They try to invent a new religion—but it's all in vain. Islam cannot be changed, cannot be transformed," he said. "The future of Tunisia can only be seen in the whole of the Muslim nation—and Islam is now in the state of advancing. They're the only Arab country to pretend that the veil is not part of Islam, and that all the Muslims from the dawn of history to nowadays are wrong and only the Tunisian government is right. What an arrogance! They are just foolish."

The Tunisian conflict, he believed, was just a small part of the post–September 11 existential struggle between Islam and the domineering West. "For the West led by America, combating against so-called extremism is the first goal—and democracy and human rights are seen as nonsense for the Arabs and the Muslims. The only important things for the West are Israel and petrol," Ghannouchi sighed. I could see why this could be a convincing argument for many Tunisians—who witnessed Western backing for Ben Ali, as well as Western rewards for his conciliatory attitude toward Israel.

I asked Ghannouchi about the bombing in Djerba. He said he didn't approve of such violence but saw it as inevitable: "As long as there is lack of freedom in Tunisia, hundreds of young Muslims will be attracted to the violent groups."

The real enemy of the Muslims, however, was not in Djerba or Tunis.

Islamic revolution could succeed only on a global scale, Ghannouchi came to believe. "Tunisia is not a superpower or a center of the world. I'm not foolish to think that Islamic change can happen in a small country like Tunisia. Only the change in the global balance of power can help."

Then he opened up with a smile of a man who's confident of knowing the future. "The global balance of power now is not in favor of Islamic change—but it is not stable and is not forever," he said. "The hegemony of America is not forever." His smile grew broader. "History is moving."

YEMEN

You're Here to Pinpoint Air Strikes
against Our Mosque

First a blot of saliva landed on my windshield. Then a mob of short, angry men, sporting red skirts and outsize curved daggers atop their private parts, started rocking my car outside the Kheir mosque in Sanaa. I was tired and sweaty. It was less than forty-eight hours since I'd arrived in Yemen, and I had already dealt with enough mischief: detention in a lockup, a swarm of mustachioed spooks, and now a crowd of knife-wielding lunatics.

I traveled to Yemen, and then to other parts of the Arabian Peninsula, on a mission that in retrospect sounds like a death wish. In October 2001, I came here to interview Arab jihadis, the young men who had abandoned normal lives to fight in a war against the West. I wanted to understand what exactly moved these people to dedicate themselves to a simple cause: murdering people like me.

That month was a peculiar time to visit Yemen, the vast and mountainous land where Bin Laden's father was born and where jihadis from around the world have found a refuge. Just before arriving, I spent eight interminable days aboard the USS *Carl Vinson,* a nuclear aircraft carrier that is as long as the Empire State Building is tall.

The Navy had flown me and a handful of other journalists to "somewhere in the northern Arabian Sea," off Pakistan's shores, to witness the opening salvos of the October 2001 strike on Afghanistan. Coming weeks after September 11, these were literally the first shots of the West's still-continuing campaign to transform the Islamic world, by sword if necessary.

In the name of eleventh-hour secrecy, we weren't allowed to witness the first rounds. Instead, Navy minders herded us into a windowless dining room just as Tomahawk missiles lit the horizon, streaking toward Kandahar and Kabul. At the historic moment, I was chewing spring rolls and guessing when the bombing might start. (Some believed it was still days away.)

Soon there was no escape from the noise of war. Day and night, bomber jets roared away from the ship's flight deck just above my head, a deafening *screech-clunk-screech* rhythm marking their catapult launches into the sky. Confined to a room most of the time and required to have a Navy escort even for toilet trips, we watched on TV the green-hued night-vision footage of how these bombs—lovingly assembled by sailors in the ship's innards a short walk away and, before launch, smelling like a new car—were becoming giant fireballs in Kabul. We also watched a defiant video of Bin Laden's spokesman, Suleiman Abu Ghaith, urging Muslims to retaliate by attacking Americans across the Persian Gulf. Three days later, I learned from a brief CNN item that a Canadian employee of a U.S. defense contractor, later identified as Luc Ethier, was duly gunned down in Abu Ghaith's home country, Kuwait.

From inside the aircraft carrier, this war seemed devoid of suffering and death. Back from their first combat missions, pumped-up pilots shared the excitement of finally blowing up stuff for real. "Tonight was about giving America back its confidence," breathed out a squadron commander when he returned from the first sortie over Afghanistan. Just in case Qaeda might get to their families, many pilots covered their name patches with duct tape and insisted on being identified only by their call signs. In between missions, they unwound over rounds of root beer and overcooked hot dogs in the ship's neon-lit cafeteria, with the steady hum of Fox News in the background.

Unlike the lethal insurgencies that ground troops and chopper crews would come to face in Afghanistan and Iraq, these pilots' mission was relatively safe: the Taliban had no way of hitting back at the planes that fired satellite-guided bombs from far away in the skies. So the airmen mostly whined about getting sore behinds on bumpy flights and about cockroach infestation in the cockpits—a natural development considering the number of Twinkies and Twizzlers they'd consumed inflight. On one of the walls in the recreation area, a cartoon summed up the ship's mood: a large map of the Middle East, and a caption "Lake Afghanistan" in the space occupied by the country. Even among most reporters, shocked by September 11, a similar bloodlust was palpable. A Serbian cameraman for a major TV network who had filmed the 1999 American bombing of Belgrade, up close from the blazing ground, was a rare holdout. "It's interesting to see it all from the other side," he muttered one day.

✦ ✦ ✦

Thousands of mujahedeen, the Arab holy warriors who fought with Bin Laden against the Soviets in Afghanistan, had been invited to Yemen in 1994 to help President Ali Abdullah Saleh crush a Socialist rebellion in the separatist south. Many of these jihadis remained in the country, often in positions of power—and in close contact with Qaeda. In the fall of 2001, scores of them were reportedly trickling back to Afghanistan to join the Taliban fight against the United States, and there was growing talk that Yemen itself might be next on America's bombing list.

"The ideal would be for you to catch a ride on a boat on which these mujahedeen are sailing off," an editor in New York helpfully suggested to me once a creaky Navy plane brought me ashore from the *Carl Vinson* in an eventful flight that, because of a hydraulics malfunction, involved an emergency landing in the United Arab Emirates. "Yeah, and they'd probably start by throwing me overboard," I joked back. But, of course, I would have eagerly gone for the ride had I found such a boat. This was three months before my *Wall Street Journal* colleague Danny Pearl was kidnapped in Pakistan and beheaded precisely by this kind of jihadi. In 2001, risky encounters with militants were still the norm. Cocooned in the misguided belief that our supposed impartiality would offer protection, as it had in conventional wars in the past, few Western journalists realized at the time that they, too, had become targets of choice. I bought a plane ticket to the Yemeni capital city, Sanaa, from Bahrain, the U.S. Navy Fifth Fleet's home base, and flew on.

✦ ✦ ✦

My quest for the mujahedeen hit the first of many stumbling blocks on arrival in the Sanaa airport. I was taken for one.

Our scrappy Yemenia airliner touched down in the first hours of Thursday, the first day of the Muslim weekend. Two American reporters for a tabloid TV network show, along with many Yemenis toting bulging bundles, flew with me on the plane. As we discovered minutes later, all three foreigners carried with them a major liability: Pakistani visas in our passports. (I had procured mine just in case, although the closest I had come to Pakistan that year was the *Carl Vinson*'s flight deck.)

Yemen's security services were concerned with more than simply local mujahedeen going to Afghanistan. They didn't want cowardly Qaeda militants not yet ready to embrace martyrdom by American bomb to sneak into Yemen. At least, not through the main international airport in plain view of the Westerners.

That week Washington demanded that the Yemeni government crack down on Islamist radicals it had protected, including those in a Qaeda offshoot that killed seventeen American sailors in the city of Aden in 2000. The Yemenis' lack of cooperation with the United States on that case caused much anger in Washington even before September 11. President Saleh, for years the main regional backer of Saddam Hussein's Iraq, seemed scared—and so rapidly reinvented himself as America's newest ally. The result was that most of the resident mujahedeen were told to disappear from sight. And, under new antiterror guidelines, everyone suspected of arriving from Afghanistan was to be detained until further notice. A Pakistani visa in my passport meant that this detention instruction included me.

After the rest of the passengers walked out of the terminal to head for soft beds that, I imagined with envy, awaited them in their homes, I found myself sitting on a broken chair in one of the airport's tiny holding rooms, separated from my suitcases and my traveling companions. The run-down Sanaa terminal doesn't quite have the shopping-mall look of airports in the West: in the dead of night, apart from us and our guards, there was no one in the cavernous building. And, of course, we weren't told why we were detained and how long we would be held.

Eventually Yemeni soldiers roused a somnolent officer with enough authority to rule on our case. By dawn he had made up his mind that we weren't Afghan terrorists after all. The TV crew, however, had to leave the cameras behind. "You can pick them up on Saturday afternoon in the Information Ministry, when the workweek starts, *Inshallah*" ("God willing"), the officer said and walked back to bed. The TV crew, stuck with two days of enforced holiday, eyed me enviously. "You are TV, you are more important, millions of people watch your show," I offered as a consolation to the reporter. "Yeah, and unlike your *Wall Street Journal* readers, they all live in trailer parks," he snapped back.

✦ ✦ ✦

It was too late in the morning to hit a soft bed by the time I arrived in my new Sanaa home, the Indian-run Taj Sheba Hotel. The hotel looked as though it came straight out of a bad spy movie. The tourists had long since run away. In the clouds of cigarette smoke that replaced them in the lobby, almost every couch was taken up by a stocky man with a stubby mustache. Clone-like, they would all raise their heads from newspapers when the rare foreigner walked by. Regularly, they huddled together with the Colonel, the man with the biggest mustache and slicked-back gray hair. There was no Fox News at the Taj: instead, Al Jazeera broadcast nonstop close-ups of charred Afghan toddlers.

I was just in time for a scheduled meeting in the hotel's lobby with Ahmed and Ahmed, the men who would drive me around and "fix"— a correspondent's term for showing someone around and setting up meetings in an unfamiliar land. The Ahmeds came recommended by a fixer who had worked for a colleague. That man was no longer available because, after a brief but unpleasant detention by security services interested in the secrets of the journalistic craft, he was determined never again to have anything to do with Western reporters.

The first Ahmed, an English-language student and the baby-faced son of a senior officer, had no such hang-ups. Neither did the second Ahmed, who promptly informed me that he was a relative of the imam, Yemen's monarch deposed in 1962, and that he was soon going to study in Germany. Both stopped by for a friendly handshake with the Colonel in the lobby before expressing horror that I had just taken a two-block stroll outside the hotel. Didn't I know that every Westerner was a target for kidnapping by Yemeni tribes that have turned hostage taking into a bargaining chip to secure more funding from central authorities? In a country where gun controls are unthinkable, there were three assault rifles per Yemeni, including newborns. A European diplomat's son was recently killed in a botched attempt right outside the hotel—and, in a testament to the new shortage of Western targets, a Chinese guest worker had just been seized in the city.

Their concern for my safety wasn't altogether altruistic. The Yemeni authorities were desperate to make sure that their country didn't get stuck with the label "hotbed of Qaeda militants." Even more important, the government wanted to ensure that its declared crackdown on Islamic militants was taken at face value. The official line was simple and clear: there are no jihadis here, period.

To my luck, even a cameraless TV crew attracted the bulk of the attention of Yemen's security officers, who were keenly aware that even a potential picture is worth a thousand words. "For your own safety," the Colonel said softly, the TV people shouldn't go outside without a large gun-toting escort, ensuring that no right-minded Yemeni would dream of straying from the official line. On the plus side, the TV reporter told me later, he got to see plenty of pleasant tourist spots and picturesque mountain hideaways. Too bad the tourists were too scared to visit.

✦   ✦   ✦

I began my exploration of Yemen with some honey tasting.

A shop in central Sanaa had just been listed by the U.S. Treasury Department as a Qaeda front. Honey is no ordinary product in Yemen: thick, perfumed, and often spiced with unusual ingredients, it is expensive and considered a remedy against many diseases, as well as an aphrodisiac. All over town, merchants operate special stores dis-

playing delicate jars of honey costing upward of $12, alongside some-
times pricier skin creams and rose water.

The store just blacklisted by the United States was called Al-Shifa,
and the owners' religious puritanism was evident from the fact that
all faces gracing the boxes of imported cosmetics had been blackened
out. The manager, Mohammed Ali al-Usra, wore a green jacket with a
Cartier label still on the cuff and a traditional Yemeni skirt underneath. He dismissed American accusations of links with Qaeda with
one word: "silly."

But one of his aides, Abdulghani, was more vocal about his own
beliefs. "America is killing innocent children, women, old people in
Afghanistan, but it is not really looking for culprits of September 11,
who must be the Americans themselves, or maybe the Jews who
wanted America to serve Israel better," he said with conviction. Most
Yemenis, he went on, are proud that Bin Laden's family hailed from
their country: "Anyone who fights the Americans makes the Yemenis
proud. If our Islamic scholars tell us to go to Afghanistan to join the
jihad, we'll go, too."

I tasted a spoonful of jihadi honey. With a slight whiff of ginger, it
was the best I ever tried.

Over dinner at the hotel, I told the TV crew about the place. They
rushed to the store once their cameras were returned on Saturday—
and came back disappointed. In the company of government minders,
Usra and Abdulghani were soft-spoken and quiet, insisting that they
were America's friends.

✦ ✦ ✦

From the honey store, I headed in Ahmed and Ahmed's beat-up Mercedes to the old Sanaa souk, once a magnet for the tourist trade. Sanaa
could easily rate as the most beautiful Arab capital, with its bizarrely
shaped mud skyscrapers rising off a rocky plateau. At dusk the arched
multicolored windows radiate with flickering lights. In those moments
you almost forget about the acrid smell of rotting trash and the suffo-
cating mist of laterite dust.

It was in Sanaa's old town that I innocently asked a smiling trinket
vendor by the name of Abdullah Hussein what he thought about the
war in Afghanistan. His face turned in an instant. He stepped closer to

me, pulled out his *jambiya*—the curved dagger worn by nearly all Yemeni men, in a scabbard atop the groin—and started stabbing an imaginary target a few inches from my shoulder. "I'll kill Americans like that, like that, in the heart," he yelled theatrically, his veins bulging. "If I can, I'll go to Afghanistan tomorrow, because Osama is defending God and Islam." As a crowd assembled around—something that happens instantly in many Arab towns whenever a Western reporter starts asking questions—a schoolteacher of English, Mohammed Juweiber, announced with quiet determination: "Nobody will be late for jihad."

Clearly alarmed, Ahmed the aristocrat tugged at my sleeve. "It's time to go," he insisted. "You're making them all too worked up." As I reluctantly walked back through the old town's maze, a beggar hissed at us from the main mosque's steps. "Leave him alone, he's not an American," Ahmed had to retort.

✦ ✦ ✦

While hatred of the United States seemed to seep through every conversation I had on Yemeni streets, not everyone in the country subscribed to the brand of Sunni radicalism preached by Bin Laden and Qaeda. For most of its history, in fact, Yemen was ruled by the Zaydi sect, an offshoot of Shiite Islam; until 1962, Yemen's monarchs were also the imams, or top clerics, of the Zaydi hierarchy. As the last imam's relative, Ahmed the aristocrat was a Zaydi, too; so is about one-third of Yemen's population.

But in the decades since monarchy ended, a puritan *salafi* current of Islam, influenced by neighboring Saudi Arabia and the Gulf emirates, increasingly took hold among the country's Sunni majority. Most of the Yemeni mujahedeen who had fought in Afghanistan, or who still had connections with Qaeda, were *salafi*. The natural place to find them in Sanaa, the two Ahmeds told me, was at al-Kheir, a large *salafi* mosque also reputed to be a recruiting ground of volunteer fighters for wars in Afghanistan, Bosnia, or Chechnya.

It was Friday morning, just before the noon prayer—the main Muslim gathering of the week. As a non-Muslim, I couldn't set foot inside the mosque itself. So we parked on a street two blocks away from the mosque and settled in for the wait. A ten-year-old child cradling a Kalashnikov rifle about his own height sat on the porch of a house nearby, a common sight in this gun-crazed country. As I looked at him, I thought about my own son, not much younger, who dislikes even toy guns and whom I couldn't imagine entrusting with a loaded high-velocity weapon. For the Yemeni boy, the Kalashnikov seemed a natural outgrowth of the body, something he must have learned to handle with his first steps.

The walls in Kheir's neighborhood screamed with graffiti in Arabic and English. Unlike the flowery Arabic phrases, the English versions usually carried succinct, focused messages. "Fuck America. Fuck Jews," said one. Ahmed showed me the day's newspapers. The official organ of the Yemen Armed Forces carried a banner headline: "FBI Arrests Zionist Agents for Blowing Up World Trade Center." The honey merchant's ideas were, after all, perfectly mainstream.

Children circulated through the gathering crowd with trays of Bin Laden posters and rousing audiotapes for less than $1 apiece. Around the car, I talked with the faithful as they headed to the mosque, wearing traditional Yemeni outfits and scrubbing their stained teeth with a desert root used as a toothbrush by the *salaf,* Prophet Mohammed's seventh-century companions. The first man introduced himself as Abu Osama, which meant that he has named his firstborn after Bin Laden. The second insisted that I should come along to the mosque and convert to Islam on the spot. I asked for time to consider the idea. "What's to think about?" he wondered, puzzled. "You either get salvation with us, or burn in hell." The third potential interviewee just spat at my infidel feet and walked on.

I thought I'd reserve my inquiries for after the prayer. A crowd of tens of thousands gathered by noon, packing every space in the three blocks around the mosque. Cars were abandoned in the middle of the road and prayer rugs spread on the melting asphalt. Everyone settled down to listen to the sermon—for many in the Muslim world, the week's main source of guidance and political news.

The imam, Sheikh Hazza al Masswari, made a stirring speech. "O almighty, punish the Americans for slaughtering our women, children, and the elderly in Afghanistan," he intoned through a powerful loudspeaker. "O almighty, destroy the Christian and Jewish monsters, and give victory to the noble mujahedeen and Sheikh Osama. The Afghan mujahedeen are like a mountain that can't be moved, battling those who want to destroy Islam and combat God. Help them fight the terrorists." (The terrorists, Ahmed explained helpfully, were meant to be those in charge of the American government.)

After the prayer, Masswari announced that there would be a collection of money for Afghanistan: "If you as a Muslim don't support your brothers in Afghanistan, God will take everything from you and will make you suffer." On the plus side, every Muslim fighter martyred in Afghanistan, Masswari promised, will go straight to heaven, where he will enjoy the eternal delights of seventy-two virgins.

At exactly this point in the speech, I stopped furiously scribbling in my notebook, looked up, and saw dozens of Yemenis slowly and silently massing in a circle around the car. They inched up, tighter and tighter. It looked almost like the attack of the cadavers in a creepy horror movie. I'm not sure seventy-two virgins were on their minds, but panic clearly flashed in the Ahmeds' eyes. "You're an American spy," one of the Yemenis suddenly screamed, and pushed the car. Others joined in rocking the vehicle, gently but perceptibly. "You're here to pinpoint air strikes against our mosque," shouted another. Considering that I had just been on an aircraft carrier that was in fact launching real air strikes, and that a Navy Fifth Fleet press badge was still in my pocket, this was too close for comfort. "Air strikes," the word passed around, "Air strikes." Heads rose up to scan the skies for American bombers.

I had to think fast. As the first spit landed on the windshield, I yanked my Italian passport from the shirt's breast pocket and waved it in the air. "La Amrika, Italiya"—"Not America, Italy"—I offered, trying to smile and stay calm. Cold sweat trickled down my nose. "Italia, pizza, pasta!!!" I continued, rattling out the names of Italian soccer clubs and players.

Such a defense probably wouldn't work today, as soldiers from Italy and other European nations have joined U.S. forces in Iraq and Afghanistan. In the months after my Yemeni trip, Islamist militants in both places have shown no qualms about murdering Italians, including reporters. But in Sanaa in October 2001, it was still sufficient not to have the words "United States" stamped on the cover of my passport. The menacing mob receded in a flash, losing interest just as quickly and quietly as they had gained it. The prayer ended a quarter of an hour later, and we were able to drive off. "That was dangerous, very dangerous," Ahmed kept repeating.

Later, a U.S. diplomat in Sanaa told me that there was indeed an American agent that day inside Kheir—as well as thirty-two other Yemeni mosques. The agents taped the sermons for intelligence analysis, not in order to pinpoint air strikes. The U.S. government, wisely, didn't send conspicuous foreigners on those missions. The agents were Yemenis, indistinguishable in the crowd. For all I know, one of them might well have been rocking my car.

✦　✦　✦

To rest after the adventures at Kheir, Ahmed and Ahmed took me to the sumptuous nearby home of a powerful tribal sheikh, President Saleh's adviser, and prominent entrepreneur. Abdullah al Gawsi's inlaid *jambiya* broadcast his wealth. He had just returned from the Kheir mosque, where—like me—he had listened to the sermon. But Gawsi wasn't interested in killing Americans. He wanted to make money, and, dazzled by the words "Wall Street" on my business card, he invited me to an afternoon social event at the Yemeni Federation of the Chambers of Commerce.

This can mean only one thing: qat.

After lunch, men and women, children and the elderly, clog Yemeni streets as they carry bundles of the green leafy branches of *Catha edulis,* as the plant is known to botanists. The poor buy the rougher, cheaper stuff. The rich have the fresh luxury variety. But until late evening, Yemenis of all means unite in masticating the tender buds of qat leaves. The saliva-soaked green lumps grow inside their bulging cheeks, while occasionally the pressure builds up too much and they are forced to spit out the green goo—on the floor, into spittoons, or simply into empty plastic bottles.

A mild but addictive drug with effects similar to amphetamine, qat is illegal in much of the Arab world. But in Yemen, almost everyone chews it. The upper-floor most-ventilated rooms in Yemeni homes, called the *mafraj*, are reserved for qat sessions. Qat is big business and is probably the staple of the country's agriculture. While coffee's Yemeni roots are clear from the word *mocha*—from the name of a coffee-exporting port on the Yemeni coast—little coffee is grown in the country nowadays. Qat is more profitable, and, as a side benefit, it reduces appetite.

Naturally, everyone brought a bundle to the meeting of the Yemeni Federation of the Chambers of Commerce. As the prominent delegates sat cross-legged around a stained carpet and prepared to spit, Sheikh al Gawsi introduced me and, out of pity, offered me a bundle to graze on. "It's good, the best," he winked.

It takes a lot of experience to enjoy qat. Its leaves are bitter and, to a novice, it feels odd to keep a lump of half-chewed stuff inside the cheek for more than a few minutes. I ended up spitting it all out quickly and feeling none of the expected buzz. My failure to observe proper procedure destroyed whatever respect the Federation of the Chambers of Commerce may have had for my person. The delegates giggled and turned to their own business. Nibbling more and more qat, they grew increasingly agitated, talking excitedly about how poor Yemen is about to emerge as the region's commercial powerhouse. With every green leaf, the nation was getting closer and closer to becoming the cornerstone of the global economy.

✦   ✦   ✦

That same Friday, I recklessly tried my luck finding the mujahedeen at Yemen's most famous landmark in the global jihadi geography—Iman University. The school's founder and rector is Abdelmajeed Zindani, number two in Yemen's powerful Islah Party (number one heads the Parliament) and Bin Laden's long-time associate in the Afghan jihad against Soviet occupation. While I was in Yemen, Zindani, a loud man with a nearly orange hennaed beard, was hiding from sight and refusing interviews. In 2004 he would be designated as a "global terrorist" by the U.S. government.

President Saleh, saved by Zindani's Arab–Afghan veterans in the 1994 civil war, allowed the cleric to establish in Yemen one of the most radical academies in the Islamic world. Funded with Saudi money,

Iman University is based in a walled military-style compound on Sanaa's outskirts and preaches a militant ideology of jihad developed in the twentieth century by Islamists from Sayyid Qutb to Bin Laden. While traditional Islam holds that only a Muslim ruler has the right to proclaim a jihad—a holy war to defend Islam—this modern ideology of *takfir*, or excommunication, proclaims that most Muslim regimes are apostates because of their dependence on the West and reluctance to implement Islamic law to the fullest extent. The logical conclusion of this view is that, if no ruler can be deemed truly Muslim, individuals must organize themselves and embark on jihad wherever an Islamic cause is in danger. This is the religious underpinning for a universal brotherhood of freelance jihadis who shift from war to war, providing a global army to any Muslim group in need of external support and ready to accept rigorous Islamic dictates in exchange.

Among thousands of foreign students indoctrinated at Iman University was the then-unknown California teenager John Walker Lindh. A couple of weeks after my visit to Sanaa, he would be captured by the CIA while fighting alongside Qaeda militants in Afghanistan and would go on to earn international fame—and a U.S. prison sentence—as the American Taliban.

After September 11, President Saleh, in theory, shut down Iman University as a sign of goodwill toward the United States. Men with Kalashnikov assault rifles guarded the entrance and no journalists were allowed inside. But Ahmed the driver walked into the guards' shed, talked to them for a minute, and returned with a broad grin. For us the road was clear.

Forbidden, dangerous places often look disappointingly boring and featureless once you arrive at them. So was the desolate campus of Iman University. As we drove around, it was obvious that the classrooms and physical training facilities weren't all empty. Here and there, groups of students clustered together. Most of them wore bushy beards, let their red-checkered headdress fall down on the sides, and hitched their skirts or pants to midcalf, *salafi*-style.

The students, who all insisted they're Yemenis, didn't hide their admiration for Bin Laden and hatred for the West. "It has been said in the Quran that the global war is coming—and we should do what has been ordained by the Quran. We should fight them," one student told me. But this conversation didn't last long. Upon hearing that I'm a reporter, another student recoiled, exchanged worried looks with his comrades, and told me to wait: he had to fetch a supervisor. Ahmed, again, pulled my sleeve. "We have to go," he murmured intensely. "Now!!!" I couldn't understand why, but we climbed back into the car nevertheless. Ahmed the driver pushed the gas pedal into the floor, and, raising clouds of dust, careened the Mercedes back to the gate as if it were a racing car. The guards raised the barrier and let us out. A mile down the road, the Ahmeds stopped the car and exhaled with relief.

To gain entrance at the Iman University checkpoint, my driver told the guards a brazen lie: I was supposedly visiting a friend who taught there. At the campus of Yemen's state university across town—an innocuous institution compared to Iman—it was just discovered that the administration used a railway container on the grounds as a private jail. People whom university bosses didn't like were incarcerated in that container for months. The news was buried on the inside pages of Yemeni newspapers.

Iman itself didn't stay closed for long. While the government finally imposed controls on foreign students, requiring them to register with their countries' embassies, an unrepentant Zindani continued to preach his jihadi worldview. The following year one of Iman's Yemeni students showed up in a Baptist-run rural hospital in the town of Jibla with an assault rifle and proceeded to gun down three American medical workers. That same year another Yemeni man educated at Iman assassinated a prominent secularist opposition leader.

✦ ✦ ✦

Back in the hotel, the Colonel was not happy. He berated Ahmed and Ahmed for our trip to the Kheir mosque, seeming to know what had happened to us before we could tell him. He told me that he cared very much for my safety—and that I should go and see Fares.

Fares? I asked my fixer. Fares al Sanabani was the editor of the *Yemen Observer*, one of the country's two "independent" English-language newsweeklies. That week, much of the paper was taken up by an op-ed written by David Duke, the former Klan leader from Louisiana. I had already interviewed Fares's rival at the *Yemen Times* and had figured that one English-language editor was probably enough.

But there was more to this man. In addition to being a leading independent journalist, Fares was the PR handler for Yemeni security agencies—and, when Vice President Dick Cheney arrived in Yemen the following year, an official government spokesman. Obviously, conflict of interest was not a familiar concept in these parts.

A handsome, tall man with a steady stare and a quick smile, Fares spoke reassuringly fluent English as he greeted me in his office. His two young sons popped in, and they spoke English, too.

Fares had done his homework. He pulled my recent articles from the Web and criticized the piece about honey merchants as providing ammunition "to some crazy Republican senator." Yemen didn't really have many Qaeda sympathizers and nobody was going to Afghanistan, he assured me. There were no mujahedeen. The country was a budding democracy and America's real ally.

After this lecture, Fares took me to a fish restaurant and then for a stroll through the city's luxury shopping district—the Libya–Yemen Friendship Shopping Mall, so named because it had been funded by Colonel Moammar Qaddhafi.

As I sprinkled my grilled Red Sea grouper with lemon and listened to how Yemen is the land of the free, I mentioned to Fares that a fellow reporter was complaining about being tailed everywhere he went, including the local museum. A clumsy cop stayed just behind him, assiduously copying down in a notebook the title of every exhibit he viewed. Another reporter in the Taj Hotel had just sneaked out to visit Bin Laden's ancestral hometown in the eastern Hadramawt mountains; when the police learned about the trip, they dragged the journalist out of his room in the dead of night, shouting threats and abuse. Fares was nonplussed. "Oh, that's unfortunate," he said with a shrug. "But you must know we've punished those responsible."

Then he suggested I visit a new government school that combats terrorism by teaching moderate Islam to future preachers. "This is the real Yemen," he said.

✦ ✦ ✦

As instructed, the next morning I went to the Higher Institute for Preaching and Guidance. The school's director, Mohammed Hassan al-Ma'amari, wore a suit and tie and no dagger—a rare combination in Yemen—and sat under a large portrait of President Saleh. Islam is a religion of peace, he told me, and should not be misinterpreted by imams who haven't had the right training.

He took me into a classroom to demonstrate what the right training looks like. As we passed the lobby, I saw a display of colorful posters that showed exploding Israeli buses and praised suicide bombers from Palestinian movements like Hamas.

The bearded instructor, Galeb al-Khourayshi, started out by telling his international-relations class of future imams that terrorism should be condemned. Having heard a somewhat unorthodox definition of terrorism in the sermon at the Kheir mosque, I asked him to explain the term's meaning. "Oh, that's simple," he replied. U.S. bombing in Afghanistan, for example, is a clear act of terror—and should be avenged. "Those who target us, we have to target them—this is self-defense," Khourayshi said. "Every Muslim who has the ability to defend the Afghans should do so." Ma'amari, the director, grew increasingly uncomfortable. Catching a worried look on his face, the instructor quickly changed tack to show his moderation. "All this, of course, does not mean that we should attack civilians in America," he said, looking at me.

✦ ✦ ✦

With Yemeni officialdom insisting that no one in the country supported Qaeda, my search for the real mujahedeen neared a dead end. Then, by chance, I discovered that one of Bin Laden's leading former associates, an Egyptian veteran of Afghan wars, worked as a teacher in one of Sanaa's elementary schools. "Let's go," I told Ahmed and Ahmed, excited by the break.

The Ahmeds stayed silent for a moment. Then the aristocratic one had an idea. "My friend used to study in that school," he said. "He'll show us around." And so we arranged to pick up his friend, a skinny youth with wispy hair and a wrinkled shirt. The friend was all too eager to be of assistance and took us to the walled school compound in the middle of a field that looked like a trash dump. We arrived just minutes after classes had begun. Ahmed's friend walked in to inquire about the Egyptian. A guard was reclining by the locked gate to make sure the children stayed inside to learn how to read and write. But the kids had other priorities. Just a few yards from the gate, they jumped one after another across the wall and outside. Some bought dirty sweets from a street vendor and lingered on the field; others just disappeared into the dusty alleys. The watchman, Ahmed explained, was responsible only for the gate. It wasn't his job to make sure that students don't climb over the wall. No one cared about the wall.

It was a neat, perhaps too neat, parable for the rest of the country. Yemen's government carefully watched the nation's main gate, the airport. But, as we have come to know in recent years, it did little, if anything, to stop the jihadis from coming and going via porous land borders or the vast unguarded coastline.

After a half hour of waiting, Ahmed's friend walked out with the school's headmaster. The man was shaking his head. "Egyptian? We have no Egyptian here!" he told me with nervous laughter. "Nobody from Afghanistan. Nobody. You have wrong information."

I wasn't allowed to go inside. We drove off to other interviews scheduled for that day. Ahmed's friend tagged along for most of the time, listening carefully. Then the day before my departure from Yemen, I saw him again in the Taj Hotel lobby, huddling with security officers near the Colonel. Clearly the purpose of the charade at the school had been to make sure that I didn't get to document the Egyptian jihadi's presence in Yemen. "Ahmed, is your friend with *mukhabarat*?" I asked my fixer, using the Arabic word for political police. I was tired, my senses were dulled; I was beyond anger at that point. "Mr. Yaro," Ahmed answered, averting an embarrassed gaze. "I don't want to lie to you."

✦ ✦ ✦

My options exhausted in Sanaa, I wanted to try my luck in the Yemeni countryside, although I had been warned not to go to the northern provinces like Marib and Saada, home to the world's largest open-air arms bazaar and the capital of kidnappings where even government troops didn't venture. Instead, my sights were set on the city of Amran, just an hour's drive from Sanaa on a paved road. While the government barred political demonstrations in the capital, I read in the *Yemen Times* that one had recently occurred in Amran. The march had been led by the Islamist leader who headed the Yemeni Parliament; the demonstrators carried Bin Laden's portraits.

Before I could set foot in Amran, there was a big hurdle to overcome: any visit outside Sanaa required formal permission from the Ministry of Information, a giant bureaucracy that, in most Arab countries, combines censorship of the media with the disbursement of money to writers, academics, and artists. Such ministries' main function is usually to suppress information rather than release it. For the permit, I had to see the minister of information himself, Hussain Awadi.

His excellency kindly agreed to meet me shortly after midnight. I had to wait while he entertained a far more important guest—a once-famous Egyptian actor whose career had faded after he'd spent several years in an Egyptian prison on heroin charges. Finally I was ushered in, and we talked over the empty glasses and half-eaten food of the actor's entourage. The minister, who wore a crumpled suit and spoke basic English, gave me his business card—with a Hotmail address. He started off with a long speech about Yemen's friendship with the United States and Yemen's peace-loving people. "Well, most people I've seen here don't quite think this way," I disagreed politely. "Oh, but they don't mean it," he assured me and angrily stared at Ahmed and Ahmed. "People have this wrong superficial perception," he said. The minister was especially angered by the connection the world was drawing between Yemen and Bin Laden: "When he was a rich man, he was a Saudi, and now he's suddenly a Yemeni. Bin Laden didn't spend a single penny in this country!" he exclaimed.

I started prodding again: "Mister Minister, it would be great if I could go and visit some of your beautiful country—say, the city of Amran."

"There is nothing to see there," he waved dismissively.

"Well, I've heard there was a demonstration and I really want to see for myself."

"You need a permit from the Information Ministry."

"Well, Mister Minister, but you *are* the information minister."

He puffed for a minute and then gave in. "Yeah, you can go," he said. Turning to the Ahmeds, he listed the rules. The permit would await us the next morning. I couldn't go on my own; a car with ministry minders had to trail us throughout.

That was better than nothing, and I thanked him profusely. The following day, the minders arrived and we set out on the trip in a two-car convoy. I looked forward to exiting Sanaa, with its smog that brought on a throat infection, and to seeing the green hills of Arabia Felix, as Yemen was once known. But first my crew had to eat. The Ahmeds and the minders clambered with me into a downtown restaurant, where food, instead of plates, was heaped right on the plastic tablecloth. (Dishwashing consisted of wiping off the previous customer's leftovers with a wet rag.) The minders enjoyed every morsel, ordering double portions of spicy chicken, rice, and steaming Yemeni bread.

Digesting the lunch, we finally headed toward the checkpoint at the exit from the city, where things got complicated.

A *mukhabarat* officer in a red skirt, qat dropping out of his cheek bulge, grabbed his Kalashnikov and ran toward us. With a permit personally issued by the minister, I didn't worry. What could go wrong?

But that's not how things work in the Middle East, where the secret police often outrank ministers, prime ministers, and various other officials with important-sounding titles. To my amazement, the qat-intoxicated officer at the checkpoint simply tore my travel permit in half. "Amran? I don't care who gave you an authorization, even the president himself," he yelled. "This is my road, and you are not going anywhere anymore."

The unhappy Information Ministry men were unceremoniously dragged from their car and, prodded by Kalashnikov butts, locked up in a shed. "Go back to the hotel now if you don't want to end up like them," the officer barked. I did, with the two frightened Ahmeds staying silent until we reached downtown Sanaa. Then I phoned Fares. He managed to arrange for my two Information Ministry escorts to be freed by the end of the day. They didn't enjoy the experience and were still shaking when they appeared at the hotel. Fares couldn't get me a new permit to leave town. "I guess you're not going," he said. There was no point in insisting.

✦   ✦   ✦

In the following months, the last of 2001, scores of Yemeni jihadis were captured in Afghanistan and Pakistan. Others would be found, alive or killed after setting off suicide bombs, in Iraq and beyond. Documents seized in Afghanistan showed that well after my visit, some senior members of the Yemeni administration remained on Qaeda's payroll—while officially helping the United States.

Before I flew out of Yemen, I called a well-known human rights activist in Aden. The southern port city, according to local reports, was the main point of embarkation for prospective mujahedeen heading to Afghanistan. The activist must know something, I hoped, as he paused to answer my questions. Having composed his thoughts, he issued a quiet reply. "I can tell you two things," he said. "First, my telephone is bugged. Second, everything is excellent in our wonderful country."

5

KUWAIT

To Tora Bora and Back

In October 2001, while I looked for jihadis in Yemen, Hadi al Enezi and his fifteen-year-old son, Mohammed, got into their car and drove south from the opposite end of the Arabian Peninsula. For them, it was supposed to be an unremarkable trip. Hadi, a forty-year-old Kuwaiti, told his wife that he and Mohammed would visit Mecca for a quick pilgrimage, or *umra*. Five days later, Hadi called home. The two were now in Kabul, under American bombs. Hadi informed his stunned spouse that they had decided it was their duty to help the Afghans' fight against American infidels.

Before the year was over, Hadi was dead, killed in the U.S. onslaught on Qaeda hideouts in eastern Afghanistan's Tora Bora mountains. His son was captured by American forces, which is how I met the rest of the family.

After my thwarted quest for mujahedeen in Yemen, I refused to give up and instead focused my attention on Gulf petro-sheikdoms such as Kuwait. This emirate, with its First World infrastructure, skyscrapers, and glinting shopping malls, is one of the most prosperous nations on earth. On the surface, at least, it has little in common with Yemen, a wild and violent land living in a qat-induced drug haze. Even Yemeni laborers have been kicked out of Kuwait because of Sanaa's long-standing support for Saddam Hussein.

But tiny Kuwait has produced probably as many jihadis as populous Yemen, in part because impressionable youths in the emirate have enough cash in the bank to act out their fantasies and travel to wars in Afghanistan, Bosnia, Kashmir, or Chechnya. Psychologically, these Kuwaiti jihadis interested me much more than the dagger-carrying men in red skirts in Sanaa.

I had long wondered what drives men with seemingly normal, settled lives to embrace death in a holy war. People like Hadi al Enezi must have led an existence not unlike mine: paying bills, worrying about children's successes at school, taking holidays abroad. How could a man who enjoys the comforts of life in a peaceful and relatively free country drop everything and travel to war thousands of miles away? Kuwait, with its boisterous Parliament and freewheeling press, is not Saudi Arabia, where citizens are killed just for slapping back a prince. After all, Kuwait owes its very existence as a state separate from Iraq to an American military intervention merely a decade earlier.

As I've learned in Yemen, the real jihadis—as opposed to the big-mouth sympathizers—aren't the kind of people who particularly like to share their experiences with a Western writer. So when I spotted a Kuwaiti newspaper article that mentioned the fifteen-year-old Mohammed and his detention in Afghanistan, I jumped at the opening. I imagined the Enezis would talk—unlike other mujahedeen families—because they'd be eager to secure the teenager's release.

✦ ✦ ✦

I landed in Kuwait City on a drizzly December afternoon just before Christmas—a normal working day here. It was cold, and the aseptic landscape of endless suburbia separated by six-lane highways instantly put me in a gloomy mood. Not knowing anyone in the emirate, I relied on Danny Pearl; he e-mailed me several local contacts he had gathered on an October trip to Kuwait. On Danny's list was Saad al Enezi, an easygoing TV journalist who headed the local office of Al Jazeera. Kuwaiti authorities would ban the station—deemed too critical of the emirate's rulers—the following year.

I guessed correctly that Saad—who hailed from the same huge Enezi tribe as the dead jihadi—had already met Mohammed al Enezi's relatives. He volunteered to set up a meeting for me at the house of Hadi's cousin Saleh, not far from my hotel. The family agreed the very same evening.

My suitcase still unpacked in the hotel, I waited for Hadi's two brothers in Saleh's *diwaniya,* the airy reception room where Kuwaiti men gather regularly to discuss politics and current affairs. Saleh started telling me about the man who had just died in Afghanistan. The discourse sounded almost comical, similar to what is said by neighbors surprised to discover that a serial killer has been living next door. "Hadi was a normal person, so quiet. He had good relations with everyone," Saleh mused. "We couldn't believe he went there. . . . We were all in shock. . . ."

It was soon my turn to be surprised. Hadi al Enezi was neither a firebrand preacher nor a sociopath. He was, in fact, a pillar of Kuwaiti society, serving, until leaving for Afghanistan, as a lieutenant colonel in the Kuwaiti police by the Saudi border. "He never said: I hate America," Saleh recalled. Quite the opposite: Hadi fought side by side with American forces against Iraq back in 1991. Saleh insisted it was all a mistake: "He just went to help fellow Muslims, as a humanitarian. Any Arab they catch in Afghanistan, they say he's Qaeda." The truth was that nearly every Arab fighter captured at Tora Bora and elsewhere in Afghanistan claimed to be a humanitarian aid worker. It was all a matter of definitions, of course. In an ideology that sees America as the enemy of mankind, killing Americans can be easily described as humanitarian work.

As tea was offered, Hadi's two brothers finally arrived: thirty-year-old firefighter Freih and twenty-seven-year-old sports teacher Abdullah. Dressed in traditional Bedouin garb, they were eager to please, smiling and interrupting each other as they answered my questions and fingered their brand-new cell phones.

"Hadi's never been involved in politics," Abdullah said. "He's the kind of guy who goes straight home from work, and straight to work from home."

"If we knew he'd be going somewhere like Afghanistan, we would have stopped him," Freih injected. I asked them whether Hadi had ever mentioned Bin Laden, Qaeda, or the United States. "When September 11 happened, he was very angry and very sad. He was saying that civilians should not die like this," Freih replied. "But afterwards he wanted to help the Afghans. He didn't believe that it would be a short war and that the Americans will crush Afghanistan so fast."

After a pause, Abdullah exploded: "It's really not normal to take a baby there. So irresponsible." Hadi's son Mohammed, he explained, was a regular Kuwaiti kid. He was good at school, liked watching TV and driving around the desert on sand buggies. He also liked playing soccer with his uncles and taught them how to surf the Internet and use e-mail. "You'd love him from the moment you meet him. His father used to prefer him over all his other sons, which is why he took him along to Afghanistan," Freih said.

For weeks the boy's mother, Jamila, received no other news after taking that phone call from Kabul. Then, with despair, she glimpsed Mohammed on satellite TV, among Arab prisoners paraded by a U.S.-backed Afghan militia. Mohammed's legs were injured, and he couldn't walk. An Afghan militiaman told the TV reporter that Mohammed's father was dead.

"Some religious guys came to the house right away to congratulate her on the martyrdom," Abdullah recalled. "But she is really grieving. She's shattered and spends her time in and out of the hospital."

A few days later, the family saw Mohammed on TV again—this time in U.S. custody in Kandahar. Given the circumstances, Abdullah was determined to make sure that no one considers the family anti-American. During the Florida electoral recount in 2000, he proudly told me, they all cheered for George W. Bush because of Bush senior's role in liberating Kuwait from Iraq: "We consider the U.S. a very good friend. It's true."

To understand the family better, I wanted to see where Hadi came from, so I asked the two brothers to drive me to the man's home. Inside his car Abdullah flashed a smile and popped open the CD drive. I was expecting to hear Arabic pop music, but instead came the monotonous chanting of prayers. "Quran," he explained. "I listen to this when I drive." The drive took some forty minutes with the Quran at full blast.

Hadi al Enezi had lived south of Kuwait City, in an area of luxurious villas occupied by senior officers and public servants. A glistening Jaguar and a BMW lined the driveway. Inside, the house was surprisingly bare, almost sterile. There was nothing on the white walls of the green-carpeted *diwaniya* and only a smattering of leather-bound, religious books on the shelf. A crystal chandelier flooded the room with intense, steady light. For several minutes Freih and Abdullah loudly argued over my request to see Mohammed's room—and denied me permission on the grounds that my visit would have involved me walking near the forbidden female quarters upstairs. There was no question of allowing me to speak to Hadi's widow, Jamila, or other women in the household.

Inside the *diwaniya* Hadi's Bangladeshi chauffeur poured coffee and tea to men with long, bushy beards. I found myself doing the round of shaking their hands, in effect participating in their mourning for a man I knew to be a Qaeda militant. Surprised by my appearance, they welcomed me and then stayed silent. Mohammed's older brother Abdullah, seventeen at the time, brought out a passport snapshot of his dad. Sporting a white headdress and a round beard, Hadi stared into the camera with a boring, unremarkable look. There were no pictures of Mohammed in the house except for a photocopy of his ID card; as devout Muslims, the family frowned on photography and took pictures only for official documents.

The young Abdullah fought mixed emotions. He seemed upset that his father had bypassed him for the Afghan jihad in favor of the younger son. Yet he kept the family secret when friends and teachers called on the house, asking where Mohammed was and when he would return to school. "Until now, I told no one he was in Afghanistan," he said proudly.

On the way back to Kuwait City, we stopped at Freih's house to watch the taped TV footage of Mohammed in Afghanistan. Freih's was a much poorer home, but also more humane, without the hospital-like feel of his dead brother's vast mansion.

We sat under a tent in the inner courtyard, and Freih put on the teakettle to warm us up in the freezing winter night. After he inserted the tape and fiddled with the video recorder, I saw Mohammed on TV. The camera first showed a gaunt bearded man, one of what looked to be several Arab mujahedeen injured and captured in the fighting near Tora Bora. "*Ya ahi*"—"O my brother"—"Where are you from?" the TV reporter asked. The man, in visible pain, murmured: "Yemen."

The camera then panned to a youngster with a barely sprouting beard who appeared in better spirits. "This, this is Mohammed," Freih pointed to the screen, perking up. Mohammed, who kept asking for water, recounted how he got caught. "The American Apaches appeared and then they started firing at us," he said. "They fired and fired, and killed many people."

Freih hit the pause button and reflected. His children, he said, often ask him why their cousin Mohammed is on TV. How does he reply? I wanted to know. "I don't answer them," Freih said. "I simply don't know what to say."

✦　✦　✦

A few days later, I met diplomats at the American embassy and mentioned Mohammed al Enezi's case. Since the boy was a minor, I was told that the United States would satisfy Kuwait's request for repatriation. Indeed, Mohammed was returned to his brothers and mother a couple of months later.

As we talked about the family, a diplomat at the embassy cautioned me against taking everything the smiling Enezis had said at face value, especially their professions of pro-American feelings. The diplomat then handed me a copy of one of Kuwait's main newspapers.

There, on the back page, the Enezis had taken out a conspicuous quarter-page mourning notice for Hadi. I was jarred by how much the notice's tone differed from what I had been told by Hadi's relatives. "We joyfully announce to the Islamic nation the news about the martyrdom of our mujahed, hero Hadi al Enezi," the family's announcement crowed. "He died in the holy month of Ramadan while supporting the weak and in the defense of the faith and Islam in Afghanistan."

✦　✦　✦

I returned to Kuwait nine months later, in the fall of 2002. By then, Kuwaiti authorities announced they had cracked the case of Luc Ethier, the Canadian defense contractor gunned down as I floated on the USS *Carl Vinson* off Pakistan. Amazingly, the authorities claimed that the assassin wasn't an Islamic jihadi. Instead, Ethier had been murdered in a banal life insurance scheme—organized by his Filipina wife, Mary Jean Bitos.

After crisscrossing the Arabian Peninsula, I found it hard to take the official story at face value—both because of the Gulf nations' record of mistreating guest laborers, especially female, and because of a series of suspicious trials that had occurred in neighboring Saudi Arabia in previous months.

There, a perverse pattern had emerged. Since the late 1990s, several Westerners had been killed or injured in small-scale bombing attacks. But the Saudi police stubbornly refused to consider the most likely culprit, an Islamist terrorist network. "There are no terrorist attacks on foreigners in our country," the Saudi interior minister, Prince Nayef, assured the world as late as mid-2002, after one more such bombing killed a German engineer. "There are no Muslims, Arabs, or Saudis involved in this," he said.

At the time, Saudi police arrested, instead, several Western expatriates, some of them involved in selling illicit alcohol, and announced that the bombings had been a by-product of a turf war among Western bootlegging gangs. Tortured, some of these Western suspects confessed on Saudi TV, and two were sentenced to be beheaded at secret trials. The bombings, of course, went on unabated and culminated in massive blasts that killed dozens and devastated Riyadh residential compounds in the spring and fall of 2003, followed later by increasingly daring kidnappings, shootings, and beheadings of Westerners throughout 2004.

Saudi Arabia's culture of secrecy made it hard to investigate the kingdom's blame-the-victims policy. Saudi courts operate behind closed doors. Foreign embassies are usually informed about the sentencing of their citizens after a delay of several months, which in capital cases often means well after the heads have been chopped off.

The Ethier case seemed to me suspiciously similar—except that it was happening not in Saudi Arabia but in Kuwait, one of the Arab world's most open countries, with a relatively transparent justice system. It wouldn't be beyond some Kuwaiti officials, I reckoned, to frame a widow in the name of saving the emirate's image—and protecting the well-connected jihadi killers who still lurked inside Kuwaiti society, just as Hadi al Enezi had.

✦ ✦ ✦

I started out by visiting the shabby offices of Mary Jean's lawyer, a wrinkled Kuwaiti who showed me a picture of the couple, lovers' smiles radiating into the camera, and the crime scene reports. Next to the lawyer sat a thick-jawed, laconic Canadian who introduced himself as Ben Rivard, and who had served with Ethier as a master corporal in the Canadian military. Over drinks after their discharge, he had talked his buddy into signing up with DynCorp, an American defense contractor then servicing the emirate's Air Force and, since 2003, heavily involved in assisting in the occupation of Iraq.

After Ethier's death, Rivard—feeling somewhat responsible for the tragedy—dedicated most of his free time to pursuing the killer. He was convinced that Mary Jean had nothing to do with the murder. He drove me south of Kuwait City, past Hadi al Enezi's neighborhood, to show where it all happened: a brightly lit roundabout in the town of Fahaheel.

This was no ordinary place: dominating the emirate's most conservative southern belt and squeezed between oil fields, foul-smelling refineries, and the Gulf, Fahaheel was the former home of many on the A-list of Islamic terror. Khalid Shcikh Mohammed, the mastermind of the September 11 attack on the World Trade Center and the Pentagon, and his nephew Ramzi Youssef, the man who failed to blow up the Twin Towers back in 1993, both used to study in the nondescript Fahaheel high school just a couple of blocks from this roundabout.

I knew the place because I had visited the school and neighboring mosques while reporting on Khalid Sheikh Mohammed's Kuwaiti roots. Then, I knocked on the door of a Pakistani imam who had preached in the area for decades, including the time when Khalid Sheikh Mohammed still lived nearby. The imam, rubbing his eyes after an interrupted siesta, pretended that he had never heard about the Qaeda chieftain—but this didn't stop him from proving that he took his politics very personally. "Why are you, you, slaughtering our women in Afghanistan?" he intoned, jabbing his index finger into my chest and raising his voice as foul-smelling foam gathered at the sides of his mouth. "Why are you, every day, killing our children in Palestine? In Iraq? In Chechnya? Why are you waging war on Islam?" He didn't actually expect an answer, of course. In his eyes I was the embodiment of the West's ills, not a person possessed of individual traits. As was Luc Ethier to his killers.

At about ten on the night of October 10, 2001, the Canadian went out for a walk with Mary Jean. That evening Kabul-bound bomber jets were taking off from the *Carl Vinson*. Hadi al Enezi was preparing for his departure with his son to Afghanistan. Arab TV networks were still broadcasting an appeal by Suleiman Abu Ghaith, Bin Laden's Kuwaiti spokesman, to hunt down Westerners everywhere.

Ethier looked like an off-duty GI: he had a soldier's cropped haircut and wore shorts—a Westerner's giveaway in a region that dreads naked flesh. Holding hands, Ethier and his wife bought ice cream at a Baskin Robbins outlet, strolled across the square to a jewelry shop, and then started walking back toward their high-rise. After they passed a Burger King restaurant, the killer sprang up just behind them. Unloading his gun, he fired three times at Ethier, and three times at Mary Jean. Luc died instantly. Wounded in the chest, hip, and arm, his wife survived.

Mary Jean later told the police that she clearly remembered the attacker: an Arab man who wore the red-checkered headdress and shouted "Allahu Akbar"—"God is Great"—three times before running away. There were plenty of other witnesses on the square, but no one came forward. As we retraced the murderer's steps at precisely the same time of night that the killing occurred, Rivard pointed to a closed garment shop just a few feet away: the immigrant traders who worked there saw the shooting, he said, and fled Kuwait because they were too scared to testify.

As Mary Jean lay in the hospital, partially paralyzed, Kuwaiti police quickly rounded up several Islamist radicals known to have visited Afghanistan and Pakistan, the countries where Qaeda camps operated, and showed her a lineup. She picked out Majeed al Mutayri, a sergeant in the Kuwaiti police force that protects oil fields. An internal police report soon concluded that Mutayri was guilty of shooting Ethier "beyond reasonable doubt."

The Mutayris, like the Enezis, are one of Kuwait's biggest tribes, and tribal codes call for protecting kinsmen regardless of guilt. The sergeant came with influential backers in Parliament and the government. Islamist legislators and Mutayri's own defense team argued that he was being tortured in jail. "The police beat him, insulted him, suspended him on a skewer like a chicken, and pulled the hair from his beard," insisted his lawyer, Nawaf Sary al Mutayri. The sergeant's alibi was that he had been in the desert, at a tribal religious ceremony, at the time of the murder—a claim that the police didn't believe before political pressure built up. Then the Kuwaiti interior minister—just as Saudi Arabia's Prince Nayef had done after anti-Western bombings there—gently suggested that the police look for perpetrators outside the Islamist circles.

Immediately, police investigators barred all access to Mary Jean's hospital room. Despite her injuries, she wasn't allowed to sleep; interrogators accused and threatened her around the clock. The police went on to detain scores of other Filipinos who knew Mary Jean or Ethier, torturing several into writing confessions in halting English. A triumphant interior minister rushed to declare, in Parliament, that Kuwait's honor was safe and that this was a common crime: Mary Jean was proclaimed the murder conspiracy's mastermind and Mutayri was released to a cheering crowd that included prominent legislators. As he was hoisted on their shoulders, the sergeant shouted three times "Allahu Akbar." Then, according to local accounts, he urged God "to give victory to the fighters of jihad worldwide."

✦   ✦   ✦

Rivard met me again in the back room of another Canadian's apartment on a beachfront not far from the murder scene. A party was at full swing in the living room, with home-brewed beer, dimmed lights, and techno music. Many of the guests had known Ethier, which is why I was invited.

Rivard told me he had been accompanying Ethier's body to Canada when Kuwaiti authorities first accused Mary Jean. He was shocked by the news and, at first, didn't know whom to believe. But soon his confidence in Kuwaiti justice started to crumble. It turned out that Ethier's life insurance policy—worth 100,000 Canadian dollars—was in the name of his mother and former Canadian girlfriend. This meant that Mary Jean had no financial gain and therefore the motive alleged by the police didn't exist. The supposed murder weapon—a pistol found in the possession of a Filipino maintenance worker who had confessed to the killing—didn't match ballistic evidence. The confessions themselves contradicted each other in crucial details. And then there was the strange case of disappearing witnesses.

Rivard suspected a political coverup. "The Kuwaitis have had to reassure the population and catch someone. And it couldn't be a terrorist because, if there's one terrorist, we all know there are more," he reasoned.

The Kuwaiti court had no problems of its own in accepting the official view. The verdict read almost like a parody: no motive, no murder weapon, and no witnesses, the document said. It also mentioned that the Filipino suspects claimed that their confessions had been extracted by torture. Yet, according to the judges, no medical evidence existed that such torture had occurred. Under Kuwaiti law this meant that, even when retracted, the confessions alone constituted sufficient proof of the suspects' guilt.

I arrived in Kuwait as the case went on appeal. Mary Jean, emaciated and forced to wear a black *abaya,* was in jail, as were other Filipino defendants. Her alleged accomplice, convicted of having pulled the trigger, was on death row; three of his cellmates had already been hanged.

In a maddening effort, I spent several days trying to contact the Kuwaiti investigators, or even the spokesman for the local police. They knew what I was after, which must have been why they had invariably stepped out of the office the moment I called and never phoned back. At her appeal hearing, the police claimed they had a tape of incriminating conversations between Mary Jean and the alleged gunman—but never produced it.

Even Kuwaiti liberals seemed little inclined to help Mary Jean; Filipinos were low on the list of Kuwait's priorities. A page-one article that I wrote about the case produced a light shock at the Kuwaiti embassy in Washington and spurred at least some Kuwaiti human rights activists into action.

Then more blood was shed. Kuwaiti Islamists gunned down two U.S. Marines training on Failaka Island, and later killed another defense contractor—this time an American—who was leaving the main U.S. base in the emirate. Suddenly Kuwait could no longer claim that it didn't have homegrown terrorists. Pressured by the U.S. military, which was angry about sustaining casualties just months before the invasion of Iraq was supposed to start, Kuwait finally started arresting its own jihadis. Luckily for Mary Jean, there was no longer any political value in insisting that her husband had been killed in a Filipino conspiracy.

In October 2002 the appeals court reversed the sentences of all Filipino defendants—just as Kuwaiti authorities announced that they had unraveled yet another plot to kill Westerners, this time arresting two members of the Enezi tribe and one member of the Mutayris. Mary Jean was finally allowed to go home to the Philippines.

In the following months, Rivard continued sending me updates on his quest to punish Ethier's real murderer. But, in fact, I lost interest. Looking back on this case, I realize that it marked the end of a period that, while bloody, elicits something akin to nostalgia nowadays. Back then, the killing of just one ordinary person, and the injustice done to another, still seemed like important news in the Middle East.

The next year, as war began in Iraq, body-count inflation set in. Beheadings, videotaped and distributed via the Internet, took the place of anonymous street shootings. Starting in the spring of 2003, insurgents and jihadis in Iraq, Saudi Arabia, and neighboring lands started murdering people, Western and local, every day. Western bullets and bombs killed thousands of Muslim civilians, too. It was no longer unusual for the daily toll to reach into three digits. Through all of this, Ethier's case remained unsolved. And, apart from a narrow circle of parents and friends, nobody cared.

6

IRAQ

Tell Mr. Bush That I Have Dirty Clothes

Like so many who should have known better, I worried about all the wrong things when I returned to Kuwait in February 2003. The war on Iraq was about to start and—remember?—it was supposed to be about weapons of mass destruction. Like hundreds of other journalists, I brought bulky suitcases filled with thousands of dollars of gear. On my first night back in the emirate, after a dinner sprinkled with morbid discussions among depressed colleagues, I barely managed to sleep. In the cocoon of my luxury hotel, I kept waking up in the middle of nightmares about blister agents turning my skin into putrefied flesh and nerve gas forcing me to drool and choke on my saliva.

Weeks earlier my editors had sent me to a bucolic English village for a one-day course on how to try surviving a chemical war. The instructor, a British military veteran, didn't put much of an effort into his performance: after grimly announcing that "try" was the operative word, he explained that our chances would be slim no matter what we did. Holding up an army-issue chemical suit, he made a farewell remark: "Remember one thing: the military always buys this stuff from the lowest bidder."

In Kuwait, I had set up house in a brand-new Hilton resort on the southern seashore, complete with looped New Age music piped

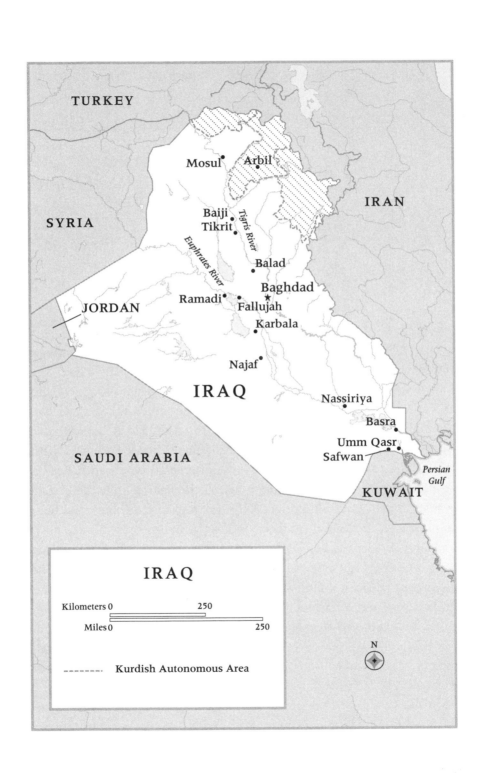

TURKEY

SYRIA

IRAN

JORDAN

Mosul

Arbil

Baiji
Tikrit

Tigris River

Euphrates River

Balad

Baghdad ★

Ramadi
Fallujah

Karbala

Najaf

IRAQ

Nassiriya

Basra

Umm Qasr
Safwan

*Persian
Gulf*

KUWAIT

SAUDI ARABIA

IRAQ

Kilometers 0   250

Miles 0   250

-------- Kurdish Autonomous Area

N

through corridors and an (initially) discreet U.S. military press center. As we waited and waited for the fighting to start, hordes of reporters, military PR officers, and U.S. government civilians in khaki safari vests converged on the overwhelmed hotel. The pack of reporters filled their days with the quest for illicit alcohol, teenage amusements such as all-night go-karting, and shopping for nifty gadgets we all imagined we'd need up north.

✦ ✦ ✦

At the *Journal*, as in many other news organizations, the division of labor was resolved by the time fighting started. Reporters from the Washington bureau took all the "embedded" positions, while full-time foreign correspondents like me prepared to drive to Baghdad on our own, as "unilaterals," either from Kuwait or from autonomous Kurdistan in Iraq's north.

Unlike the bulk of my colleagues, engaged in elaborate plotting to secure slots with units likely to end up on the "tip of the spear" of the invasion, I didn't want to enter Iraq in a Humvee or a tank, or cover actual battles. Instead, I was fascinated by the way ordinary Iraqis would react to the war and the way their lives would be changed once the tip of the spear moved farther north. This required an independence of movement that embedded reporters didn't have.

I crafted a simple plan: I'd drive in just behind the tanks in a rented four-wheel-drive and move from Kuwait's Hilton to what friends assured me was a perfectly pleasant Sheraton in Basra, Iraq's second-largest city, located a few dozen miles north of the border. After cajoling the local Hertz agent, I obtained the keys to a brand-new GMC Yukon that, we both pretended, wouldn't go anywhere near Iraq. I then spent weeks of frenzied shopping outfitting my Yukon with a pair of spare tires, contraptions for independent power supply and satellite links, jerry cans with enough gas to drive to Baghdad and back, and water and food sufficient to survive for weeks.

✦ ✦ ✦

The morning after the first U.S. bombs fell on Baghdad, I drove toward the Iraqi frontier with a *Journal* colleague. Suddenly the soft rock on our radio was replaced with an air-raid siren. Iraq had just started lobbing missiles into Kuwait, thankfully of the less-than-accurate kind. An American convoy passed us on the road, and I realized with a chill that all these soldiers were now wearing chemical suits and gas masks, looking like aliens fresh off a spacecraft. I sniffed the air, remembering from my British class that lethal gases smell like rotten eggs or freshly cut grass, and looked out the window to see if birds were falling from the sky. We leapt out of the car to don our gas masks and to shroud ourselves in chemical suits, gracelessly squeezing into heavy rubber boots and gloves. If there had been a real gas attack, of course, we'd have been long dead by the time we were done zipping up.

In the desert, once we reached the four-lane highway toward Iraq, a tableau of American military might unfolded before our eyes. Thousands of tanks, Bradley fighting vehicles, Humvees, and transport trucks emerged from desert tracks on both sides of the highway, joining it as smaller blood vessels converge into a throbbing vein. Whipping up clouds of sand, this armada slowly inched toward Iraq, halted only by the occasional traffic accident or an engine breakdown. On all four lanes, the traffic was northbound only.

✦ ✦ ✦

In the months before the war's start, I overdosed on Iraqi satellite TV's incessant odes to Saddam, performed by pudgy singers who waved assault rifles in the air and wore mobster-style leather jackets. The similarity to 1980s Soviet broadcasts I had watched as a teenager in Kiev, down to the poor film quality, was stunning.

Many of the same Washington officials who spearheaded Reagan's successful crusade against the "evil empire" now pushed for war on what President Bush branded the "axis of evil"—starting in Iraq. It was obvious to me that the parallels between eastern Europe and most of the Islamic world were misplaced: unlike the former Communist lands, where largely pro-American peoples suffered under anti-American rulers, in the Muslim world the opposite was true. Pro-American regimes like Egypt, Pakistan, and Saudi Arabia lorded it over increasingly anti-American populations.

But Iraq was different. It was one of the few Muslim nations ruled by an openly anti-American dictator—and here, I thought, was a chance for the United States to demonstrate that it could be a force for good in this part of the world, as it had been in Eastern Europe. Among the Iraqis I had met abroad, few seemed likely to weep for Saddam.

My optimism may seem hopelessly naive in retrospect, knowing how tragic the invasion and its aftermath turned out to be, but I wasn't alone in my expectations. The U.S. government was still widely assumed to be competent, and many Arabs I interviewed in the prewar months agreed with the rosy predictions of Iraqi gratitude that I heard from American military PR. Often educated in America, and universally exposed to Hollywood movies that tend toward happy endings, these Arab intellectuals usually opposed U.S. domination of the region for political reasons. But on a human level, many believed that the Iraqis would be infinitely better off under American rule. "Anything is better than Saddam. For now, the interests of the Iraqis coincide with those of the Americans, and the Iraqi people should take advantage of this before the Americans change their mind," Najeeb al Nauimi, the former justice minister in the Gulf emirate of Qatar, told me in early 2003. This, he added at the time, was a highly unusual admission for a self-professed Arab nationalist who represented several Arab terrorism suspects detained by the United States at Guantánamo Bay.

There were other opinions, often tinged by prejudice. When I asked non-Iraqi Arab intellectuals about what they expected to happen in Iraq, many ended up reciting the same speech made in the year 694. Delivered by a governor who had been dispatched to run Iraq for the Umayyad caliph in Damascus, the speech is held up as proof that, from time immemorial, only dictatorship can work in Iraq; until 2003, Iraqi schoolchildren were required to learn it by heart.

"By God, people of Iraq, people of discord, dissembling and evil character. The Commander of the Faithful has emptied his quiver and bit his arrows and found me the bitterest and the hardest of them all. Therefore, he aimed me at you," the governor, al-Hajaj bin Yusuf, allegedly told a crowd of his new subjects. "I see heads before me that are ripe and ready for plucking, I am the one to pluck them, and I see blood glistening between turbans and beards. By God, I shall strip you like bark, I shall truss you like a bundle of twigs, I shall beat you like stray camels." Of course, I never heard that speech from Shiites who were at the receiving end of al-Hajaj's oratory and of Saddam's guns more than a millennium later.

In those months leading up to the war, I also read a prescient forecast in an article by Raghida Dergham, a columnist for the pan-Arab newspaper *Al Hayat*. As a Lebanese citizen, she knew firsthand the psychology of a people living under foreign occupation. "Iraqis might view an American invasion as salvation from the status quo, and greet the soldiers with roses and cheers. They might also do the opposite, and deem invasion and occupation the worst of all worlds for them. Or they might combine both attitudes and rise against both their leadership and the U.S. administration, and stage an amazing revolution to seize control of their fate," she wrote a few months before the war.

The basic truth was that—as long as Saddam remained in power—nobody really knew what was happening inside Iraqi heads. Once the war started, my job was to get across the frontier and find out. Now that, for the first time in decades, Iraqis were free to speak out, I could ask them whether their hatred of Saddam actually translated into sympathy for America and the West. Were they really grateful to be "liberated"?

✦　✦　✦

Back at the Hilton, the mood was exuberant. Even as air-raid sirens sent us packing for the hotel's bomb shelter every few hours, military PR officers were making plans to fly their favorite TV personalities to a liberated Basra. From there, the networks were supposed to beam to the world pictures of British and American troops showered with flowers and kisses by a grateful populace. My room in the Basra Sheraton was booked, just in case.

On the second night of the war, I banded with several other journalists and set out for Iraq in a convoy of seven SUVs. A detachment of U.S. Marines blocked our passage at the main border crossing. Our military-issue press cards screamed "UNILATERAL" in huge red letters—and the Marines had been told not to let anyone so branded across. As we idled for hours at the Marine checkpoint, watching helicopters hover in a combat mission just to the north, another colleague called us from her cell phone: British troops had bulldozed a hole in the frontier sand wall a short drive away. Revving up our four-wheel-drive monsters and U-turning in front of the puzzled Marines, we raced east across the sands and followed British armored personnel carriers that roared through the opening. A cheerful sign pronounced: "The First Royal Fusiliers welcome you to Iraq."

Driving past the sand berm and into rising clouds of fine dust, we turned right to see "liberated" Umm Qasr. The road was roped off with warning notices in English and Arabic, and anguished Iraqis stood by the side, waving white flags made from bedsheets and asking for news from the city. Gunfire crackled in the distance. We plowed ahead nonetheless, until we found a mud-covered Marine amphibious vehicle parked by the side.

As we dismounted to don our flak jackets and helmets and to make large "TV" markings with duct tape on the cars, a couple of journalists' SUVs sped up in the other direction. French photographers yelled out that they had just escaped from Umm Qasr, where—despite triumphant reports of the city's fall—fierce fighting still raged. As we tried to talk to the jumpy Marines, an ancient white-and-orange Iraqi taxi slowly passed by, its driver gathering courage to follow in our tracks. Seeing the vehicle, the Marines suddenly opened up with a volley of heavy machine-gun fire, aiming just in front of the cabbie.

Not yet understanding where the fire had come from, most of my colleagues dropped to the asphalt, cowering behind their flashy SUVs. The terrified Iraqi hit the brakes and froze in sheer panic. He was lucky to stay alive. Military orders in the days following would be to treat any approaching Iraqi vehicle as a potential suicide bomb, a policy that took the lives of hundreds of Iraqi civilians. Frazzled by such a stressful beginning, we turned back toward the west, trying to find a "liberated" town from which we could report. Our choices were limited: ahead lay a clover-leaf intersection of highways, with the right turn leading to Basra, the left to the town of Safwan and back to Kuwait, and the road straight ahead to Baghdad.

At the intersection, British troops had organized a small camp, picking up disoriented Iraqi soldiers who wandered in from the fields and putting them behind coils of barbed wire on one of the clover's leaves. One Iraqi soldier surrendered to us under the overpass, just a dozen yards from the nearest British officer, before kissing a *Newsweek* reporter on the cheek. The Iraqi was afraid he'd be shot on sight without our protection. Unlike the POWs, a British captain at the intersection didn't appreciate our appearance. "It's dangerous here, and I strongly urge you to go back to Kuwait," he said. "But I can't make you do it."

Iraqi civilians from Safwan, the nearest town to the intersection, started trekking toward the underpass, curious to see firsthand the invaders, be they soldiers or reporters. The first Iraqi I spoke to, a young man in a white gown, came up with a 250-dinar banknote featuring a smiling Saddam etched in blue ink, and tried to swap it for one dollar, or several times its value. Here was my chance to find out what Iraqis themselves thought about the invasion that America launched with the promise of bringing them freedom, and of turning their country into an example of democracy and prosperity in the Middle East. I bought the 250-dinar note and asked a simple litmus-test question: "So, is this liberation or occupation for you?" The Iraqi, seventeen-year-old student Jasem Abdelaziz, smiled shyly and gave me an answer that he thought I wanted to hear: "It's freedom, of course. Saddam was very bad. He waged war on everyone." Soon he was rewarded by British soldiers with two packets of rice pudding. "Does this contain pork?" he asked anxiously.

Right then, a Toyota pickup truck sprinted up from the direction of Umm Qasr. Inside, a middle-age woman in a black dress screamed in pain, blood gushing from her shredded leg. As British military medics rushed to bandage what they said was a shrapnel wound, another battered pickup roared in, with another wailing woman in the back. On her knees she held two young men—her brother and her husband, she said. They seemed asleep, with flies feeding off their closed eyes. "The Americans murdered them, the Americans did," she kept repeating.

Suddenly, this war seemed a lot more complicated.

✦ ✦ ✦

My plans to install myself in Basra's Sheraton had to wait—the city wouldn't fall to British troops for almost three weeks. Fighting continued to rage just north of the Safwan clover leaf and, unlike a TV crew from Britain's ITN, I listened to military advice and didn't go that way. Instead, I headed north on the Baghdad highway, clogged by American military columns. Nobody was using the southbound lanes, so I just drove across the median—helpfully flattened by a tank—and raced up the wrong side.

My passenger, a French reporter who had covered plenty of wars, took a deep breath. "It's so liberating," he exhaled. "There are no more rules." War, with its suspension of conventions and its adrenaline rushes, was proving intoxicating—both for soldiers and for us, the privileged onlookers who didn't have to kill.

Our path to Baghdad was blocked by an immense traffic jam of American tanks and Humvees, waiting their turn while battles still raged for bridges across the Euphrates into the city of Nassiriya. The traffic would last days, and we decided to head back toward the Safwan clover leaf, expecting that Basra would fall first. The return wasn't easy. On a stretch of highway we'd just passed, a British armored personnel carrier smoldered, disabled by a roadside bomb—the first appearance of the devices that would take hundreds of American and British lives during the occupation. More bad news followed: the ITN crew had been caught in a crossfire on the road to Basra, with one journalist killed and two others, who have not been found, missing and presumed dead.

Once again, at the improvised media camp under the highway overpass, we found some colleagues in tears: a *Newsweek* reporter and photographer were also missing, caught in an Iraqi ambush; they would be rescued hours later by Marines. Half of our little convoy decided it was just too risky driving around in a soft-skinned vehicle that could turn into an instant fireball should bullets hit the jerry cans in the back, and returned to Kuwait. I chose to stay in Iraq, sleeping inside the car so I would be ready to rev up and sprint away on a second's notice.

The next morning those of us still remaining gathered our courage and headed north toward Basra, following in the path taken by the unlucky ITN crew. The first thing we saw up the road was abandoned Iraqi barracks which two British soldiers guarded at gunpoint while four Iraqis kneeled under a colorful mural of Saddam Hussein and

Jerusalem's al Aqsa mosque. The young Iraqis with Saddam mustaches under crewcut hairstyles were probably members of the regime's Fedayeen militia, the soldiers said. "We're not Baathis or soldiers, we're just looters, we only came to steal some doors," one of the Iraqis shouted in his defense.

The orgy of looting, which would cause more damage to Iraq's economy than the war's fighting, had already begun. A few minutes farther to the north, we reached the town of Zubayr, where the road was lined with dozens of Iraqi tanks, artillery pieces, and ordinary civilian vehicles carbonized in the invasion's maelstrom. Occupants' body fragments, helmets, gas masks, and unexploded ammunition lay on the ground in lakes of soot-covered diesel fuel and oil.

The local food depot's manager, Mohsen Galban, ran up to us to complain. The depot, which contained thirty days' worth of supplies, was, he blurted out, being looted as we spoke—and the American military was just shrugging off requests to restore order. "We ask the Army for help, but nobody helps us," he said with open anguish on his face. "American soldiers are simply encouraging the thieves."

This was the perception that, from the first days of the invasion, Iraqis would have of their liberators. Just as they did in Zubayr, American and British forces would later stand by and watch as looters destroyed and torched government buildings, hospitals, museums, and hotels across the land—culminating in an April 9, 2003, looting free-for-all in Baghdad. "Stuff happens," Defense Secretary Donald Rumsfeld shrugged it off at the time, explaining that looting was an acceptable price for "freedom." Not in Zubayr, a middle-class home to many oil industry workers, where, barely three days into the war, the breakdown in civil society was already seen as a bigger evil than repression under Saddam. Despite U.S. prewar assurances that Iraq's infrastructure would be spared, water and electricity were knocked out in Zubayr and much of the rest of Iraq—and would stay that way for months.

As I flipped open my notebook, schoolteacher Majid Kaddoum stepped forward from a gathering crowd, his voice shaking: "We are Iraqis, and we will defend our country and defeat the aggressors." Ismail Hantush, a local oil industry engineer, seethed, too: "The Americans are destroying our country. There will be a fight."

Trying to reason with them, I mentioned the massive humanitarian aid that, according to Pentagon announcements, was about to be rushed into Iraq. "We don't need any assistance," an oil worker in the crowd snapped at me. "If you let us live free and export our oil, we'd be richer than you."

I was inclined to take this anger and defiance with a pinch of salt, aware that fear of the regime and reluctance to support the United States openly had not yet dissipated. But when I walked away from the crowd, a local tailor came up to me with a sheepish smile. He pushed a bicycle, holding a baby boy propped on the seat. Looking straight into my face, and then pointing at wrecked cars on the road, he repeated almost entranced, in a quiet, murmuring voice, "We hate you. You are all criminals. We hate you. You are all criminals."

Not that long ago, as bombs were falling on Afghanistan, and I was surrounded by a mob near a Yemeni mosque, I felt righteously outraged by their hostility. But here, and for the first time in the Middle East, I was overcome with guilt. So much for the kisses and roses, I thought. I came to this man's country more or less as part of an invading armada sowing death and imposing foreign rule. It didn't matter, at least in his eyes, that I didn't personally carry a gun, or wasn't embedded. I was part of Them, the People Who Have Come to Harm Us. "The Criminals . . ."

✦   ✦   ✦

We had to retreat from Zubayr a few minutes later because shooting had begun in the side alleys. Already in the first days of the invasion, the conventional war that the American and the British militaries knew how to fight was morphing into an intractable insurgency. "We don't know if it's the Iraqi Army or the civilians picking up guns and firing at us," the British sapper Robert MacLeod told me in Zubayr, as he took a defensive position under a red banner that proclaimed, in the Arabic language, which he could not read: "Every last droplet of blood we'll give for you, O Saddam."

By dusk the highway intersection turned into a media circus, with about a hundred cars packing the strip and TV networks doing their "Live from Iraq" feeds. Across the road the British set up a mobile medical services tent. As I walked up, an Iraqi woman was screaming at the top of her lungs, ripping up her clothes and exposing her breast: her son, she said, had been wounded by American soldiers and then taken away, somewhere. "Where is he, where, where?" she yelled, pushing away her husband, who gently tried to cover her up and to steer her toward the car. The British didn't know and, I realized, would probably need days, or even weeks, to find out.

In Safwan, the nearby town, things were getting out of hand. The only gas station was being looted. Several journalists joined in the frenzy to help themselves at the pump, climbing atop the SUVs and siphoning fuel with a rubber hose attached to a tank above. By the mosque, past a Saddam mural destroyed by the Marines and an unscathed sign proclaiming "Palestine is Arabian from the river to the ocean," mourners were gathering to bury townsfolk who had been killed by American and British troops hours earlier. As I arrived, two more dead farmers were brought in. I asked a passerby, a farmer by the name of Majid Simsim, the same question: "Is it liberation or occupation?"

He gave me a sophisticated reply. "How can we be happy? They are killing our people here," he said, pointing at the mosque. "We want our country to be independent again, and the Americans to leave under a United Nations guarantee." This, I thought, in a supposedly pro-American Shiite town long oppressed by Saddam, while barely a slice of Iraq was under allied control.

✦ ✦ ✦

As night fell, a British captain who presided over the clover-leaf intersection sent out sentries to summon one person from every car. Things are real bad, he said in a hushed voice: a hostile crowd from Safwan was supposed to attack the intersection any time now, with Kalashnikov assault rifles and rocket-propelled grenades, or RPGs. Our retreat to Kuwait was cut off: we must immediately vacate the area and head up the highway toward Baghdad, he said. "After about fifteen klicks [kilometers], you can stop and spend the night." There would be no escort.

Suddenly everyone rushed to their cars. Italian journalists abandoned the pasta they'd been cooking on a portable stove; TV networks left behind generators and satellite dishes. Somehow, I ended up in the front of the convoy, driving toward Baghdad in pitch-black darkness. I tried to slow down, letting others take the lead, but they would slow down with me and pass up the chance to be the first victim.

I knew from the previous day's drive that the Marines and the British had set up small positions along the road to Baghdad. I also had no illusions about their likely reaction at seeing a column of unmarked SUVs approach unannounced in the middle of the night. We frantically called fellow reporters in Kuwait, trying to get the Marines to tell the units on the road that we're not a bunch of Baathi militiamen out to shower them with RPGs. After a good hour of calling—while curious Bedouins watched us from the desert's darkness, according to a colleague who scanned the fields with night-vision goggles—we found out that a reporter was staying with a British unit a dozen miles up the road. Through him the British were told we were coming.

Their faces blackened with camouflage paint, the British soldiers were in a somber mood. They whispered instructions: switch off all electronic equipment, wear helmets and flak jackets at all times, keep your voices low, and, above all, don't leave your vehicles. A U.S. truck convoy going in the opposite direction halted in the same spot, switched off its lights, and went silent. This was the evening Jessica Lynch and several other American soldiers were ambushed, just a little to the north. Near the Safwan clover leaf, insurgents' bullets and RPGs meant for our evacuated encampment killed, instead, a British patrol.

After a couple of hours, British officers spread a new message—it was too unsafe to stay, and we should continue farther north. To avoid ambushes, we had to drive without using headlights—and without hitting the brake pedal, so as not to be given away by brake lights. As I turned on the ignition, my Yukon's antitheft alarm suddenly went off, ringing across the desert. So much for being invisible.

After an hour of driving in moonless darkness, we finally arrived at the next British outpost, where once again we were gathered for a briefing. "Above all, don't go walking in front of where you just parked your cars—it's a mine field," we were warned.

Just a few seconds later, a Kuwaiti TV journalist—who spoke almost no English—plowed right ahead for a pee in the sands. We screamed at him with horror, bracing for an explosion. Unperturbed, he answered with a "What? What?" from afar and slowly returned, stepping evenly and deliberately. He lived.

✦ ✦ ✦

Umm Qasr fell later that week, and finally I had an entire "liberated" city to cover. Unlike tiny Safwan, Umm Qasr was a place of some size and contained Iraq's main port. I started out at the local Baath Party headquarters, an imposing building on a sandswept road. Like every other government office in town, it had been looted. Colorful membership certificates of the Palestine Liberation Brigade, showing Saddam firing a rifle in front of Jerusalem's al Aqsa mosque, spilled out on the ground outside. All the windows were wrecked. Inside, the once plush movie hall was thoroughly gutted.

A skinny twenty-nine-year-old lawyer, Ali Yasser, was surveying the damage inside, shaking his head. "Why, why do we have all this occupation and all this destruction?" he asked. I didn't answer and, somewhat uncomfortable with being alone in this empty, cavernous building, walked toward the sunshine outside. Yasser was eager to talk and followed me there. Then, in a moment of frankness, he lifted up his stained Bedouin robe. Underneath, he wore a T-shirt emblazoned with Saddam's smiling face. "People love him because he's a strong man," he said. Then he added nostalgically: "Iraq will never have someone as strong again."

Just then, another young man walked up to me, politely disagreeing. He thrust forward a crumpled black-and-white photograph. The images, he said, were of his relatives—killed when Saddam put down a Shiite uprising in 1991. "Saddam is a criminal and a crook," he said.

The week without water and electricity was beginning to take its toll. Children ran after our car, and after that of every other journalist, yelling out the only English words they knew: "Water, mister, water." Every time I stopped, a crowd of adults gathered around me, with the usual litany—no water, no electricity, no security, why? Then, inevitably, someone would ask to borrow my satellite phone to call relatives abroad and let them know he had survived the war. The images beamed across the Arab world by stations like Al Jazeera suggested that the entirety of Iraq lay in ruins, so the conversations on my Thuraya were amusingly similar.

"I'm okay and our house is okay," the man would shout to his relatives in Europe or the Gulf. "No, I'm not lying. It is okay. And Ahmed is also okay. And Uncle Ali is also okay. And Uncle Mohammed is also okay. No, it is true. No, I am not lying. No, really, we are all okay. Thanks be to God. Yes, Uncle Jaffar is also okay."

Initially, I would toss a water bottle out of the window, and let an Iraqi use my phone. But then I had to stop—my water reserves started running dangerously low, and, of course, everyone in every crowd ended up asking for a free overseas call, making work impossible. I soon caught myself becoming increasingly irritated and rude every time someone said "Water, mister, water" or pointed at my Thuraya. Mere days later, I was snapping back. If I had been a shellshocked Iraqi, emerging from decades of misery and suddenly colonized by extraterrestrial-looking armies, I'm sure I would have hated me.

✦ ✦ ✦

Umm Qasr, a rare Iraqi city with a permanent foreign presence, was the home of a United Nations liaison compound, once almost identical to the parallel UN outlet I had visited the previous year on the Kuwaiti side of the border. Now only a carcass of a building remained, with every window frame and air conditioner removed, every toilet bowl smashed up, and even the plaster ceiling brought down by looters.

Abu Ali, a dignified bank teller in a country where most banks were now closed to all but looters, greeted me in the UN's courtyard. "I'm ashamed," he said, furtively glancing at the building's destruction. Others loudly disagreed, only momentarily suspending their search for valuable items in the UN's trash—empty Heineken bottles, used batteries, a box from a Siemens cellular phone. "These people here, they had air conditioners and were living a good life—while we haven't seen such things since the 1980s," said one of the men, a port worker who introduced himself as Abu Hussein. "We live in an oil-rich country, and look at what shoes I'm wearing," he said, raising his foot to display an ancient sandal. "I've never had a refrigerator in my house. We can take all these things from here because it's our right."

A neighbor joined in the crowd. "Before, the secret police would not even allow me to approach here. If they ever saw us talking to foreigners, this would be it," he said, making a throat-cutting gesture. A British-educated seaman, Salman Ishak, took me aside. "These people are not savages," he said. "It's just that there is no law anymore." He spoke in a polite, measured voice with traces of BBC English, thrusting his finger into my chest and finding it surprisingly hard because of the bulletproof plate. "Now, if someone beats or rapes someone, who will take action? The Americans? I can kidnap you now and no one will care."

Half an hour later, I walked into the UN building again, stepping over staff schedules and old newspapers. This time, Abu Ali, the bank teller, was not so ashamed as to be watching from the sidelines. Together with his wife, he busily chipped at a divider wall, extracting wooden planks from the plaster. Cooking gas was no longer available, and his family would use the planks as firewood to prepare dinner, he said. "Anyway, this UN, they did nothing to prevent the invasion," he muttered. His wife, Hennan, had no feelings of guilt. She stared at me, smiling and showing off streaks of dirt on a dress that she was now unable to launder. "Where is freedom?" she asked. "We have no power, no water, no gas. Tell Mister Bush that I have dirty clothes."

◆　◆　◆

She wasn't the only one. Stuck in Umm Qasr, we slept in our cars, smeared with dust and using precious bottled water to clean teeth and wash hands. The Umm Qasr port was controlled by the military and out of bounds for us unilaterals; we parked overnight by the giant garbage pile near the port's gate.

In the morning we took the short drive from the dump to what had become a peculiar frontline on the outskirts of Basra. The British Army had seized a bridge across a canal leading into the city and positioned a few armored personnel carriers on both ends. But civilians were allowed to cross as if there were no war, circulating for weeks quite freely between Saddam-held territory and invaded areas to the south. As black clouds from oil fires hung above Basra, everyone heading into the city seemed to be carrying ripe Zubayr tomatoes—in trucks, cabs, bicycle baskets, and simple black plastic bags.

Basra was supposed to fall early on in the war. Predominantly Shiite and long oppressed by Baghdad, it's where the 1991 uprising against Saddam's rule began—with an Iraqi Army officer fresh from defeat in Kuwait lobbing a tank round into the local Baath Party headquarters. The United States initially encouraged that uprising, but then—fearful that Iraq would fall under the sway of Shiite Iran—relaxed the cease-fire terms to allow Saddam's military to use helicopter gunships. This doomed the rebellion and caused hundreds of thousands of casualties across Iraq's Shiite south. And as far as the Shiites I met on the Basra bridge were concerned, their 1991 tragedy had co-villains: America and Saddam.

"Now is not 1991. Now the Shiites hate America," one of these tomato farmers, Jaffar Shaddad, told me as he waited his turn to cross. Another farmer, irritated at the British military's thorough searches, started coughing as a British tank, the word "Carnage" daubed on its gun, passed by in a cloud of exhaust fumes. "How would the English like it if the Iraqis tried to stop them on the way from one English city to another?" he wondered. "This is occupation. Nothing else."

✦   ✦   ✦

By the second week of April, Basra fell and the bridge checkpoint was removed. But the Sheraton was no longer there. In the manner of entire neighborhoods across this city, once dubbed the Venice of the Orient because of its palm-tree–lined canals, the Sheraton had been looted, wrecked, and then set on fire. It was still smoldering by the time I arrived at Basra's riverfront. Straggling looters were loading pieces of glass and a shattered piano onto donkey carts.

The Shatt al Arab quay, near the Sheraton, was still bedecked with larger-than-life martial statues of Iraqi heroes of the war against Iran. Barely distinguishable from each other because of their Saddam mustaches, slight paunches, and similar uniforms, almost all of these iron-cast officers stood in the same defiant pose, pointing accusatory fingers at the Persian enemy to the east. Soon these, too, would be stolen and sold for scrap. At their feet the riverbank was covered with a tapestry of mortars, shells, rockets, and other discarded ammunition, free for the taking. The Basra Natural History Museum nearby was also burning. Across town, even the Museum of the Martyrs of Persian Aggression didn't survive. The museum had been dedicated to the suffering of Basra's people under almost daily Iranian bombardments during the Iran–Iraq war, with exhibition cases displaying the personal effects of the children, women, and old men who were killed. The custodian, himself a legless veteran, shook his head as he showed me the vandalized displays. The thieves even stole victims' baby shoes, wedding dresses, and toys.

Every few minutes—and almost nonstop during the night—gunfire volleys rang out. Rival gangs of looters were fighting each other in front of the Basra office of the Iraq Central Bank. All downtown buildings containing anything valuable—banks, shops, hospitals—were assailed by mobs ready to strip them bare. The smarter landlords simply mortared up, with bricks, all the windows and doors of their houses, giving the streets a blind, nightmarish look.

I searched for refuge inside the Teaching Hospital, a tall concrete block preserved because the British commandos had set up an observation point on its roof. The hospital's doctors, disheveled after many sleepless nights, were eager for Western protection and saw us reporters as their best hope, should the British commandos leave. I was offered a cot in an empty ward; occasionally, there was even cold water for showers. After the Umm Qasr garbage pile, this was luxury.

Down the corridor, limbless, quivering victims of allied bombing raids lay on urine-soaked cots like the ones we slept on. A better-off young man, Ershad Hamid, quietly moaned of pain as his mother tried to comfort him. His bandage was crimson red.

Hamid was unlucky enough to be at his job as an electricity technician of Basra Maternity Hospital, another clinic nearby, when five looters showed up the previous day. One of them had a Kalashnikov and wanted to steal the hospital's electric generator—a critical piece of equipment, considering that the main power supply had been knocked out. Hospital guards tried to fight back, and Hamid was caught in the crossfire, his arm shattered by high-velocity bullets.

"We look at the city—and we're afraid to go there," Adnan al Azzawi, the hospital's acting director, told me as he offered sweet tea. Armed bandits tried to carjack one of the hospital's vehicles right by the exit gate. Another vehicle, an ambulance, had been stolen before. Luckily, British troops had just caught it at a checkpoint—carrying an unlikely cargo of fresh fish. The medics' own apartments, in a housing complex that sat next to a military site, had already been gutted by looters. I asked Azzawi why he was only the acting director and what happened to the permanent one. The man was home, grieving over the death of his family, he answered. They had been killed in a U.S. bombing raid.

✦   ✦   ✦

That afternoon, in Azzawi's ground-floor office, I watched an old grainy TV set tuned to the Kuwaiti news channel. It was April 9, and the news led with the pictures from Baghdad. The doctors looked on in excitement as Saddam's statue on the capital's central Firdous Square was pulled down by Marines. A few hours later, a stolen Hyundai bus dragged a similar Saddam statue through Basra. Skinny, bare-chested teenagers danced on the roof of the bus, spitting on the statue and pelting it with shoes.

By nightfall, just as the Iraqi doctors expected, the British commandos left the hospital's roof for positions elsewhere. Casualties from gun battles among looter gangs started trickling in. At one point, a group of intoxicated, angry youths arrived to visit one of their wounded comrades, pulling out a live hand grenade on the hospital floor and threatening to blow it up.

Azzawi worried that, with the British gone, his hospital—the only one not yet looted in the city—would be destroyed as well. The handful of foreign reporters who took up residence on the trauma floor flocked to the roof. We joined the doctors who anxiously eyed groups of youngsters in stolen cars that, like sharks, circled around the compound, pausing by the gate and then taking off again. "We told them the British are not gone," one of the medics said. "You have to be the British."

Equipped with fancy blue-and-red tactical flashlights purchased during a prewar shopping spree, we stood at the edge of the roof, sending meaningless—but visibly alien—light signals into the darkness below. The city, deprived of electricity, still sounded like a battlefield, with red tracer rounds going up and the crackle of assault rifles interrupted by the occasional boom of a grenade. It occurred to me that, with my flashlight in hand, I made a perfect target.

Our other valuable commodity was satellite phones. Although we should have known better, someone dialed the British military's chief PR officer in the theater, a colonel with blow-dried hair. Two weeks earlier, his response to my question about military inaction during the looting spree in Umm Qasr was to straighten out his uniform, look me in the eyes, and ask: "Do I look to you like I'm a policeman?" This time the colonel simply told us to mind our own business. While the British never sent the commandos back to the hospital, they did order a patrol of armored personnel carriers to rumble by the hospital's gate—and that fleeting presence alone was enough to scare the looters away.

The next morning the hospital's doctors—most of them secular, and a great many Christian—called for more reliable help. They invited for tea a prominent Shiite cleric, asking him to protect the hospital with a religious militia. The cleric, Ali al Mussawi, was only too happy to oblige. "We don't accept the looters," he said. "What we are trying to do now is to save the property of every Iraqi—it has nothing to do with cooperating or not with the British and the United States." A few hours later, tough Shiite youths stood guard by the hospital's gate. In a few weeks such militias would become the law in much of Iraq.

✦　✦　✦

On the day after the fall of Baghdad, Basra's streets were covered with the innards of a dead state—a blanket of documents blown out of gutted government buildings, their pages embossed with Iraq's proud eagle and picked up by an occasional whirlwind. A couple of blocks from the hospital, in the home of a wealthy timber merchant, a new Iraq was in the making. Intrigued by the crowd of tribal sheikhs gathering outside, I stopped by and was quickly introduced to Sheikh Muzahim Mustafa al Kanaan, the man whom the British military would appoint as Basra province's governor.

Sheikh Muzahim, a sporty fifty-year-old with a neatly trimmed beard, red-checkered headdress, and meaty hands, sipped tea in a packed sitting room under a gilded ceiling. Pride of place on the wall was reserved for a faded picture from the old days: the host standing next to a younger, thinner Saddam Hussein. Sheikh Muzahim, a Shiite former general whose brother had been killed by Saddam, said he was only joining hands with the foreigners to stop looting and restore order. I asked him how he saw a future Iraq. "We want an independent and free country that won't have any foreign soldiers on its soil and that will govern itself as soon as possible," he said.

I also asked him what he had felt as he watched TV the previous day. The sheikh paused for a moment, presumably considering whether to tell me the truth, and then confessed that he found it hard to rejoice as he saw the Marines pulling down Saddam's statue. "I'm suffering from this sight," he said. "As an Arab and as an officer, I never expected to see foreign tanks running through our capital."

On the way out of Basra, I ran into a demonstration—probably the first in postwar Iraq—that was organized by Shiite clerics against Sheikh Muzahim's appointment. The clerics, flexing their muscle, demanded power for themselves. Walking through a putrid slum, the marchers waved a green flag and the banner WE WANT AN HONEST MAN. As our SUVs approached the march, the Shiite demonstrators reacted with a near-schizophrenic mixture of relief at the removal of Saddam and of long-standing resentment against Iraq's self-proclaimed liberators.

The handful of reporters' cars attracted immediate attention. A thousand or so demonstrators deviated from their path and ran toward us, across an empty field. Some teenagers and children immediately began to throw rocks. As a crowd surged around my vehicle, blocking off escape routes, Shiite militiamen armed with clubs pushed the mob back and cleared the exit. "Go, go now," one of them screamed at me.

Confusingly, another man pressed his nose to my window, smiling broadly and yelling in English: "Bush, Blair Good."

✦　✦　✦

I continued out of Basra and headed to Baghdad with two French colleagues. In the next town we entered, Nassiriya, we tried to report on the main square—and were instantly surrounded by yet another Shiite mob whose attitudes shifted, unpredictably, from welcoming to hostile. An ambulance cruised by, its loudspeakers beaming the same nonstop message: Those who have stolen dialysis machines from the hospital should please return them, as people are dying. People are dying. People are dying.

Fleeing Nassiriya before things turned ugly, we drove to an abandoned Iraqi air defense base nearby that had been taken over by the Free Iraqi Forces (FIF), a U.S.-outfitted militia of the Pentagon's then-favorite Iraqi, Ahmed Chalabi. Eager for some PR, Chalabi's handlers allowed us inside. A banker who had spent most of his life abroad and who had been convicted of defrauding a Jordanian bank, Chalabi seemed out of his element in this wrecked piece of desert, where his militiamen openly defecated among the featureless spread of rubble and waste. A chubby man dressed in a green blazer, a crumpled cream shirt, and combat boots, Chalabi passed much of the time pacing around with a Thuraya satellite phone. His retinue consisted of his Lebanese-raised daughter, a Pakistani-American spokesman, a tall American lobbyist, and, of course, a U.S. Special Forces colonel who kept complaining about State Department bureaucrats.

Chalabi—who, according to American occupation authority opinion polls, would emerge a year later as Iraq's most disliked politician—had to build up a power base now that he was back in his homeland. We followed him in the act with a minivan full of FIF militiamen, driving in a convoy to a God-forsaken Bedouin village of the Bidoor tribe across the Euphrates. There Chalabi strode purposefully into a village hall packed with tribesmen wearing traditional robes and sandals on bare feet, and took his place under a picture of a long-haired Imam Ali. His daughter settled in the adjoining chair, unveiled, prompting little murmurs of shock among the village notables. Later on, as

Chalabi went to inspect the ancient city of Ur, which is ensconced inside a busy air base, she fielded phone calls from her Parisian acquaintances. "C'est très difficile," she talked in melodious French. "Il n'y a rien ici, mais absolument rien." There is nothing here, but absolutely nothing.

To the sheikhs of Bidoor, Chalabi delivered his usual stump. "Baath is finished, and there will be no return for Baath and Saddam," he promised, describing at length how he, and the Americans, will revamp Iraq. The sheikhs, however, seemed more concerned with pressing day-to-day matters. "We have no water, no electricity," one of them insisted. Instead of responding, Chalabi simply got up and led the way to a sumptuous lamb and rice banquet served on the carpeted floor outside. Like everyone else, I dug in with bare hands, washing the food down with water of unclear origins passed around in a communal zinc cup. This was my first hot meal in a long time.

The tribesmen seemed genuinely puzzled by Chalabi and his foreign entourage. "Dr. Ahmed is very good," said Karkan Msir, a biology student, pointing by way of comparison to the fact that Saddam used to cut off the ears of those suspected of disloyalty. His own earlobes were still intact. "But there is one problem," Msir mused. "We don't know anything about Dr. Chalabi."

Nearby, another tribe member, Hardan Abbas, spotted a small badge with a blue, green, and yellow flag on the shirt of Francis Brooke, Chalabi's Washington lobbyist. "What is this?" he wondered. Brooke summoned a translator and answered that this was the flag of a new Iraq. "But we already have a flag, and we don't want to change it," Abbas said, genuinely puzzled.

An angered translator retorted that the current Iraqi flag contained the words "Allahu Akbar" ("God is Great")—allegedly written in blood by Saddam's own hand. "I don't care who wrote it—Allahu Akbar is what we all believe," Abbas said, flashing a watch decorated with Saddam's portrait. Then he looked in Chalabi's direction and shrugged. "Who is he? It is the Americans who now decide everything. Is this freedom?" On the way home to the base, our cavalcade lost its way. Chalabi and the Free Iraqis had to stop by an American checkpoint to ask for directions.

Later that evening, a platoon of FIF militiamen returned from its first patrol in the area. As the troops jumped from their trucks, waving Kalashnikovs in the air, they gathered around a gleefully smiling Chalabi.

"With our spirit and blood, we'll redeem you, O Ahmed," they chanted—borrowing the wording that had been used for decades to praise Saddam. Then one of these militiamen decided to engage in another ancient Iraqi custom and fired his gun into the air. Showing who's in charge, an American officer screamed at the Iraqi, pushed him and the gun away, and unloaded a string of obscenities.

Within a few weeks, the FIF—transferred to Baghdad—earned a reputation for looting and seizing private homes at gunpoint. A few weeks later, disgusted with such a power grab, the U.S. military finally moved in to disband Chalabi's FIF—and repossess many of the properties for themselves.

✦   ✦   ✦

From Chalabi's Nassiriya encampment we headed north to Najaf, the burial place of Imam Ali and the holiest shrine of Shiite Islam. Listening to BBC radio along the way, I heard that a pro-American cleric had been hacked to pieces on the steps of the golden-domed Ali mausoleum. All along desert roads to Najaf and Karbala, another holy Shiite city and the burial place of Ali's son Hussain, clusters of pilgrims walked in the baking sun, often barefoot. They carried banners—red, or green, or black—that fluttered in the wind, intense flecks of color in a gloomy, ocher-colored flatness.

As I drove into town and past a giant cemetery where Shiites from the world over want to be buried, I couldn't help noticing that we were the only foreigners for miles. Heads turned at the sight of my SUV, probably the first of its kind to enter Najaf. It was a more tense, nervous city than Basra or Nassiriya. I didn't see anyone smiling or waving at us. Remembering how we'd been mobbed in previous days, I decided it was too dangerous to stop. We headed on to Karbala, hoping for a warmer reception there.

By then it was already getting dark, and we had nowhere to sleep. I saw a dismounted U.S. patrol on a Karbala street and approached, asking for shelter. A friendly lieutenant sent me to a school occupied by troops three blocks away and—after long radio negotiations with his superiors—the company commander let us inside.

It was the first time I had spent the night with American soldiers during the invasion. The troops, from the Eighty-Second Airborne Division, had just fought their way up through the city of Samawah, halfway between Najaf and Nassiriya. Now they had to deal with another foe, diarrhea. A bug had gotten into the troops' food supply, and now most of them, including the company commander, were curled up with fever and downing antibiotics. To deal with the bug's effect, the soldiers had taken three chairs from the classroom, punched football-size holes through the seats, and set them up in the garden as improvised toilets. Although the school courtyard was surrounded by a wall, whatever the soldiers did was perfectly visible from the surrounding Iraqi buildings. Only a thin camouflage net partially shielded the latrine from dozens of Iraqi families living near the school.

Occasionally, some locals would come to the building, yelling in Arabic to uncomprehending troops that they wanted the school back. I looked at a pile of textbooks on the terrace, leafing through Book 5 of the *New English Course for Iraq,* with the obligatory full-page picture of Saddam, on page 3. Next to a drawing of two unveiled ladies wearing fairly short 1950s style Western dresses, the book had a typical piece of dialogue:

"Hello, Layla."

"Hello, Shatha. Oh, what a pretty dress. Are you going to a party?"

"No. It's Students' Day, you know, and there is a good play on."

"Oh, what is the subject of the play?"

"It's about the role of students at home and in society."

Here the transition from pretty-dress talk to politics is abrupt. Layla replies: "Oh, this has often been stressed by our Beloved Leader President Saddam Hussein. In one of his speeches, he says, 'We do aspire to see students initiate in their homes a new pattern of life arising from the Arab Baath Socialist Party principles.'"

As a form of rent in exchange for our relative safety in the Karbala school, we gave the soldiers satellite phones so that they could call home. For most, this was the first call since the war began. Often as young as eighteen, the troopers were still reliving in detail their last battle, against a group of Saddam Fedayeen in Samawah. "Remember, when I shot that guy, he just went like this—*wheesh, wheesh, wheesh,*" one of the younger soldiers recalled over dinner of a Meal Ready-to-Eat. As his MRE was being warmed in a self-heating chemical liquid, he stood up and mimicked the convulsions of a body falling on the ground, torn asunder by high-velocity rounds: "Yeah, that was really cool."

An older soldier with unsettlingly steady, fish-like eyes and an exceedingly polite demeanor told me he also once lived in Italy, serving near Vicenza with the U.S. Army's 173rd Airborne Brigade. He left the Army a few years earlier and moved to Texas to work as a death row prison guard. "But I got really bored waiting for them to die," he explained with a disarming smile. "So I thought I'd go back to the Army to get me some myself." In the morning the soldiers wished us good luck, and we set off for Baghdad.

✦ ✦ ✦

On the way to Baghdad from Karbala, thankfully unscathed by the stomach bug, we drove through towns that had yet to be seized by American troops. In a war without clear frontlines, it was easy to wander into the wrong side—and several Western reporters had mistakenly driven into regime-controlled areas in previous weeks. (Saddam treated these captives rather nicely, taking them all from the south to air-conditioned rooms in Baghdad's Palestine Hotel.)

As we pressed north, the towns and villages halfway to Baghdad were bustling and, unlike the south, showed no trace of war. I suddenly realized that men wearing green Iraqi fatigues still lurked in some corners, following us with puzzled looks and trying to figure out whether we belonged to the invading forces. Large posters announcing "International Press" in Arabic were on every window of our car, which had no license plates. That's probably what allowed us to get through that swath of as-yet-unconquered Iraq without getting shot.

On the outskirts of Baghdad, the picture began to look grimmer. In one town Saddam hid tanks in narrow side alleys between homes and shops off the main avenue. The United States bombed them anyway, hitting some of the houses, too. Driving through town was like following the tracks of a bush fire. Coagulated asphalt was buried under oil and soot, and cars maneuvered carefully to avoid running tires over unexploded shells. In a palm grove just outside Baghdad, a few hundred yards to our right, full-out war still raged. As helicopter gunships lobbed missiles at an unseen enemy, fireballs were popping up above the tree line in straight succession, one after another.

Holding a ridiculously (and probably deliberately) inaccurate tourist map of Baghdad, I tried to navigate toward the Palestine and Sheraton hotels, a compound where most foreign reporters were based. Picking the shortest route, I drove to Saddam's huge palace grounds, then just seized by tanks of the Third Infantry Division. The tired, grime-covered lieutenant in the first tank at the gate saw my military press pass and just waved us across. So did the second, and the third tank up the road. Zigzagging to avoid shells and jagged shrapnel, we drove by Saddam's palace, a gaudy block decorated on every roof corner with four giant heads of the dictator wearing a Babylonian helmet. Then we approached the fourth tank. Seeing my Yukon, its officer jumped off, grasped his pistol with both hands, crouched, aimed at me, and began shouting words I couldn't understand from the distance. I hit the brake as hard as I could, and then slowly, slowly, stepped out of the car, making sure I held nothing except the yellow press badge in my hands. Then I walked the several dozen yards separating us. The lieutenant kept aiming at me until he could read my credentials. Then, without emotion, he just waved: "Okay. You're good to go."

Baghdad opened up from a bridge across the languid, decaying flow of the Tigris. Camouflaged by dust, the city's expanse of low-rising houses seemed color-matched to American soldiers' desert-style uniforms. Almost all the taller buildings scattered around—most of them government ministries—had been gutted by looters and bombs. Like chimneys, they emitted clouds of intense black smoke that rose to the skies.

Ten minutes later, we drove up to the Palestine gates, where helpful Marines chased away a throng of Iraqis, flung open the coil of barbed wire, and let us—privileged foreigners—inside. Earlier that week one floor of the hotel had been blasted by a U.S. tank shell, killing two foreign reporters. Underneath the hotel, a fleet of dusty SUVs just like mine competed for space, some still bearing the stickers of Kuwaiti rent-a-car agencies. In the lobby the former Iraqi Information Ministry booth was still plastered with cartoons showing long-nosed Zionists pushing their American puppets to defile Arab honor. Newspapers of the defunct regime lay on the floor. I bumped into journalist friends who had spent the entire war in Baghdad, sleeping in beds, eating in restaurants, and regularly using flush toilets and showers. Suddenly, I realized just how dirty and disheveled I was.

7

IRAQ

One Saddam for Every Neighborhood

Baghdad's Palestine Hotel, from which the Marines briefly tried to run the eastern half of the city, instantly turned into the occupation's most visible symbol. On the square in front of it, where Saddam's statue once stood, thousands of Iraqis pressed all day against barbed wire, trying, usually in vain, to get into the hotel with requests for jobs, aid, and information about missing relatives.

By the second week of Baghdad's occupation, anti-American demonstrations replaced the supplicants. I went to one of the first such protests, held by a group of Sunni tribal sheikhs, and started writing down the already familiar chants calling for Americans to leave Iraq. A thin, finely featured woman in a black veil interrupted one of the sheikhs and told me in good English: "Actually, I think we need the Americans to stay. We need them to help transform our country." I turned toward the woman and asked her to wait for a minute while I finished interviewing the protest's organizer. Fixing hostile stares, some of the men in the crowd stepped forward to upbraid her in feverish whispers. A few seconds later, she was gone. I would never hear similar words in public again.

Inside the Palestine lobby, a man with a stubby beard and shifty eyes was holding court. Aides whispered to reporters that this was the new governor of Baghdad. The man, Mohammed Mohsen al Zubaydi, was vague about his credentials apart from the fact that he had been associated with Ahmed Chalabi. Soon he started addressing reporters, who dwelled on his every word at packed press conferences. Baghdadis were so disoriented and traumatized by the sudden collapse of Saddam's authority that, within days, thousands flocked to Zubaydi's office to fill out applications for jobs, a process that required the deposit of a fee. It was only after Zubaydi declared that he intended to travel to the next OPEC meeting as a representative of Iraq that the U.S. military noticed and briefly detained him. Nothing was heard about the "governor" again.

Outside the hotel's barbed wire perimeter, I bumped into the woman who would help me penetrate Iraqi society in months to come. A retired university professor of English, Samira stood out in the crowd, dressed with an elegance I had not yet seen in Iraq, except on the pages of Book 5 of the *New English Course*. She told me she was bored out of her wits after hunkering down at home during the war. Blessed with a healthy curiosity, she was eager to work with a journalist to figure out for herself what was happening to her country.

Samira was a Kurdish Shiite, belonging to a once-thriving minority that had been decimated by deportations and killings under Saddam. Raised in Baghdad, with Arabic as her mother tongue, she had survived all these years by blending in and pretending to be Arab. She and her husband, Jaffar, a former driver of an Iraqi general, were elated that Saddam was gone. One day several weeks later, Jaffar looked at my handheld global positioning system device, which mapped our routes with a precision of a few yards, and shook his head to marvel: "And Saddam thought he could beat the Americans who have all this. . . ."

On the same afternoon that we met at the square outside the Palestine, Samira invited me home to have lunch with Jaffar and their daughter, Baan. As we waited for Baan to finish cooking, Samira switched on the TV. With Iraqi transmitters destroyed by American bombing, TV offered only two choices—a grainy U.S. propaganda reel showing looped footage of President Bush's speeches about bringing freedom and democracy to Iraq, and the Al-Alam station from Iran.

Iran had set up this Arabic-language news channel before the war, investing in powerful transmitters that could beam the signal all the way to Baghdad. Now, in the critical first days when Iraqis were making up their minds about their American rulers, Al-Alam enjoyed a near-monopoly over news. Its slant was obvious from the promo: a shot of a Marine firing a weapon, superimposed on the footage of an Iraqi mother cradling a dead child.

Unlike her secular mother, Baan wore a veil. And after days of watching Al-Alam, she was increasingly angry with the way the United States was behaving. Her six-year-old son showed me his drawings: they were of him shooting down American planes. His dad, an officer in the Iraqi military, wisely chose to stay home during the invasion.

A slender, soft-spoken schoolteacher, Baan was also a sharpshooter who participated in national competitions. After lunch she fetched the family's arsenal, about average for Iraq. Atop the closet, she picked up a Kalashnikov AK-47. From the attic, she brought out a sports air gun and a shiny 9-millimeter pistol. Another AK-47 had been loaned to a neighbor. "Careful—it is loaded, and it hurts," she warned me in a melodic voice as she passed the 9-millimeter, over tea and cookies. "I know how to fire them all," her son boasted as he raised his head from a Lego game.

With her school gutted by looters, Baan was spending her days shopping for a perfect handgun at the open-air weapons markets that sprouted up after the war. She wanted a mint-condition 5-millimeter that she could easily conceal in her purse. "I liked the weapons before because I liked the sports. But now we need them for survival," she said.

With Samira, I went the next day to have a look at the gun fairs. We drove to the central square of the New Baghdad neighborhood, a middle-class, predominantly Shiite area not far from her home. Technically, these gun markets were illegal—American occupation authorities banned the carrying of weapons in the streets and limited ownership to one gun per household. But the gun merchants at New Baghdad made little effort to conceal their wares, which they sold among carts full of cucumbers, tomatoes, pickled mango, and counterfeit whiskey. Every few seconds, a shot or a burst of automatic gunfire rang out as prospective customers tested the quality of goods on offer.

I walked into the middle of the crowd in the square and struck up a conversation with a cab driver by the name of Ibrahim Ali. He told me his neighbors' home had been looted days earlier. "It is very dangerous here, so I need protection," he said, inspecting a Hungarian-made Kalashnikov. The vendor, a young man with a trimmed beard, ended up selling the gun for 100,000 dinars—a bagload of bills bearing Saddam's beaming likeness that, at the time, was worth around $35. I asked the man about the rifle's origin. His reply was frank: "We looted it."

I turned to another merchant, Ali Abdulhussein. He showed off a 25-millimeter Russian-made machine gun with a melon-size round clip—a weapon that is usually mounted on a rooftop to mow down crowds. Abdulhussein, a twenty-eight-year-old dressed in a canary-yellow shirt, had sold three such guns in the previous three days, at a profit of 50,000 dinars apiece. "People will do anything these days to protect their families," he said. But wasn't he afraid of the Americans? I asked.

Abdulhussein's mouth widened in a grimace of scorn when I mentioned the U.S. military. Yes, he said, an American patrol rumbles by, about three times a day. "But when they come, everyone hides the weapons behind their backs and looks at the Americans with a wave and a smile," he said. "They never stop and never seize anything."

I recalled this conversation later that year, after hearing about the occupation authority's new measure of its own popularity on Iraqi streets: the so-called wave factor, measured in the level of response U.S. officials received when they waved at Iraqi bystanders from their shotgun-riding convoys.

At the New Baghdad market, the waves of Iraqis clearly masked mounting hatred. Buyers packed in a circle around me, jostling to speak out first. "You know why we are buying these weapons?" shouted Alaa Habib, a fifty-three-year-old oil company worker, as he pointed at Abdulhussein's machine gun. "So that we could kill American soldiers if they don't leave our country."

Abbas Ali, an unemployed government worker, interrupted him. "The American Army is very, very bad. All they do here is murder children and women," he yelled. He said he had personally witnessed Marines shooting up a car, with women and children as passengers, that failed to stop quickly enough at a Baghdad checkpoint. Samira whispered, unflinching: "We should go."

◆ ◆ ◆

From the gun market, we crossed the Tigris to the huge compound of Iraq's dreaded military intelligence. Since the 1980s, thousands and thousands of Shiites suspected of dissidence, as well as other assorted foes of the regime, were taken into the walled riverside complex to be tortured and often to disappear forever.

In the fall of 2002, Saddam had flung open the gates of his prisons, freeing most detainees. But countless inmates, often taken away decades ago, were still missing. Many families were convinced that their loved ones continued to rot in secret underground jails in the military intelligence compound. A crowd had gathered at the gates, guarded by an American tank. By the time I arrived, men were banging on the metal and demanding to be let in to dig the ground and search for the buried dungeons.

"Give us back our prisoners," the protesters started chanting. One man, Ahmed Fellah, raised his voice, telling the crowd he had worked as a painter inside the compound the previous year. His assertion that he had seen stairways leading to secret underground cells prompted gasps and another volley of insults against the American troops. "I have heard voices from the ground. Our people are there," shouted Moaz Saheb Walid, who told me that his cousin had been arrested in 1981 and was never seen again.

An American sergeant stepped out of the gate to tell the crowd, in English, that no such underground cells existed. His words were drowned in jeers.

It was clear to me then, and would be made abundantly clear by the discovery of mass graves all over Iraq in the following months, that these missing prisoners were most likely dead. Yet their Iraqi families shied away from the searing truth and instead prowled the streets, starting to dig at the slightest rumor. On the way back, we bumped into one such crowd blocking the highway underpass of Baghdad's central Tayaran Square. Someone claimed to have heard tapping on the side wall, and suddenly all traffic was stopped and sweat-soaked men were tearing away slabs of concrete with their bare hands. In a few minutes they ripped out a metal door that led to a ventilation duct and entered a narrow tunnel parallel to the road.

An hour later, a two-Humvee patrol of Marines showed up, accompanied by an Iraqi police car. Because the Marines had no interpreter, Samira stepped in to explain what was going on. The patrol commander set up the perimeter and, wielding a green chemical light, sloshed through the mixture of sewage and mud to inspect the pitch-dark opening. I and Samira, in her elegant shoes, followed suit. What we discovered was a young man who had entered earlier to look for prisoners; there was no trace of secret dungeons. If any voices had been heard in the tunnel before, they were drowned out by the rumbling of thousands of mostly Shiite men outside.

Back on firm ground, Samira volunteered to help the Marines. A few months later, such interaction would become impossible. But back then, many Baghdadis still viewed American soldiers as potential allies. Samira climbed on a cinder block and, with professorial authority in her voice, talked to the crowd—addressing the ruffled, wide-eyed men with a maternal "shebab," Arabic for "boys." "Move back and be quiet, please. We can't find anyone if we can't hear anything," she urged them. The mob seemed to obey for a few minutes, moving back a dozen steps, but then someone would start pushing and shoving again, the tentative order would collapse, and the crowd would expand to brush up against the Marines.

Putting his hand, black from mud, on my notebook to prevent me from writing down his words, the patrol commander told his Marines that he couldn't find anything in the tunnel but that he would search a little more "just to appease the masses."

Then his commander radioed in that an unrelated anti-American demonstration was marching our way. The Marines, guns pointed at the crowd, ran back to their Humvees and roared away. The Iraqis started heckling and booing. "The Americans are like Saddam. They don't want to free our people," someone shouted.

I was beginning to see how the Shiites' hatred for Saddam and their growing dislike for the American occupiers were melding, creating increasingly fanciful conspiracy theories. Soon I would hear, more and more often, that Saddam had been an American agent who invaded Iran and then Kuwait so that the United States would have an excuse to colonize this part of the world and control its oil supplies. By the next year, many Shiites would end up hating the United States more than Saddam.

In early 2004, I was given a lecture on this subject in Nassiriya by Aws al Khafaji, a prominent Shiite leader for southern Iraq. I had asked him about the 1991 Shiite uprising, and whether Republican Guard generals who had crushed the rebellion at the time should be able to regain prominence in a new Iraq. "We can forgive our brothers from the Republican Guard who want to help rebuild our country," he answered. "But we will never forget or forgive the Americans, whose planes were circling overhead, helping out, as Saddam's helicopter gunships were mowing down our people."

✦ ✦ ✦

Khafaji belonged to an organization that calls itself the Bureau of the Martyred Sadr. The martyred one was Ayatollah Mohammed Sadeq al Sadr, a populist Shiite cleric who commanded wide respect among Iraq's poor, especially in the giant Saddam City slum on the northeastern edge of Baghdad. Ayatollah Sadr, while stridently anti-Western, sought to remove the taint of collaboration with Shiite Iran that has always hung over Iraq's Shiite majority. So, just like the Hezbollah in Lebanon, he had adopted a fierce Arab nationalist language, deliberately blurring the Shiite–Sunni divide. The ayatollah was killed in 1999, apparently on Saddam's orders. His son Muqtada—by all accounts younger than thirty—was now in charge of the movement, and his ambition was to represent all Iraqis, not just the Shiites.

A baby-faced overweight cleric with bad teeth and an unkempt black beard, Muqtada was an unlikely leader. Wearing the black turban of a *syed*—a descendant of Imam Ali—he spouted uncompromising anti-American rhetoric in frequently ungrammatical Arabic marred by a nasal, lower-class accent. While Muqtada clearly lacked a basic education, from the very first days after the war his organization displayed its strength: a militia of several thousand impressively disciplined thugs who regularly descended on downtown Baghdad from Saddam City, now renamed Sadr City, in looted buses and atop garbage trucks, to march and chant at the top of their lungs. Their favorite slogan, simple and catchy, was "*La Amrika, la Saddam, naam naam la Islam*"—"No to America and no to Saddam, Yes, yes to Islam." This militia, well armed and called Mahdi's Army, quickly moved on to intimidate Muqtada's two rivals for supremacy in the Iraqi Shiite world: the septuagenarian Grand Ayatollah Ali al Sistani, and the Iranian-backed Hakim family of prominent clerics.

Ayatollah Mohammed Baqr al Hakim, exiled in Iran until the war, had taken part in the U.S.-sponsored Iraqi opposition. The fiery name of his movement, the Supreme Council for Islamic Revolution in Iraq, didn't stop Hakim from joining the American-created interim authorities. Sistani, according to the U.S. military, had also come on board and issued a *fatwa* urging Iraqi Shiites to cooperate with the American effort. Unlike these two senior clerics, Muqtada was virtually unknown outside Iraq until the collapse of Saddam's regime.

Muqtada and Sistani lived a few blocks apart in Najaf. The day after meeting Samira in Baghdad, I decided to return to Najaf as a passenger in her husband's beat-up Toyota rather than in my Yukon, a magnet for unwanted attention. Jaffar was eager to go—although his enthusiasm had more to do with restocking his supplies of *torshi,* the discolored pickled vegetables for which Najaf is famous. Burnt-out remains of Iraqi tanks, truck-mounted rocket launchers, and artillery pieces lined the road, a testament to the lethal efficiency of American firepower.

Built around the shrine to Imam Ali, who was killed here, and surrounded by a giant cemetery, Najaf is a city that lives off mourning and death—somber, bitter, and submerged as it is in the Shiites' millennial sense of having been wronged. The streets are filled with the black turbans of Ali's descendants, dressed as if to add to the sense of a permanent funeral.

The holy city seemed even more tense than when I had driven through, without stopping, the previous week—just after the macabre slaughter of Abdelmajeed al Khoei, the most pro-American of Iraq's Shiite hierarchs. The son of Sistani's predecessor as grand ayatollah,

Khoei had lived for years in London exile. Even before the fall of Baghdad, the U.S. military flew him to Najaf on a special plane as part of a grand plan to recruit Shiite support for the occupation.

Under Saddam, a loyal supporter of the Baath regime was serving as *kalidar,* or custodian, of the blue-tiled Imam Ali mosque, the center of Islamic jurisprudence, pilgrimage, and learning across the Shiite world. After Najaf's seizure by the United States, that man, known as Haidar al Kalidar, went into hiding, fearing retribution from Shiite clerics who had been persecuted by Saddam.

Khoei saw a chance to reconcile the city and to cement his stature by offering shelter to the *kalidar,* and invited Saddam's appointee back to the mosque. Feeling that Khoei's protection essentially meant protection by the United States, the *kalidar* accepted. But within minutes, the two men were surrounded by an angry crowd inside the mosque's courtyard. Khoei fired a pistol into the air, trying to disperse the mob. A group of armed men—by most accounts, Muqtada's supporters— then broke into the shrine compound, setting off a long gun battle with Khoei's bodyguards. After protracted negotiations, another group of Muqtada's supporters escorted Khoei and the *kalidar* outside. There a crowd unexpectedly closed in with knives, swords, and axes. Kalidar was dismembered and hacked into small pieces. Khoei, who wore a flak vest under his robe, proved harder to kill. He was stabbed more than thirty times and his remains were dragged across the city, leaving behind a trail of blood on the streets.

By the time we arrived in Najaf, Muqtada's supporters had switched their ire to Sistani. An ultimatum demanded that the ayatollah leave Najaf or else. Sistani, whose popularity was incomparably greater than Khoei's, responded by calling on supporters from across Iraq to flock to the city. A defiant, suspicious crowd of those backers met us by the entrance to a narrow alleyway that led to Sistani's modest home. Nearby streets were bedecked with tribal banners of solidarity. Alarmed by Muqtada's threats, the spiritual leader of Lebanon's Shiites, Ayatollah Mohammed Fadlallah, had just issued a ruling urging Iraqis to protect Sistani. So, too, did a Shiite leader in Kuwait, Mohammed al Mohri.

Nervous guards checked our bags and let us into the alleyway. Samira, dispensing with her 1950s ladies' wear, was wrapped in a black *abaya* for the occasion. Even so, her presence was unsettling to Sistani's aides. Couldn't I bring a male fixer with me? they asked. After a long theological argument, Samira persuaded the aides that it would be acceptable for her to be in the same room with me if Jaffar, her husband, joined us, too. Finally we were ushered in and sat, cross-legged, on the carpeted floor. A quarter of an hour later, Sistani's son, Mohammed Reda al Sistani, came out to talk, sitting down on the carpet but avoiding any direct contact with Samira.

The ayatollah—who would maintain his mystique by shunning all public appearances and refusing to meet with American officials—was in hiding "somewhere in Najaf," his son said. "Blood is flowing everywhere and guns are shooting everywhere," he explained quietly. "Until the situation improves, my father will not appear." While he wouldn't openly criticize Muqtada, Mohammed Reda was worried by violence in the city after Khoei's death. "I expect anything," he said. "I feel very pessimistic."

I asked him whether it was true that Sistani had issued a *fatwa* urging Iraqi Shiites to cooperate with the American occupation. "It's all lies, lies, lies," the ayatollah's son exploded. He was clearly disturbed by suggestions that Iraqi Shiites—and especially Iranian-born Sistani—were somehow unpatriotic. "Look at the war—where were the heaviest battles, the heaviest resistance?" he asked, and then answered himself by proudly listing the Shiite cities of Umm Qasr, Basra, and Nassiriya. "It took the Americans more time to seize Umm Qasr than Baghdad," he exclaimed, "let alone Tikrit," the former dictator's birthplace.

Sistani's position was clear—the Americans should leave Iraq immediately. "There shouldn't be an occupation authority here even for just one day," his son announced, and got up to signal that the interview was over. Yet for more than a year after Mohammed Reda's declaration, the occupation officials in Baghdad operated on the premise that Sistani would end up endorsing American plans for Iraq.

✦ ✦ ✦

From Sistani's alley we walked to Muqtada's home, just across the square from the Imam Ali mosque. Like Sistani, Muqtada was refusing visitors at the time, fearing for his own life. After waiting in a crowd of agitated young men, many hurrying by with stacks of freshly printed leaflets containing Muqtada's *fatwas,* I was told to come up the stairs and into a bare room with two brand-new computers looted from a government building in Baghdad. The host who welcomed me was Riyad Nouri, Muqtada's brother-in-law. A man in his late twenties, Nouri introduced himself as the new supervisor of teaching at the Imam Ali mosque.

I asked him about Muqtada's anti-American fervor. After all, wasn't the cleric grateful that the United States had ousted his father's killer? "Americans say that they will release the Iraqi people from injustice. If this is true, we will thank them," Nouri answered, carefully measuring every word. But, he added quickly, Muqtada's men will fight if they see that one dictatorship has been replaced with another. He kept his word. A year later, amid bloody battles between Muqtada's militia and American troops for control of Najaf, the U.S. military captured Nouri—describing him as the Shiite militia's chief battlefield commander.

Politely, I inquired about the killing of Khoei. Nouri started out by portraying his brother-in-law as an innocent victim. "They all try to weaken him with their rumors," he said. "Now I believe these enemies are trying to kill Muqtada." Of course, he hastened to say, he didn't quite mourn the former *kalidar.* Unlike Khoei, Muqtada had refused the man's request for protection. "Kalidar was a member of the regime. All the people here wanted to kill him, to drink his blood," Nouri explained, making a sucking noise for greater effect.

An older tribal sheikh, Adnan Shehmani, interrupted him. The unfortunate incident happened because everyone hated the *kalidar,* and not because Muqtada or others nurtured any hostility against Khoei, he said. "Nobody could control the crowd. They were in extraordinary anger. Many plunged their knives into Khoei's body without even knowing who he was," he said. "We couldn't do anything. And now everyone is saying that followers of Muqtada al Sadr killed him. It's not true." I was almost convinced.

✦　✦　✦

Later that day, in another dusty alley of Najaf, I sat down on another old carpet with yet another black-turbaned cleric, Mohammed

Hussein al Hakim. In his back room he uneasily fingered worry beads and told me more about Khoei's murder, which he had witnessed.

Muqtada's men tricked Khoei into surrendering arms and leaving the mosque with a false promise of safe passage, he said. Once outside, unarmed and surrounded by a bloodthirsty crowd, Khoei tried to appeal to Muqtada, who was surveying the scene from a porch a few dozen yards away. When Khoei tried to break away, and ran toward his purported protector, Muqtada simply turned his back on the man. Seconds later, Khoei was dead.

Hakim was shaking his head as he complained about the mounting violence. Then a visibly distressed aide stepped inside and locked the door behind himself. "Three people whom we don't know just forced their way into the house, and we fear they want to harm you," the aide whispered into Hakim's ear.

Unnerved, the cleric looked at me and said: "Our situation is unsafe, and there are weapons and bandits everywhere." Eighteen members of the Hakim family had been executed by Saddam's regime, and sixteen others never returned from prison. "I fear that the current situation will cause a bigger death toll in my family than what happened before," he said and stood up. "Now, if you excuse me, I have to leave," he concluded and slipped out through the back door.

I walked back to the crowded front room and peered through the door. A hundred or so Muqtada supporters—the by-now-familiar breed of disciplined young thugs—were demonstrating in front of the house, waving banners with saccharine paintings of Shiite saints and chanting in an accusatory tone: "Yes, yes to Islamic unity." Unity, of course, meant submission to Muqtada.

Hakim's premonition of more bloodshed proved correct. In August 2003 a powerful car bomb went off in front of the Imam Ali mosque, just a few yards from where Khoei had been slaughtered. The nearly one hundred people killed by the bomb included Hakim's uncle and the clan's chief, Ayatollah Mohammed Baqr al Hakim, as well as other family members. The culprits were never caught. Then, twice in 2004, Najaf and Karbala became lethal battle zones in a guerrilla war between Muqtada's militia and the United States. Much of downtown Najaf was reduced to rubble, and even the Shrine of Ali itself was damaged by indiscriminate fighting before Ayatollah Sistani brokered a tenuous cease-fire.

✦   ✦   ✦

Intrigued by the source of Muqtada's power, I returned to Baghdad and, the following morning, headed to Sadr City. As in Najaf, Samira wore her *abaya,* while Jaffar kept sizing up shiny new cars on the streets and clicking his tongue. "Looters, they're all looters. Look at this car, and at this car. They were all stolen," he would say after examining the license plates.

At the entrance to Sadr City, painters were busy replacing a huge Saddam mural with an acrylic picture of the two Sadrs. I was looking for the Hekma mosque, the Sadr organization's headquarters at the time, on the outer edge of the neighborhood. The area was one sprawling traffic jam, with children wandering up to the cars to sell, for a few cents apiece, blank military documents and passports just looted in downtown Baghdad.

The mosque was a pleasant shaded oasis amid trash-cluttered roads and haphazard mud houses. A man in an ample white gown, Sheikh Abdelzahra al Sweyadi, sat on a soiled sofa in the courtyard, surrounded by dozens of the faithful. The mosque's imam, Sweyadi had been wounded by Saddam's Fedayeen militia in previous weeks and still had trouble getting up. An aide gave me a tour of the premises. The ground floor storage room behind the sofa was crammed with dusty computers, typewriters, and printing machines, equipment looted from one of Iraq's official media organizations. The courtyard's corner was occupied by the anti-American banners and placards that I had seen waved in front of the Palestine Hotel earlier that week. A room upstairs was packed with phones, tires, medicines, and electrical equipment. Five looted vehicles were parked outside, including a red double-decker bus and a repainted army truck. On the gate hung a poster with the clergy's request for the looters to return goods that had been stolen from the French ambassador's residence. According to the list, these included ten expensive Persian carpets, one red Jacuzzi, one fridge, one oven, and five air conditioners.

The cars outside and the goods inside storage rooms, Sweyadi told me, had been brought to the mosque after the Shiite leadership appealed to the faithful to return what they had stolen after the fall of Baghdad. But once placed in the mosques, the loot became too valuable for the clerics to simply return it to legitimate owners, except in politically expedient cases, such as to help out the French embassy. Instead, Muqtada's men, who often organized the looting in the first place, redistributed the goods to buy political loyalty. Sweyadi was refreshingly frank about his mission.

"The people looted because they felt angry with the Saddam regime," he said. "Now we told them it was not Saddam's money, it is the people's money, and that they should bring it all here. We will return the cars and the equipment to the offices. But we will distribute the food and the medicines to the poor people here ourselves," he said. I sat down next to his sofa and watched the proceedings.

A young man named Hammad Jabbar, who silently knelt to kiss Sweyadi's hand, was dismissed with a gentle wave. An aide led him to a room filled with food stolen from government storage facilities and handed over a two-gallon can of cooking oil and three black plastic bags with tea, sugar, and beans. "These people here are the only ones who care for us. No one else does," Jabbar said appreciatively as he accepted the gifts, tears in his eyes.

Food and medicines were not the only things given away. Another petitioner, Moayed Abbas, a twenty-nine-year-old unemployed man in a gray nylon shirt, explained his case to Sweyadi. Abbas said he was one of the looters himself and had already returned his booty to the mosque. Now his car battery had died and he needed a replacement. Couldn't he just take a battery from one of the cars parked outside? Sweyadi slowly pulled out his notebook, its cover decorated with garish flowers, and scribbled a chit. "Go take it," he said, waving the man away.

I asked the cleric how it felt to be the only real authority in the neighborhood now that the Iraqi state had collapsed. "We don't want to be involved in politics. We only want to establish a religious society in Iraq," Sweyadi answered modestly. He paused and added: "But now that there is no government, we have to rule." The petitioners, who hang on his every word, grinned obligingly. "It's best to be governed by the mosque," one of them said, clutching his now-full shopping bags.

On the way back, Jaffar was shaking his head. "Before, we had just one Saddam," he said. "Now we have one for every neighborhood."

✦ ✦ ✦

After inhaling for hours the putrid, smoky air of Sadr City, Jaffar and Samira wanted me to see a nicer part of Baghdad. So they took me to a shaded street of riverside villas facing green pastures across a placid bend in the Tigris. This area, once out-of-bounds for mere mortals and protected by a checkpoint of secret police, used to house Saddam's closest relatives and associates in the Baath hierarchy—all next to each other, to keep potential rivals under watchful control.

These homes had, of course, been thoroughly looted in the previous week, with anything valuable carted away, to Sadr City and elsewhere. But because the thieves didn't much care for documents and other printed matter, there were plenty of interesting things for me to scrutinize. As I walked into the first villa, I felt almost like an archaeologist, sifting through the remains of a vanished civilization in a man-made Pompeii.

Some houses were now guarded by the Shiite militias that had seized the properties. Others were protected by neighbors or by the families of the original owners, who had been forced to surrender their homes to Saddam's elite. The most recent inhabitants—the majority of them featured on the U.S. military's deck of "most-wanted" cards—were now either in hiding or behind coils of razor wire in American detention camps. Nobody objected to my coming inside and having a look.

The first house on the block belonged to Saddam's half brother, Wathban al Tikriti. I stepped into the monumental living room, pieces of smashed mirrors cracking under my boots, and picked up the books that had once filled the stolen shelves. Wathban was no lover of fine literature—the books were either collections of Saddam's writings or the paranoid Arab nationalist pamphlets written by an earlier generation of Iraqi politicians, such as Saddam's uncle Khairullah Tulfah. I leafed through the titles. *Jews Are Behind Every Crime*, read one. *Why Arabs Are Better Than Iranians*, explained another.

Inner rooms showed that, despite such nationalist feelings, Wathban and his family had quite an affection for the latest Western goodies. On one floor, broken CDs of American video games were swept into a corner, together with faded photographs of Wathban's pampered children hugging horses and cows. I picked up a printout with an auction-house description of a piece of furniture that had once decorated the bedroom. "Impressive dressing cabinet in walnut wood, German neo-baroque style, 19th-century," it said. I wondered how that cabinet improved the looks of the Sadr City hovel where it now probably stood.

Wathban's family clearly liked to dress well: I counted twelve pages in just one bill for fashionable clothing from France's 3 Suisses mail-order firm. To circumvent UN sanctions, these shirts, coats, dresses, and pants had been shipped to a front address in Paris. Wathban also apparently wanted more progeny: the looters left behind a box labeled: "Discretest—Tells you when you are most likely to conceive."

In the garden, next to a broken sculpture of Wathban, I found a pink leg cast. Wathban had to wear it, the guards explained, after Saddam's psychotic son Uday shot up his half uncle in a fit of rage. Uday's own palace towered just a few hundred yards down the road. This closeness, I reckoned, must have been unnerving to Wathban all these years. Uday's abode, dominated inside by a large mural depicting Saddam's happy family, was occupied by the Marines and not yet looted. It would be gutted a couple of weeks later, in the few hours between the Marine pullout and the redeployment of an Army unit into the area.

I went for a look into Uday's private playground next door, the Iraqi Yacht Club, where the dictator's son, with his taste for white suits, torture, and pet lions, had organized infamous sex-and-drug orgies. A pink statue of a lascivious woman, now lying in the grass, greeted visitors. The looters had worked hard to mutilate her groin and breasts. Pieces of kitsch chandeliers were everywhere. Only small shards of glass remained on the formerly all-mirror walls, testifying to the enormous energy expended to wreck the place. I peered into a shed stocked with piles of the club's correspondence.

One undated letter addressed to the yacht club's president, Uday, informed him that 2,192 bottles of Turkish beer had lapsed beyond the expiration date. The author, fearing punishment, quickly added that the beer had expired under his predecessor and asked for permission to destroy the stock. I broke out laughing when I read the scribbled answer: "Please transfer these items to the tourism board," for consumption by tourists.

I picked up another circular, sent by the Administration of Presidential Palaces in 1999. "By order of President Saddam Hussein it is strictly forbidden to put any nylon tablecloths on the tables in the palaces, unless specifically ordered otherwise," the stern circular said, promising retribution to those who would disobey. Like most files in the shed, it was marked "top secret." A regime's paranoia can be measured by what it chooses to classify.

Other pieces of correspondence were tragic: petitions for help from the families of people imprisoned by the regime. I didn't see a single one that had been marked with instructions to respond. As I was leaving the yacht club, a group of officials from Chalabi's Iraqi National Congress appeared, hanging their green, blue, and yellow flag at the entrance and claiming the premises. "Uday stole from the people, and so now the people must get it back," the group's leader told me. I didn't argue.

The next home to visit was that of Tarek Aziz, the former foreign minister and prime minister, a Christian and one of the most educated and articulate figures in the regime. His manicured garden was dominated by tilework proclaiming, "Long live our leader." But Aziz's study showed that he was a man of cosmopolitan tastes. The floor was carpeted with recent issues of American magazines unavailable to ordinary Iraqis, including *Newsweek* and *Foreign Affairs.* Apparently Aziz was also a movie fan. His collection of DVDs, untouched by looters, included *Thirteen Days,* a film about how John F. Kennedy handled the Cuban missile crisis—presumably a tool in drafting Iraq's WMD policy.

While all the furniture was gone, the living room's floor was littered with books, mostly in English. The house was soon to become the property of a prominent Shiite cleric, and his militiamen didn't have any use for the alien literature. Seeing that I was interested, one urged me: "Take what you want. We're burning these books to cook, anyway." I picked three: a pamphlet of Aziz's speeches, a memoir of a Lebanese Christian militiaman who had switched his loyalties from

Israel to Syria, and the first edition of *Baghdad Sketches,* a 1937 trav-elogue by the British writer Freya Stark. In the following years, I read Stark's book several times, often wondering how the green volume, purchased in Delhi in November 1937 and probably brought into Iraq by a British colonial officer, had ended up in Aziz's possession.

A Marine unit had come into Aziz's house just before the looters, seizing important documents and cash. The unit's men, who also guarded my hotel, told me they were impressed by the cheetah skins that covered the walls, the number of weapons inside, and the whiskey bottles stashed all over the residence. "There was booze everywhere. More than you can drink in a year," crowed one of the Marines, Lance Corporal Donald Mischke. Soon Aziz's aged whiskey was being traded to the hotel's journalist guests, for phone calls to the States. Within weeks the mansion would be taken by Abdulaziz al Hakim, the Shiite leader whose relative had fled from a meeting with me in Najaf.

Jaffar and Samira took me to a few other houses outside Saddam's immediate compound. One, seized from a Kurdish Shiite family that had been deported to Iran, belonged to the Palestinian militant Abu Abbas. He masterminded the 1985 hijacking of the Italian cruise liner *Achille Lauro*—an operation remembered for the terrorists' decision to throw an elderly, wheelchair-bound Jewish American passenger over-board. Saddam had given Abu Abbas a VIP welcome and was using his faction, the Palestine Liberation Front, to settle his own scores abroad. Abu Abbas, detained by U.S. forces right after the fall of Baghdad, would later die in captivity.

As I wandered through the villa, which had been protected from looters by a sympathetic neighbor, I marveled at how Abu Abbas seemed to have settled into whatever passed for a comfortable upper-class life in Iraq. While ordinary Iraqis went to jail for putting up a satel-lite TV dish, Abu Abbas had enjoyed free access to CNN and Al Jazeera. The bedroom contained a year's supply of Herbalife diet potions. The kitschy coffee table featured the book *The Art of the Faux.*

It was only after I looked at Abu Abbas's hastily abandoned desk that I recalled his true profession. Place of pride was reserved for the *Handbook on the Use of Personal Weapons,* written by Lieutenant

Colonel Abu Tayeb of Yasser Arafat's personal protection service, Force 17. Beside it was a plan for future action: a research paper, "The List of Electrical Generators in Israel," that meticulously outlined every Israeli power station, providing surreptitiously taken snapshots and recommending the best access routes for an attack.

✦   ✦   ✦

The more we crisscrossed Baghdad, documenting its postwar convulsions, the more Samira soured on the American effort. Her husband was more upbeat. "Iraqis were quiet as Saddam spent thirty years to destroy the country. And now they don't want to give the Americans thirty days to fix it?" Jaffar would say.

But Samira, who, like many Iraqis, expected the Americans to be omniscient and all-powerful, was increasingly frustrated with how ignorant of the local ways, and how incompetent, most American officials we'd come across seemed to be. She finally blew up after I took her to the Baghdad Convention Center, a mammoth hall built by Saddam, across the street from the Rashid Hotel, for a nonaligned summit. The convention center and the adjoining presidential palace compound were out-of-bounds to the locals. Samira could enter only because I, a foreigner, was her escort and only after submitting to a thorough search. Weeks later, this vast part of central Baghdad became the occupation authority's Green Zone, an isolated but, for a while, relatively safe American bubble in an ever-more-hostile land.

We had driven to the convention center, its mosaics depicting American planes bombing peaceful Iraqis, for the first public appearance by Jay Garner, the retired American general tapped to run the occupation authority—then known as ORHA, the Office for Reconstruction and Humanitarian Assistance. Before the war, I had bumped into Garner and his staff in the Kuwait Hilton, a place that now seemed to belong to a distant past. He and an ORHA forward team had just arrived in Baghdad, half a month after the city's fall. Samira was itching to see the man who would run Iraq for the world's only superpower.

Struggling to speak in grammatical English, Garner crowed about how the United States ran the war with "merciful" weapons and how "the infrastructure is still in good shape." It was a dazzling statement in a city where most residents had no electricity, tap water, or telephone service—a state of affairs that would persist for months.

Testy journalists challenged Garner's rosy presentation. One asked the general to explain the anger against Americans that was being voiced so often on the streets of Baghdad. He attributed the feelings to a misunderstanding. "Iraq has been in a dark room with no light for thirty-five years and, two weeks ago, we opened the door and pushed them out in the sunlight and they cannot see yet," Garner responded. I saw Samira emit a gasp. She was insulted by such a patronizing attitude. On the way out of the press conference, as I was buttonholing a thoroughly useless military PR officer, she vented her feelings, as "an Iraqi citizen," to an Abu Dhabi TV crew that put her on prime-time satellite news. "The Americans are the ones who're in darkness and can't see here," she fumed. "They know nothing about the Iraqis and Iraq."

✦ ✦ ✦

On Saddam's birthday, April 28, Samira took me to Baghdad's Sunni heartland. Until then, I spent most of my time talking to Shiite clerics who had stepped into the void created by the occupation and started running parts of the country as an alternative government—while Garner was still by the Hilton pool in Kuwait. Saddam's fellow Sunni Arabs, about one-fifth of Iraq's population, remained eerily quiet. The Sunni elite, which had ruled Iraq since its independence from Britain in 1932, seemed too stunned by the speed and magnitude of their country's defeat.

Unlike the Shiite areas of Baghdad, relatively untouched by ground fighting, the hard-core Sunni Aadhamiye neighborhood in the northern part of the city was visibly scarred by house-to-house combat that had lasted days. It was here that Saddam made his last public stand, on April 9, waving an AK-47 before vanishing into the ignominious hole near Tikrit from which he would be fished out eight months later. Buildings on Aadhamiye's main square were pierced with large holes from artillery fire. At the cemetery that started on a side street, dusty graves were pockmarked with bullets, while some had been bulldozed away. Residents' cars, flattened like empty cans by the tanks' treads, were carefully arranged on the sidewalks. Most noticeably, the clock tower of the Abu Hanifa mosque, which dominates Aadhamiye, was tilting like the tower of Pisa, with the jagged impact of a missile strike instead of the clock. Miraculously, everyone kept repeating, the halogen sign marking the word "Allah" atop the tower survived, undamaged. So did a sign with the word "Mohammed" on a half-destroyed back gate.

At the entrance to the mosque's courtyard, I asked the guard whether I could come in—and was offered a seat among a group of old men, dressed in neatly pressed shirts, subdued ties, and suits that must have been fashionable among colonial gentlemen when Iraq was still under British rule. One of these men, stricken with grief, was the son of the master who had constructed the missing clock.

Settling in my chair and accepting sweet tea, I listened to the old man, Saleh Mahsoub, who still spoke the formal upper-class French he had learned as a law student in Geneva in the early 1950s. Everyone in the neighborhood called him simply Abu Saa, the "clock's father." The man's own father, the famed Abdelrazzak Mahsoub, spent much of his life building the complicated timepiece that used the same type of mechanism as the one developed by the British horologist Lord Grimthorpe for Big Ben.

Those had been the heady 1920s, when Iraq tried to throw off British occupation. Mahsoub was dead-set on proving that the Iraqis could build a clock just as well as the British. "There were no foreign parts and pieces in it. The clock is 100 percent Iraqi," exclaimed a proud Fouad Rashed, Mahsoub's seventy-year-old grandson. During the past three decades, he and his uncle Abu Saa climbed up the steep staircase to clean and maintain the precious mechanism at Abu Hanifa. "It's very precise. Really," Rashed said.

Once Iraq became independent, the clock was displayed at the Baghdad Fair and commended by the king. But—just as Lord Grimthorpe didn't live long enough to see his clock atop Big Ben— Mahsoub died before his clock found a permanent home. It was only after the overthrow of Iraq's monarchy that the new government decided to erect the Abu Hanifa clock tower as a symbol of an independent, self-reliant Iraq. "This was the Big Ben of Baghdad," Rashed sighed.

Choking on tears, Abu Saa looked up at the gaping hole. I reasoned that the U.S. helicopter that fired the missile must have feared a sniper atop the tower. No, the men loudly disagreed, that's impossible. The spiral staircase leading up to it was disused and the gate was locked during the attack. The military later had a hard time removing the unexploded missile that had been stuck inside.

Abu Saa, in his crisp white shirt and fishbowl eyeglasses, wondered quietly. "Why, why did they do it?" he said. "You know, after this, I cried for eight days. This was not a clock. This was my life." Rashed, his nephew, shook his head: "It would have been better if the Americans bombed my house instead."

Everyone in that courtyard seemed incredulous at how quickly the entire Iraqi state had come crashing down. Walid al-Aadhami, a seventy-three-year-old writer, recalled with pride the previous time that Western forces fought for Baghdad—in 1941, when the British Army dislodged Iraq's pro-Nazi strongman Rashid Ali. "Great Britain was still great then, and we fought a whole month before they could take Baghdad," he said. "This time around, it fell in just two days."

I asked them what they intended to do now. Will you try to coexist with Iraq's new rulers? In contrast to the Shiite regions of Iraq, there was no hesitation in Aadhamiye. Rashid al Obaidi, a professor of Arabic literature at the Islamic University next door and a member of Aadhamiye's self-rule committee, spoke in hard, clear words: "No nation will accept to be occupied, so a relationship between us and the Americans is impossible."

An imam walked into the courtyard from the mosque itself and asked me if I wanted to have a look inside. This was no ordinary house of worship: the mosque contained the tomb of Abu Hanifa, the eighth-century scholar who founded one of the four main schools of Sunni Islamic jurisprudence, the Hanafi *maddhab*. Usually, non-Muslims are not allowed inside mosques in Iraq, nor in most other Arab lands. But Anwar al Aadhami, one of the mosque's elders, made an exception for me and showed me around, retracing the steps of the Marines who had burst into the compound weeks earlier. First he pointed to a door, blown off its hinges, that led to Abu Hanifa's gilded crypt. A bullet grazed the tomb's outer fencing inside the crypt, but the holy remains were intact—surviving the invasion just as they had survived the Mongol hordes almost a millennium earlier, my guide told me. From there we walked on soft prayer rugs to the women's section. A stray piece of ordnance had flown in through a window, smearing the white wall with a black streak of soot. In neat Arabic calligraphy, someone had written nearby: "Look, this is what U.S. missiles do to us." Aadhami told me the damaged wall would be preserved for posterity, so that future generations could remember what had happened here: "The Americans hate us. They just hate us," he muttered.

As we stepped back into the sunlit courtyard, I was going to object, but we were distracted by a commotion outside the gate. A convoy of two Bradley fighting vehicles and two Humvees rolled up to the mosque, their occupants nervously pointing guns at the Iraqis around them. The soldiers' mission was to tear down a banner on the outer wall that surrounded the wrecked clock tower: WE PROTEST THE AMERICAN DESECRATION OF OUR HOLY PLACE, it proclaimed. As angry worshippers gathered near the soldiers, I instinctively crouched under the wall, expecting a shootout. But the mosque's leaders, postponing their fight for another day, allowed the banner to be taken down.

I was puzzled: Why did the banner have to be removed in the first place? The lieutenant in charge of the mission, Tyler Arnold, was surprised to see a Westerner—alone? unarmed?—inside the mosque's courtyard. But he volunteered to explain his task: "We're taking down any sign that's against U.S. forces. What they're saying is not true. We are here not against the people. We are here for the people." The innocent simplicity of this response was mind-boggling. Surely the gaping hole in the clock tower incited far more anti-Americanism than the banner underneath.

As the lieutenant's Bradley roared away, with the banner safely secured inside, a businessman named Hussam Ahmed followed the troops with a bitter stare. Then he turned to me. "Didn't they say that they are a democracy and that they'd make our country free?" he asked. I didn't know what to answer.

When I returned to the hotel later that day, I flipped on the just-installed satellite TV receiver, a sign of Iraq's new freedoms, and saw a newsflash. Troops of the Eighty-Second Airborne Division—the one whose soldiers sheltered me at a school in Karbala three weeks earlier—had fired into a crowd of children protesting the seizure of a school building in the city of Fallujah, west of Baghdad. Soldiers in Fallujah insisted that they had been attacked by some demonstrators, a claim that witnesses interviewed on Al Jazeera denied. The screen filled up with mangled teenage corpses. I recalled with discomfort the excited discussion I heard about the *wheesh, wheesh* sound of killing back in Karbala. But it had been only a week or so since the troops entered Fallujah, and I thought this was one of the final incidents of a war that was drawing to a close. Samira was not so sure. "These people there in Fallujah, they're tough," she said. "Believe me, they'll seek revenge."

8

IRAQ

We Don't Count Their Bodies

Tired and relieved to have survived the war, I found it unexpectedly difficult to adjust to peaceful life once I returned to Rome. It was the first week of May 2003, just a few days after the Fallujah shootings and three months after I set off to Kuwait with my gas masks.

Witnessing war up close altered the scale of my existence: after seeing how easily humans and the fruits of their labor can disintegrate, I had trouble taking seriously a leaky faucet or a child's runny nose. Emotional numbness, so necessary to keep shooting photos and writing notes while people are dying around you, just wouldn't go away. Other war habits played tricks, too. At home I kept ducking each time a car engine backfired, and instinctively looked for land mines on roadsides as I drove to the beach. I developed an intense dislike for fireworks. My wife didn't appreciate that I watched a war movie every time there was one on TV. In spirit, if not in body, I was still in Iraq.

By late May, I volunteered to go back. Bearing gifts for Samira's grandchildren—a doll and a battery-operated toy car—I hired a vehicle to take me across the desert from Amman, Jordan, to a Baghdad that seemed even more dusty and desolate than when I left it. On the week of my arrival, the U.S. military, which had enjoyed a month of relative quiet, lost five soldiers in separate ambushes. One of these attacks was in Fallujah, the city where schoolchildren had been killed by American troops the previous month. On my second day back in Iraq, I packed flak vests and a supply of Red Bull, and got Samira and Jaffar to take me there.

Before the war, Fallujah's flat cityscape of concrete two-story homes surrounded by mud-brick walls was known for two things: the piety of its inhabitants and the succulence of its kebabs, which, Jaffar reluctantly admitted, were better than the ones he proudly cooked himself. Soon Fallujah would become the byword for bloody anti-American insurgency—"the Americans' grave," as Fallujans began calling their hometown, without exaggeration. A year later, in the spring of 2004, Fallujah, bombed into rubble by American forces, would become the first part of Iraq fully controlled by insurgents, an area where neither American troops nor Western civilians dared to tread for several months.

In town, I looked for the site of the latest attack on American soldiers, at a bridge across the Euphrates. Two or three dozen taxi drivers, wearing cream-colored gowns, huddled at a traffic circle near the bridge. Breaking out in quick smiles, they were eager to recount the attack's details. The assailants fired rocket-propelled grenades from the thick reeds that stretched along the sides of the road. The explosions damaged two Bradleys, killing two soldiers and wounding nine. A medevac helicopter that arrived on the scene was destroyed, too. Al Jazeera had already broadcast, throughout the Arab world, the footage of Fallujah residents dancing with the helicopter's debris and waving V signs—one of the first of many such scenes that would be filmed across Iraq as the war dragged on.

"This is a message to America. The attack is part of a jihad that we are preparing. The popular resistance is beginning," said one of the taxi drivers, Khalid Hilal, who used to be a mid-ranking bureaucrat under Saddam. "We're going to blow ourselves up like the Palestinians are doing it in Israel," interrupted another cabbie, Mahmoud al Issawy.

Having heard a different story from the U.S. military, that the assailants had fired from a neighboring mosque, I went there to talk to the imam. But, unlike the Shiite clerics in Baghdad or Najaf, the man refused flat out to meet with an infidel reporter. As the faithful trickled in for the noon prayer, one man took me aside and explained the Fallujah mind-set: "Every Iraqi is a bomb against the Americans. And every day will bring more attacks." When I asked why, he got angry. "Why? Why did they have to kill our kids?"

The April killing of schoolchildren was clearly a watershed in the city—which, after all, had surrendered to American forces without a fight. I went looking for the pockmarked street where the killings took place, in a grim industrial zone on the edge of the town. The school building where paratroopers from the Eighty-Second Airborne had bivouacked was now empty and locked. Curiously, I couldn't see any bullet marks on the school, despite the military's insistence that the soldiers had come under sustained fire from demonstrators.

The picture was different across the narrow street. The villa in front of the school was riddled with large-caliber holes, its outfacing garden wall transformed into Swiss cheese. A woman invited us inside. "The Americans, they fired like mad," she said, and—suspending Muslim propriety for a nobler, nationalist, cause—let me examine her bedroom and kitchen. The bullets, which effortlessly pierced the walls, were lodged inside the fridge and the sink; one punctured the water tank above the heater. Others etched a bead-like scar just above the alcove. "One of the people who were killed, he stumbled all bloodied right into our living room and died in front of our eyes, as the children watched," she said. "What do you think these children will do when they grow up?"

I asked how she felt about the ambush against American soldiers the night before. An eight-year-old boy who was listening intensely to our conversation, Seif al Mussa, blurted out an answer before his mother had a chance to speak. "We were so happy, all of us in school. We told the headmaster that the Americans should leave not just Fallujah but the whole of Iraq, because we are Muslims and they are not." As his mother smiled proudly and patted Seif on the head, I asked what was the headmaster's response. "He agreed with us, of course," Seif said.

✦ ✦ ✦

On Fallujah's main road I walked into the City Hall building, which was now surrounded with barbed wire and packed with American soldiers. Just a few hours earlier, insurgents had fired RPGs at the building from across the street. An Iraqi policeman ran out to tell us that the mayor and other notables had gone to meet "an American general" in the farms near the city. If I was interested, he'd show me the place.

Together with a couple of other reporters who happened to be in Fallujah at the time, I followed the police car on rutted village roads while thinking that the thick reeds and palm groves on each side presented ideal ambush opportunities—highly unlikely back country for an American general to travel so deep into. By the time I was almost determined to turn around, we arrived at the huge white mansion of a local tribal chief. The general would come soon, we were told, and welcomed inside.

The sitting room was crammed with more than a hundred tribal chiefs, some of whom clearly mistook me for an American envoy and shook my hand with exaggerated politeness. The host offered us sweet tea and said we were welcome to witness the meeting. The host's corpulent brother, Taleb al Hasnawi, was itching to pour his soul out. The Americans, he said, had broken their promise not to enter Fallujah and have now set off a blood feud by shooting schoolchildren. Things were heading to a war, he said. "Everything is getting worse day by day. We can no longer control our people, and so more and more attacks against the Americans will occur."

One of the sheikh's aides told us that the American general had finally arrived but wouldn't enter the hall as long as reporters were present. I stepped outside, where three Special Forces Humvees had just parked. The "general" was a young Arabic-speaking American in a blue T-shirt and a baseball cap. He refused to say who he was and what part of the government he represented, demanding that we leave the area immediately. When I said that I had been invited by the sheikh, the "general" summoned an Iraqi aide, whispered into his ear, and then walked back to his Humvee. The heavy-set Iraqi, a Thuraya satellite phone in his hand, turned to another reporter's driver and uttered a few words. The driver looked at us with anxiety. "We have to go now. Otherwise they'll burn our cars," he said.

Fallujah's mayor told me, later that afternoon, that the "general" issued a warning to the town: American reconstruction aid will be halted if attacks on the troops continue. This pragmatic ultimatum, echoed at scores of similar meetings across Iraq between American officers and tribal chiefs, struck me as hopelessly out of touch with the Iraqi psyche. How could the United States hope to buy off—with promises of improved sewage and funds for roadworks—people who had been raised in a culture that avenges blood feuds and sees suicide as a means of preserving honor? The mayor didn't last long. In November he fled Fallujah, after anti-American protesters ransacked the City Hall and torched his office. He was lucky. Others in the U.S.-installed local administration would be tortured and killed on videotape by the Islamist insurgents who, beginning in early 2004, transformed Fallujah into a Taliban-like enclave.

✦　✦　✦

Back in Baghdad, I wanted to check up on the leaning Abu Hanifa clock tower. It was still standing, cracked and tilting more and more to the right. Outside, I spotted a two-Humvee patrol stationed by the mosque's gate. Just a day earlier, insurgents attacked another patrol on the same spot, killing one soldier.

The gentle old men I had met inside the courtyard were now gone. Instead, a muscular swimming trainer in a polyester track suit, who identified himself by the same nom de guerre as Yasser Arafat, Abu Ammar, was giving a pep talk to a dozen teenagers. His hand was bandaged—the result, he said, of a wound sustained in a firefight with American forces. "If all the people were fighting the Americans like we are doing in Aadhamiye, none would be left in Baghdad today," he said bitterly. The streets nearby were already covered with fresh graffiti promising a "hellish war" to the occupier, and death to Iraqi "traitors" who collaborate with the invaders. This time, the soldiers did not even attempt to remove the anti-American signs.

In a symptom of the city's darkening mood, one such sign was now daubed on the pedestal where Saddam's statue, dragged down by the Marines, had stood in front of the Palestine Hotel. Addressed in English to American soldiers camped behind barbed wire across the square, it proclaimed, ungrammatically, in bold red letters: ALL DONNE. GO HOME.

✦   ✦   ✦

Almost every day in late May and June, I traveled across central Iraq to the scene of another just-completed anti-American ambush. It would all soon become drearily similar—the chants, the bodies, the bullet-ridden homes, the Iraqis' accusatory questions to which I had no answer. President Bush's triumphant declaration a month earlier that "major combat" in Iraq was over seemed, at best, premature: more blood flowed now than during the conventional phase of the war.

In June, I received a glib news release from the military PR office, now settled in the Baghdad Convention Center and holding perennially upbeat press conferences. Unlike the famous Five o'Clock Follies in Saigon, Baghdad briefings were scheduled at varying times so as to prove themselves a more difficult target for insurgent mortar attacks. In an Orwellian twist of language, the military frequently used the label "anti-Iraqi forces" to describe anti-American Iraqis firing these mortars. The press release that I found in my e-mail inbox said that twenty-seven Iraqi "terrorists" had been killed in just one day in a "successful textbook-style" operation that involved air assault teams, riverboats, and ground forces in the so-called Balad peninsula north of Baghdad. At that time, in the first weeks of the insurgency, it was a strikingly high body count. I decided to verify the story and drove to the area of the fighting, a lush bend of the Tigris with a mixed Sunni and Shiite population near a major American air base.

Navigating by the black mourning notices hung along the roads— the ones for people killed by Americans included the designation "martyr" before their names—I crossed the Tigris and entered the village of Dhuluiya, a stronghold of the Jabbouri clan. The story I heard from the villagers, in Dhuluiya and elsewhere, was hard to reconcile with the U.S. Army's account.

The Jabbouris, one of the largest tribes of Iraq, traditionally made up the elite of the nation's officer corps. After some Jabbouri officers plotted to kill Saddam in the 1990s, the regime purged many tribe members from sensitive jobs, prompting some leading Jabbouris to collaborate with the U.S. military during the invasion. However, no such sympathy remained in the village after the "textbook-style" operation. Upon arrival, I was directed to a huge mourning tent where hundreds of leading tribe members from all over Iraq gathered to commemorate the village's dead, over boiled rice and lamb. As it turned out, only three men had been killed—not the twenty-seven mentioned in the press release.

As I sat on a plastic chair in the tent, Khaldoun Jassem Rmayedh, a twenty-six-year-old ice cream vendor, told me what happened. The American military, he said, arrived shortly after midnight, blowing up his front door and bursting inside as they cordoned off the entire village. Women were cuffed and herded off into one courtyard. Men, and boys as young as six, were thrown to the floor in another. Rmayedh's fifty-two-year-old father, who had a heart ailment, quickly passed out. The young man, who spoke English, yelled at the soldiers, telling them that his father needed to take urgent medication and must be taken to a hospital. The soldiers took the unconscious man outside.

At about nine o'clock—after a night in which some of the handcuffed children wet themselves in the courtyard—Rmayedh, his fifteen-year-old brother, Zeidun, and scores of other villagers were driven to detention cells at the sprawling Balad air base. American interrogators believed that Ali Hassan Majeed, Saddam's top general, who is better known as "Chemical Ali" for gassing the Kurds in the 1980s, had been hiding in the village. Rmayedh dismissed the idea with a chortle, saying that only an overzealous informer eager for bonuses could have thought up such nonsense. Zeidun listened quietly to the conversation. He said he didn't speak much while in detention: soldiers sealed his mouth with duct tape after he started screaming: "Where is my father?"

The teenager was released a day later, his brother after three days behind bars. Eventually, almost everyone seized in the roundup was let go because of what the military called a lack of "intelligence value." When Rmayedh came home, he discovered that his father had never been taken to the hospital or given his medication; he died on the night of the raid. Next to him lay the body of Rmayedh's uncle, fifty-three-year-old teacher Mehdi Ali Jassem, who, villagers told me, had been rifle-butted to death during the assault.

According to the villagers, the only shooting in Dhuluiya on the night of the raid came from a man who mistook the commotion outside his home for looters and fired a hunting rifle in the air; the man was killed by return fire. American soldiers camped in the Rmayedh and Jassem homes for days. Hekmat Ali Jassem, Mehdi's brother and an American-badged lieutenant colonel of the new Iraqi police, made sure I ate the rice and the lamb at the wake, and then took me to see his mansion by the intense-green Tigris riverside. Remains of Meals Ready-to-Eat and military debris littered the grass. All internal doors were busted off hinges and barely a speck of glass remained in the windows. Hekmat's six-year-old son, Hamzeh, played his favorite new game: sitting on the floor, head down, holding his hands behind the back, just as he had been tied up by U.S. soldiers.

Hekmat himself had not been detained. But the military took into captivity two of his other brothers, Baghdad-based former generals who had come home to mourn Mehdi's death. With a sweet smile, Jassem insisted he would forgive the Americans because he believes they acted on misleading intelligence. "We pinned so many hopes on the Americans when they entered our country," he said. "If some American soldiers humiliated us, it doesn't mean that all American soldiers are bad. The officers who talked to me later were all very polite, very respectful."

As we left Dhuluiya, Samira made fun of Jassem's words. "Very polite, very respectful—he's lying through his teeth," she sneered. "His one brother was just killed, his other two brothers are in jail—you don't think he's already plotting how to take revenge? Come on."

On the way out of the village, we bumped into a patrol, and I spoke to the commander. Captain Dave Gray, an intelligence officer of the Fourth Infantry Division, said he participated in the raid on Dhuluiya. The American troops did come under hostile fire but sustained no injuries there, he said. The house searches turned up "a lot of weapons" such as Kalashnikov assault rifles. Aren't the Iraqis allowed to own these, in accordance with new American policies? I wondered. Well, yes, the captain replied. Did you find any rocket-propelled grenades? I pressed. Well, no, he said. "We're here to try to stabilize the area. That's what we're here to do," he said.

✦ ✦ ✦

I crossed the Tigris again, continuing to follow mourning notices; they led me into the sunbaked village of Yathrib, a few miles to the south. At first the village seemed deserted—not a single person or moving car on the streets. We cruised through the main square and stopped by the Town Hall, a small squat building with concrete steps. More than a hundred men, peasants in tattered sandals and with calloused hands, stood on the porch.

I offered the usual Arabic greetings—"Salamu Aleikum," or "Peace be with you"—and walked inside. The crowd followed us in, and I found myself sitting in a corner of a large bare room, with all exits blocked by a throng of Yathrib tribesmen. They studied me with piercing eyes, undecided whether to treat me as a foe. I beamed a smile and slowly reached for my notebook, showing that I was ready to write down whatever grievances the villagers had. Samira quickly realized we could be in trouble and switched to her Arab-nationalist mode. "Here is a journalist, a friend who came here to us all the way from Italy," she said with her widest smile. Unlike many American reporters, who often found safety in pretending to be Canadians, I could at least avoid outright lies in potentially dangerous situations. From an ethical standpoint, it was essential to identify myself as a reporter. But in places like Yathrib, which was in a blood feud with Americans, it was better not to volunteer the name of my newspaper. Usually nobody asked.

Samira pressed on. "Let's tell him what is being done to us. He's here to listen to us," she said—using the Arabic word *jama'atna*, or "our community," and subtly making herself part of the same "we" as the men of Yathrib.

The men had plenty of things to say. Their tribe, the Bu Hashman, was related to Saddam's, and the villagers were still loyal to the former dictator. "We're all here followers of Saddam," said the village elder, Ali Khalaf Hussein. He went on to demonstrate how an American soldier pinned him down with a boot on the head during a recent search, a common practice that is seen by most Iraqis as a grave insult. "The Americans treat us like dogs, and we'll fight them all the way. We'll kill them like dogs, too," he said, waving his fist, as other villagers cheered.

I asked him about the two men mentioned in the roadside mourning sign. They were Sheikh Hussein Abbas, the twenty-eight-year-old imam of the village mosque, and his aide. Respected for his piety and dedication to religious studies, Abbas never belonged to Saddam's elite. But two days earlier, he didn't return to the village from a trip to Aadhamiye, in Baghdad. Instead, he hid in a roadside ditch and detonated an explosive device under a passing American tank. After the bombing, Abbas and his aide emerged from the ditch, firing RPGs at the convoy. They were cut down by response fire before they could kill anyone.

The two bodies were now at the Balad air base, and the villagers asked me for a favor. They were too scared to approach the base, fearing they'd be shot on sight, and they wanted me to inquire as to when the bodies of Abbas and his aide could be claimed for burial. In exchange, they promised to show me the site of the attack.

Eager to get out of the room, I agreed. In Iraq, the American and the local versions of events rarely matched—and, to figure out what had really happened, I needed to talk to someone at Balad. I parked hundreds of yards from the base gates and walked the rest of the distance—without my backpack, so as not to be mistaken for a suicide bomber. I told the sentries that the villagers were waiting up the road for the two bodies; I also requested a meeting with an officer who could talk about the incident. After an hour's wait, I was told that no one was available. Instead, I was given a satellite phone number for a division press officer in Tikrit, more than an hour to the north, and told to leave. That satphone remained switched off for days.

Farther along the road, the ambush site was obvious. There was a large hole in the middle of the lane, hundreds of large-caliber bullet casings in the dry grass, and surrounding all of this, brown-plastic MRE wrappings. Another mourning sign pointed to a side road that led to a hamlet nearby.

There, rice and lamb were boiling in giant vats on the ground, and hundreds of mourners sat silently under the tents. Unlike the people of Yathrib and Dhuluiya, the villagers here were Shiites, of the Khazraji tribe, which didn't get along all that well with the previous regime. It was smart of the imam of Yathrib to set up the ambush here, among the Shiites he despised, and miles away from his own people.

After making sure I was fed my third dose of rice and lamb that day, Shiite villagers recounted the local tragedy. The imam of Yathrib had placed the charge just a few dozen feet from a tent containing the sheep flock of Ali Jassam, a seventy-five-year-old farmer. As the explosives went off, American troops fired a red flare—a warning to other soldiers in the area that they had come under attack. The flare landed next to the tent and ignited the grass. Jassam's distraught wife, relatives told me, rousted up the farmer and urged him to save the sheep, the family's main possession. The man, his three sons, and one grandson rushed to the scene. I could imagine the rest. Dazed by explosions and having miraculously survived a shower of RPGs, the ambushed soldiers naturally saw anyone running toward them in the dead of night as yet another attacker. The old man and his progeny were cut down in a hail of gunfire and classified as "terrorists" in the military's body-count report. Their remains had only just now returned from the base.

The dead man's cousin, Saad Hashem, told me he felt like a fool because of his previous sympathies for the United States. "We were waiting for the Americans to liberate us, but all they did was to kill five members of one family," he said. "We're still ready to forgive the Americans, and we won't avenge these deaths unless they kill our people again," he added. "But the Americans—they didn't even come to apologize." They never would. Instead, in the following months, U.S. troops destroyed the village's orchards that lined the road, in an effort to make ambushes more difficult.

On the way back to Baghdad, I reread the military's statement about the latest fighting in the Balad area. "The coalition forces took care to protect innocent civilians and respect the culture and customs of the Iraqi people," the document said.

The road was clogged with slow military convoys, and when Jaffar tried to overtake one, the rear Humvee—whose gunner initially indicated we could speed up—suddenly jerked right, almost pushing us off the road. The gunner then grinned at his joke and pointed his heavy machine gun at us. For the first time, I saw Jaffar explode with fury against the United States. "Look at me. I'm an old man in my own country, and I have to suffer this," he said. "Nobody likes to live under military rule, nobody."

Before hitting the hotel in Baghdad, I stopped by the convention center again and asked the military's PR officer on duty, a handsome captain in neatly pressed fatigues named John Morgan, about the killings of the Khazraji tribesmen. Did the Army still stand by its claim of twenty-seven enemy dead? The captain dismissed me impatiently. "We don't count their bodies," he said.

✦ ✦ ✦

On Italy's national day, June 2, I relaxed at Iraq's first postwar diplomatic reception, a grand affair in a walled-off garden of the Italian embassy, which four months later would be attacked with donkey-mounted rockets. Italy had just set up an emergency hospital, open to all Iraqis in Baghdad, and had sent its first detachment of troops to protect the facility. Sipping chilled spumante, I chatted up a group of British officers deployed to Baghdad to guard Her Majesty's reopened embassy. The Britons had had a close call with American troops the previous week. Used to treating anyone with weapons and without a U.S. uniform as insurgents, American soldiers almost shot up the embassy convoy—even though it was prominently flying the British flag. "The morons didn't even know what the Union Jack was," one of the indignant Britons told me.

I didn't quite trust the story, taking it for an exaggeration in the old British tradition of disparaging uncouth Americans. Surely the soldiers wouldn't have fired at an ambassador's car. A few weeks later, the party's host—the Italian ambassador, who ran the ministry of culture at the U.S.-led occupation authority—tried to overtake an American convoy on the same highway I had traveled from Balad. He wasn't as lucky as Jaffar and I. American troops riddled the ambassador's car with bullets, injuring the diplomat and killing his Iraqi translator.

◆ ◆ ◆

Tired of daily excursions to the latest ambush sites in the Sunni heart-land, I wanted to see the other side of the occupation—how the United States and its Western partners were helping to rebuild the country. Military PR was desperate to get out "good news," inundating reporters with press releases every time some second lieutenant distributed free soccer balls or cut the ribbon at a freshly painted school. As part of this effort, the U.S. Army's Second Armored Cavalry Regiment hooked me up with an officer who was responsible for administering a slum of 100,000 people on the northeastern edge of Baghdad.

Travis Maples, a twenty-three-year-old lieutenant from Sacra-mento, California, referred to himself as "just a pup"—and, with his cherub's face, he looked it. A lieutenant fresh from officers' school, with no management experience, he now had to run an entire town in a hostile land half the world away. To reach his zone, called Shaoura, we drove past an even worse slum, where soldiers on patrol occasion-ally fainted because of the stench.

Maples told me he used a commonsense approach to figure out where to begin his administration: on his first day in Shaoura, he sim-ply went to the biggest mansion on the road. That house, he calculated correctly, must belong to the local notable. In fact, the mansion, with a built-in mosque inside a walled compound, housed the local sheikh, Fadhel al Jenabi, and his seven brothers, all of whom turned out to be eager to cooperate with the Americans. Unlike most other residents in Shaoura, the Jenabis were Sunni; therefore, they needed American backing against the encroachment of Shiite clerics from Sadr City, just a few minutes away. Maples asked Jenabi whether there were any Baath "bad guys" in the zone. The sheikh answered that not all Baathis were bad and pointed to the large propane gas plant just across the potholed road. "There are some good people in Baath. Don't arrest them all," the sheikh urged, and sent an aide to fetch the plant's director.

Hussein Olaiwi Said, the director, used to be a ranking Baathi, as were most Iraqis in positions of authority under Saddam's regime. The Jenabis spoke about the man with palpable respect. They said Said cared about the plant so much that he had abandoned his family under U.S. bombardments, sleeping at the facility to safeguard its equipment.

Determined to preserve his plant from looters, Said, a gentle man with doe eyes and a salt-and-pepper mustache, teamed up with Jenabi and his seven brothers to mount a twenty-four-hour armed watch. By the time Maples arrived, the plant was in pristine shape, while Iraq was seized by a cooking gas shortage that prompted daily explosions and lethal burns from residents' attempts to use gasoline in their stoves. (Under American rule, gasoline, too, was rationed—in a country with the world's second-largest oil reserves, car owners had to spend days lining up at the pump.) Output from Said's plant alone could satisfy one-third of Baghdad's needs.

The American and the Iraqi quickly struck a deal. Maples's unit provided military protection for a week at the plant, and Said restarted production. On the first day, thousands of Iraqis carrying rusty 10-liter gas bottles mobbed the gates and tried to surge inside. "People were ready to trample women and children, and our warning shots had absolutely no effect," Maples's commander, Captain Ed Williams, told me. Said saved the day by climbing atop a platform and delivering a rousing speech that instantly restored order.

As anti-American attacks proliferated elsewhere, I was relieved to hear this rare success story. Maples, too, couldn't hold back words of praise for Said—words tinged by bitterness for the other Iraqis he'd met. "The biggest problem we have here is that people lie to us all the time," the lieutenant mused. Said, he added, "is one of the few whose story never changes. I want him in charge."

This harmony was quickly shattered by Paul Bremer, the new American proconsul who replaced the bumbling Jay Garner. One of Bremer's first decisions was to bar from government employment all ranking members of the Baath Party. In one stroke he fired tens of thousands of university professors, engineers, schoolteachers, and technocrats who had managed the nuts and bolts of the Iraqi government and economy, in a country where the Baath Party was in power for thirty-five years and where promotion was usually conditional on holding a membership card. Instead of a thank-you note for saving the plant, Said received a firing notice. To replace him, the U.S.-supervised oil ministry dispatched an executive who had permitted his own facility, elsewhere in Baghdad, to be looted by Shiite militias.

"Everything we're trying to do here is being knocked off at the top," Maples fumed as he drove me to one of his regular rice and lamb feasts at the Jenabis. (Some of Maples's fellow officers, with their delicate stomachs, usually downed a course of antibiotics after every such outing.)

Wondering whether Maples was naive about Said, I returned to Shaoura on my own to check out the director's past. For a good hour, I went around the village asking about Said's Baath connections, and couldn't find anyone with bad things to say about him.

Meanwhile, Maples was so determined to help Said that he trekked in his Humvee across Baghdad to the marble-floored Iraqi Oil Ministry, the only major government ministry building that the U.S. military protected from looters. Sitting in a wood-paneled office with cushy leather chairs, the American-appointed acting oil minister just shrugged his shoulders. Under Bremer's policy, "I don't have any power to make exceptions," he said. Only Bremer himself could issue a waiver.

The new manager duly arrived at the Shaoura gates to an icy reception. Plant employees simply refused to let him in, saying that Said's dismissal was being appealed. "He had his own plant looted, so we weren't going to let him destroy ours," explained Abbas al Jenabi, one of the sheikh's brothers and Said's assistant at the plant.

The following week, in consultation with the lieutenant, Sheikh Jenabi organized a delegation of some twenty plant employees, local villagers, and Sunni and Shiite clerics to plead Said's case again, in the state gas company headquarters in the town of Taji, north of Baghdad. Maples and his commander, who initially promised to accompany the delegation, traveled to the same office for a separate visit the following day—to avoid ambushes, they had to show up unexpected. Under this combined pressure, a compromise was worked out: Said was allowed to keep managing the plant, without pay, pending Bremer's decision on whether to remove him from the Baath blacklist.

I asked Maples whether he found unnatural this alliance between an American officer and a senior Baathi like Said. "I'm partial to this guy," he answered. "He's trying to make this country better—so that I can go home."

Maples would spend much longer than he'd imagined in Iraq. His regiment's mostly Shiite area of operations exploded in a deadly revolt in April 2004, leaving dozens of soldiers wounded or killed. Soldiers of the Second Armored Cavalry Regiment were then sent to other Shiite hot spots, including Najaf, and stayed in Iraq well over a year. The Iraqi government that replaced Bremer's authority in June 2004 quickly moved to restore the bulk of former Baathis to their previous jobs. After all, the new U.S.-installed prime minister, Eyad Allawi, was a former Baath member himself.

✦   ✦   ✦

Unlike American soldiers, stationed in Iraq for a year or more, I was free to leave, and, by late June 2003, I was fed up with the feeling of being an unwelcome intruder in a dangerous, disemboweled, and yet boundlessly proud land.

So, picking a place that was as different as possible, I went to California, decompressing with my family for an entire month, watching seals and sea lions off the Monterey coast, and trying my best to avoid reading casualty stories that increasingly surfaced in newspaper headlines. In August, instead of returning to Iraq, I volunteered to cover another war zone. In Liberia, people who looked like me were not among the combatants, and no one challenged my cocoon of impartiality. Liberian rebels were on the verge of seizing the capital city, Monrovia, and there was mounting international pressure for Liberia's dictator, Charles Taylor, to step down and avoid a bloodbath. Everyone—the UN, the Africans, the Europeans, and chief among them the Liberians themselves—called for an American intervention to rescue a country that had been founded by freed American slaves.

After Baghdad, Monrovia felt truly liberating—despite the complete lack of electricity, the drizzling rain, cholera, malaria, and general despair. At least there, in contrast to the Middle East, I wasn't inundated daily by conspiracy theories of Zionist plots; instead of complaining about American occupation, the people I met usually berated the United States for failing to deploy troops. Unlike Iraqis, who were raised to believe that their nation was the cradle of civilization, only temporarily impoverished by perfidious Western scheming, the Liberians knew they had made a mess of their country and now needed outside help.

One day I went up a jungle road from Monrovia to interview rebel commanders—a generally unpleasant bunch of intoxicated men wearing amulets while presiding over an army of preteen soldiers who believed themselves to be immune from bullets because they wore plastic shower caps, wigs, and white wedding dresses. Some of the rebel leaders were nominally Muslim—a fact that didn't prevent them from walking around with bottles of scotch looted from Monrovia's port.

As I waited at the rebels' checkpoint, chatting up a ten-year-old gunman, a patrol of U.S. Marines rolled up—part of a small American contingent on the ground that was deployed in Liberia for just a few weeks to support Nigerian-led West African peacekeepers. Used to seeing American soldiers and Marines in Iraq in dirty desert fatigues that displayed signs of rough living, I was surprised at how neat and clean these men looked.

It turned out that they, too, had spent time in Iraq, deployed to the city of Mosul before floating aboard their ships in the Gulf and then on to Liberia. I talked to one of the Marines, Sergeant Eric Schera. He marveled at the difference in the reception he was getting from the Liberians. "In Iraq, I felt some of the smiles were not genuine, but here when they smile at us, they mean it," he said. "They really seem to want us to be here." For a soldier—and, in a way, for a reporter—this made all the difference.

Later that evening I returned to my bare room in Monrovia's Mamba Point Hotel, the Lebanese-run refuge for journalists, aid workers, and UN staff members trying to jump-start Liberia's tentative reconciliation after decades of civil war. I found everyone unusually sullen, with several UN employees openly sobbing on the hotel's terrace overlooking the Atlantic, atop which three American warships loomed on the horizon.

The UN headquarters in Baghdad's Canal Hotel had just been blown up, killing twenty-two people—including the mission's chief, Sergio Vieira de Mello, a respected diplomat from Brazil. The world of aid workers who brave war zones is relatively tight. Everyone on the Mamba Point terrace seemed to know someone who was just killed or maimed in Baghdad. Even in Liberia, a continent away, I could find no escape from Iraq.

✦ ✦ ✦

By October, I was back in Baghdad, again. Samira and Jaffar didn't pick me up in the U.S.-run airport, and I couldn't find them for days. Instead, a driver for a departing aid group gave me a ride to my new hotel, the Hamra. As we approached town, the change in the city's landscape was striking: Baghdad had become a city of walls.

The Palestine Hotel compound on the main Firdous Square was now cordoned off by a maze of giant reinforced concrete blocks, twice as high as an average man. Similar blast barriers, surrounded with coils of razor wire, towered around several other hotels and ministries, spilling into the sidewalks and the road itself. We drove past the Green Zone, with its new perimeter walls, on both sides of the street, that stretched into the horizon. I was told that each of those blocks of blast barrier, the length of a car, contained enough cement and iron to build housing for a family—in a country where many slept a dozen to a room. The Green Zone's perimeter alone was an entire city of aborted houses, compressed into extra-hard concrete that could withstand a carload of explosives.

On my first day back in Iraq, the colleagues I found by the Hamra's pool also had concrete on their minds. The NBC team, whose small hotel had just been blown up, was buying an extra layer of blast barriers around the Hamra, and each resident journalist was expected to pitch in. Every morning we would awake to the now-familiar thud of explosions and run out to the balcony to divine the target by plumes of smoke. The blast barriers didn't always help—insurgents were using rockets and mortars, firing above the walls and even coming close to killing Deputy Defense Secretary Paul Wolfowitz, in the Rashid Hotel inside the Green Zone.

I had reported from the sites of suicide bombings in Israel a decade earlier, and was all too used to the sight of burning cars, twisted metal, and dismembered bodies lying amid the sewage that streamed into a bomb crater from blasted-out pipes. Sitting down on the ground to take notes one day in Tel Aviv in 1994, I realized after a few minutes that someone's severed finger was lying just under my shoe.

But it was different in Iraq. On the morning after my return in October 2003, a car bomb exploded at a police station in Sadr City. Several people, mostly civilians who shopped at the Shiite slum's open-air market nearby, were killed. I was surrounded by a furious crowd right after stepping out of the car. Some men were still wearing blood-stained shirts, and they weren't interested in talking. "It's all because of you Americans," one shouted, shoving me. "It's because of you that we are killed." A policeman cut through the crowd, yelling at me in English: "You! Go! Now! You! Go!"

Back at the hotel, I learned that other reporters had been roughed up that morning by knife-wielding mobs. The bombers, most likely Sunni Islamists, understood the Iraqi mentality perfectly well. Instead of prompting Shiites targeted by Sunni terror to cooperate with American occupiers against their common enemy, every new bomb simply inflamed anti-American rage. For the shadowy insurgents, this was a win-win situation. Soon a sizable part of Shiite public opinion was convinced that the United States was planting these bombs, as a replay of a *Quiet American* strategy designed to perpetuate American control.

I could understand where such paranoia came from. No matter who was responsible for each bomb, one fact was clear to most Iraqis: none of this horror was occurring before American tanks rolled in. "You've brought this on us" was an accusation I would hear again and again.

✦　✦　✦

Eventually I managed to track down Samira and Jaffar. They had just returned from a trip to visit relatives in the north, and Samira was busy reopening a bookstore that she owned on the Baghdad University campus. Her grandson instantly recognized me, bringing out the cherished toy car I had brought him from Rome.

Samira seemed distant. Well plugged into Baghdadi gossip, she knew that socializing with Westerners had become exceedingly dangerous. Insurgents were already killing "traitors"—anyone suspected of working as a translator for the U.S. military or the occupation administration. Within months, interpreters and fixers for Western news media would be tracked down and killed as well—often with their families. Samira was not willing to take a risk, especially as she increasingly shared the insurgents' bleak view of the occupation. I had to find myself another fixer.

"Things here are going from bad to worse to worst," she told me over tea and home-baked cookies. "What did the Americans bring us? Nothing. Only the looting and the killing. See—we still don't have electricity yet." We were all supposed to go out for dinner the following night, but only Jaffar showed up. He was just as sour on Americans as Samira.

Later that week, exactly half a year after the fall of Baghdad, Bremer triumphantly announced at a press conference, complete with Power Point presentations, that the occupation authority had finally managed to restore Iraq's electricity output to prewar levels. What he didn't say was that this was achieved by jerry-rigging all available generators and cranking them up to maximum capacity—a publicity stunt that produced a weeklong spike just in time for the press conference but damaged the infrastructure and made the power supply even scarcer for the rest of the year.

✦ ✦ ✦

Iraq now had its own governing body, handpicked by Bremer from among U.S.-financed exiles such as Chalabi and future prime minister Allawi, Kurdish strongmen, clerics, and tribal leaders. This docile institution, whose decisions were rare and, in any event, invalid without Bremer's signature, was officially known as Iraq's Interim Governing Council.

It was curious to hear what part of that long name people actually used. American officials would always refer to the body as "the Governing Council." Iraqis knew better. Aware that the council didn't really govern anyone, many called it simply "al-Intiqali," "the Interim One." Appointed rather than elected, the IGC members proceeded to exploit their positions for personal gain, naming sons, brothers, and cousins to top government jobs.

Depressed by daily bombings, I looked for any sign that the West was indeed trying to inculcate its values of freedom in Iraq. If successful, such an effort could have justified the entire mess. But despite all the promises of democracy, the American administrators were in no rush to institute self-rule or elections. The closest body that seemed to fit the bill for democratic reform was the new Baghdad City Council.

Since the first postwar months, U.S. troops in Baghdad had gone street to street, blaring out messages from Humvee-mounted loudspeakers calling for aid in organizing local town-hall meetings to select neighborhood councils. In some areas, thousands of people attended, packing an entire stadium in one occasion. In other parts of Baghdad, these "town halls" consisted of a handful of Iraqis who had already cooperated with the U.S. military.

By fall 2003, the neighborhood councils, in turn, elected assemblies for each of Baghdad's nine districts. Finally the district councilors elected, from among themselves, the thirty-seven members of the city-wide legislature. This complicated process, which gave the occupation authorities the power to screen out undesirables at every turn, was hardly textbook democracy. Still, the new body was billed as a huge step in the right direction.

"Part of the whole premise is to experience democracy in action, in case the Iraqis want to incorporate these processes in their constitution and city charter," Joe Rice, the project's coordinator, explained when we met up in Saddam's former palace, deep inside the Green Zone. Before deployment to Iraq, Rice, a lieutenant colonel in the Army Reserve, served as mayor of Glendale, Colorado, population 5,000. In Baghdad, he had to supervise more than six million people.

The next day I went to the bullet-scarred Baghdad City Council building to encounter this new breed of supposedly democratic politicians. While the chairman was busy meeting visitors, I struck up a conversation with an amiable woman who spoke decent English and covered her hair with the *hijab*. As we sat in a cavernous assembly hall inscribed with gilded quotes from the Quran, Shatha Hadi al Obaidi told me about the accidental beginnings of her political career. A mid-level manager at Iraq's Socialist Bank, she was cloistered at home with her family in a neighborhood right next to what would become the

Green Zone, when American troops rolled into Baghdad. While everyone was still afraid to step out on the street, Obaidi was overwhelmed by curiosity and left home to have a look at Iraq's new overlords. "Everyone urged me to stay put, but I said, 'Why would the Americans kill me? I didn't do anything.'"

Outside her home, Obaidi was stunned by a surprising sight. At about the same time I was driving my Yukon through Saddam's former palace, soldiers were gathering the dictator's extensive supplies of food. Concerned about possible poisoning, American troops in Iraq almost never ate local produce. Saddam's stock of flour, rice, and oil was meant to be discarded as trash outside the perimeter. Once Obaidi noticed the food-laden military trucks, she gathered enough courage to run up to a commander and beg him to distribute the supplies to the neighborhood's poor instead of dumping them into a landfill. The commander agreed—on the condition that she would translate for the soldiers and organize the distribution herself.

Obaidi went door-to-door, recruiting enough volunteers to help the entire neighborhood stock up on Saddam's groceries. It was these volunteers who later protected the area from looters. Using her new friendship with the American commander, Obaidi also steered some cash from the unit's emergency fund to repair postwar damage in the area. When neighborhood councils were created, she was a shoe-in.

In the district council, however, Obaidi came up against opposition from a leading cleric. Enjoying his new freedom, the cleric stood up and declared that women—who, after all, had been represented in the upper ranks of Saddam's regime—had no business sitting on government bodies. Obaidi responded that the cleric had no business telling people what to do. "If you read the Quran, you'll see many women doing important things there," she said. Thanks to tacit American support, she beat the imam for the citywide council seat.

I asked her whether she feared retribution from the growing resistance for her affiliation with the occupiers. "Now Iraq is weak, like a baby. We must take care of it, make it grow to become a child and then a man," she replied. "Even if the devil comes in to help, I'll be with him to make Iraq strong again." I asked her about Muqtada al Sadr. "Oh, he's so ugly," she giggled.

Obaidi was intelligent and courageous, and I was impressed by how she had seized on the opportunities available to her. But I couldn't get around the fact that the only reason she was on the council was that she met the right American officer at the right time. If Samira had chanced upon a truckload of American-guarded food instead of finding me that same week, she'd probably be a budding politician as well. It was great that people like Obaidi finally had a chance to get involved in politics—but how long would they last, absent American tanks?

Soon enough, I had my answer. As reconstruction funding started to trickle in from Washington, Sadr City, the Shiite slum that housed more than a quarter of Baghdad's population, received its first sizable influx of cash for neighborhood projects. The Sadr City district council was supposed to oversee this spending—and, inevitably for Iraq, some of the money ended up in the pockets of council members. Suddenly these American-created institutions—established in the midst of general apathy in Sadr City—were no longer irrelevant.

Muqtada al Sadr's movement wasn't going to miss out on such a windfall on its home turf. At meetings in Sadr-controlled mosques, the movement oversaw the selection of its own alternative district council, composed only of men. These new assemblymen then simply seized the district council headquarters, backed up by RPG-brandishing thugs from Muqtada's militia, Mahdi's Army. Muqtada's picture was hoisted under the Iraqi flag on the council's roof. Members of the American-backed assembly either defected or were reduced to meeting in secret—in Colonel Rice's office, inside the Green Zone.

On the day I went to watch the Baghdad City Council in action, the crisis in Sadr City topped the agenda. The Baghdad council's chairman, Adnan Darraji, a former chief steward of Iraqi Airways and a Shiite himself, led the charge to restore legitimacy. At his urging, the city assembly voted to call on the U.S.-supervised Iraqi police to seize the Sadr City building and kick out the unauthorized district assembly.

"It's a dangerous situation. If they are allowed to keep the building, this evil will spread all over the country," Darraji told the assembly, as Colonel Rice quietly took notes. One after another, the members agreed, ratcheting up the rhetoric. Councilman Mohammed Baqr al

Suheil, wearing the robes of a tribal sheikh, bellowed: "Muqtada al Sadr says he doesn't recognize the Governing Council. He says he doesn't recognize our council. And one day he will say he doesn't recognize God." Only one other councilman, Riyadh Nasser, tried to inject a dose of realism: "Brothers, we all know that when they had elections for the council in Sadr City, almost nobody participated. Half the people were afraid that Saddam will come back and punish them for voting, and the other half did not want to support the people who they thought to be working for the Americans."

The same day, I went to Sadr City to meet the unauthorized assembly. By chance, I arrived at exactly the same time that these new council members had begun a meeting with an American representative they knew as "Mister Peejay."

Mister Peejay, a lean man with a crew cut, was alone with several dozen Iraqis inside the Sadr City district council hall. He wore an almost invisible white flak vest under his khaki polo shirt.

I expected to see thuggish militia leaders and clerics, but this alternative district council consisted mostly of well-educated professionals. The conversation started out as polite and quickly degenerated into barely suppressed rage. Salah Erebat, a bearded lawyer, opened the discussion by saying that the U.S.-appointed body was corrupt, and threw America's own example, then in the news, at Mister Peejay. "When the people of California were unhappy with their authorities, they kicked them out and elected Schwarzenegger," he said. "So why is it that Americans can do it and we in Sadr City cannot?"

Mister Peejay, believed by all present to be a civilian, was actually an active-duty Army colonel by the name P. J. Dermer. He listened quietly at first.

"America says it is for democracy," Erebat went on. "Why can't I be on the council? Why am I denied my voice?"

"Where were you when the council was elected?" Dermer cut in.

"But there were no elections in our neighborhood!" an exasperated Erebat answered.

"That's not true," Dermer responded. "Just because someone walks in and demands change, this doesn't mean you do it. So far you've shown me nothing. You say you represent the people. Show me the people."

The unofficial council's chairman, engineer Naim Qaabi, jumped at the opening: "Tomorrow I can make a demonstration with two million people. Can you come to see it?"

Dermer remained silent.

As disapproving murmurs grew in the hall, one member stood up and, angering the American, bellowed: "Why do you hate the Iraqis?" Then, a gray-haired elder, Adbulhussein Jabr Amr, tried to offer an olive branch. "The enemies of America are also our enemies. Do not lose our friendship," Amr pleaded. "Dissolve the previous council. It's just a small group. These people were put together by the coalition without the knowledge of the people, and that council is not legitimate."

"Tell me what law is he speaking of," the colonel asked through his interpreter.

"Iraqi and international and universal law," Amr replied.

"There is no Iraqi law," the colonel shot back. "There is only one law in Iraq—it's coalition law." Nobody in the room liked this reminder of their status as an occupied people subjected to foreigners' whims.

As the meeting broke up, the Iraqis filed into the courtyard and nervously lit their cigarettes. The walls of the building, refurbished with U.S. money just weeks earlier, were now spray-painted with graffiti. "Down with occupation," said one. "America is the rapist of our country," said another.

The Iraqis all hovered in one part of the courtyard. Dermer stood alone in the other.

"We were suppressed by the old regime, and now we are suppressed by the Americans," scowled one of the Sadr-backed councilmen, Ridha Alwan. "Where is freedom?" In his corner, the colonel was shaking his head: "They just don't get it. They don't."

The following day American tanks surrounded the building, blocking for weeks the district's main road and spreading out coils of barbed wire. Within hours, they ousted the renegade council and arrested everyone found on the premises. There were no casualties. The American-appointed district council was back in office. Legitimacy was restored in what seemed like a rare happy ending.

Then, less than a month later, the chairman of the pro-American assembly was negotiating his way past tanks to reach his office. One soldier demanded to search the car, and the Iraqi started arguing. The American pulled a gun and shot him dead point-blank, one of what by now were countless such shootings. Little outcry ensued.

Next year, when Muqtada repeatedly declared an open uprising against the United States, nearly every local official and policeman in Sadr City sided with him. Hundreds, or even thousands, died. Nobody counted the Iraqi bodies.

9

IRAQ

Even if You Turn This Country into Heaven

Almost all embedded reporters, considering the story, and the war, to be over, departed Iraq a few days after the April 2003 fall of Baghdad. Six months later, as it became clear that the worst fighting was only beginning, the military was embedding again, for short stints. Until then, I spent most of my time in the country gauging the experiences of ordinary Iraqis. I knew all too well that many of them now viewed American troops as threatening and utterly alien intruders, imagining the GIs to be almost inhuman.

This was only one side of the story, of course. American troops in Iraq had to struggle with often impossible circumstances; resorting to brutality was sometimes the only way to survive. Often smart and courageous, the soldiers led harsh lives in a dangerous country where they hadn't expected to be posted for stints lasting more than a year. I was curious to see Iraq as the soldiers did, to understand the wall of mutual incomprehension that separated them from the people they were supposed to have liberated.

By the fall of 2003, one of the most perilous spots in the whole of Iraq was Ramadi, the capital of the province of Anbar, the western half of the lethal Sunni Triangle. A battalion of the Florida National

Guard controlled the city, and I jumped at the Army's offer to stay with the unit. In contrast to my previous trips in Iraq, I couldn't sit upright in the car on the road from Baghdad. This time, as we drove to Ramadi through Fallujah, I had to lie in the back seat of an inconspicuous cab driven by an Iraqi fixer, invisible to potential kidnappers; a flak vest was propped up against the curbside door to protect us from shrapnel.

The Guard battalion's commander was Lieutenant Colonel Hector Mirabile, in civilian life a genial Miami cop. Minutes after my arrival, he was scheduled to visit with the local sheikhs, and he allowed me to tag along. Sent into Ramadi without any intelligence about local society, Mirabile had been reading up, on his own, about how the British ruled the place eighty years earlier. The grandchildren of the same tribal leaders who had either opposed or supported the British were now fighting, or tolerating, Mirabile's men.

Like most officers I met in the field, Mirabile was scathing about Bremer's occupation administration, and about its high-minded goals of creating democracy in Iraq. Mirabile's priority was to make sure his soldiers, subjected to daily attacks, returned alive to their families back in south Florida. As long as the tribal sheikhs promised to curb the resistance, Mirabile was willing to steer money and contracts their way, leaving the chieftains to rule their tribe members as they saw fit. After half a year in Ramadi, Mirabile came to one conclusion: "Since Lawrence of Arabia, not a damn thing has changed here. The only difference is that, instead of camels, they now ride cars."

As we started washing down the usual rice and lamb feast with tea, a man sat next to us and proffered a business card describing himself as a human rights activist. Sweating profusely, he complained about American misdeeds—indeed, his uncle had been mistakenly killed in an air strike, he said. As a lawyer, the activist represented some three hundred security detainees in Abu Ghraib and other American-run jails, although he never had access to his clients. "The Americans are not doing things here the right way," he said gently. "For example, when they come in to search houses, why do they have to break down doors right away? Why can't they knock?" Mirabile listened, without saying a word. Once the man left, he leaned toward me to explain the local etiquette. "You know, all I have to do now is to go to the sheikh and say quietly, 'This guy just humiliated me in public, in front of a journalist.' In five minutes they'll take him to the back and beat the shit out of him."

Guard soldiers under Mirabile's command were usually adults with regular civilian jobs, often in police departments, many with children. They were reputed to be much less trigger-happy than the younger Eighty-Second Airborne troops in charge of nearby Fallujah. As a result, anti-American ardor in Ramadi hadn't yet reached Fallujah's feverish pitch.

As night fell on the city, Mirabile entrusted me to a three-Humvee patrol that would roam Ramadi from the battalion's base. Virtually every night, these patrols were attacked with roadside bombs—often hidden inside dead animals, trash bags, or pieces of concrete. I was happy to be riding in one of the few armored Humvees the unit possessed.

Donovan, the gunner in my Humvee, was on his second overseas deployment in one and a half years. Shipped to Iraq almost immediately after a stint in Afghanistan, he was bitter in a resigned, almost imperceptible way. I asked him what usually happens on these missions. He flipped a CD into his Walkman, adjusted the earphones, and laughed: "They shoot at us. We shoot at them. We kill them. No paperwork."

On the first leg of the patrol, we stopped by the local governorate building. Like soldiers all over Iraq, the ones in my Humvee referred to the natives by the pejorative "hajji." An Arabic term of respect for someone who had performed the hajj pilgrimage to Mecca, the word has been twisted by American soldier-speak into an insult akin to the "gook" and "Jap" of previous wars. It was about an hour before the 10 PM curfew, and the street was full of children and men dressed in white or beige gowns. Bored, Donovan started playing with the red laser beam of his sights, pointing it at random. Oblivious at first, Iraqi men suddenly noticed a crimson laser point on their chests. Scared, they looked up, spotted the Humvee, and then—often shaking— rapidly scuttled away. Others simply froze, watching the red spot move up and down their body. Sitting atop the Humvee, Donovan was having a good time. Me too, because I found the whole scene almost funny.

By Ramadi standards, the night was uneventful. We were fired at, once, from behind an ice cream parlor, with the single bullet harmlessly whizzing past the Humvee. Soldiers ran out to find the gunman, cursing after Iraqis on the street who claimed not to have heard the shot. Thankfully, we were not hit by roadside bombs. Dinner was back at the base, in a brand-new hall where soldiers gathered to watch DVDs and baseball on large plasma-screen TV sets. The transition between the war zone outside and the college-dorm atmosphere inside was unsettling. I picked up a Kuwaiti ice cream and a can of Bahrain-bottled juice from the fridge, and ate my cheeseburger with real Heinz ketchup.

One of the soldiers, who had already seen his business in Florida go bankrupt because he was stuck in Iraq with the Guard, told me about his latest task. To combat the black market in petrol, the troops had been stationed at gas stations in the city. There were strict orders against jerry cans—so every time some Iraqi walked in with his tattered plastic container, the soldiers would seize it and cut it up with scissors. "As you can imagine, we made lots of friends this way," he said.

Just after dawn we left the base again to sweep a riverside road—the part of town soldiers abhorred most. Running along a bush-covered riverbank, with plenty of abandoned buildings along the way, the road was ideal territory for bombs. Every few yards a crater testified to the almost daily explosions. This time the armored Humvee was taken by another unit, and I sat—feeling uncomfortably exposed—in the back of an open vehicle. A flak vest was wrapped around the backrest, providing a degree of protection against smaller blasts.

The road, usually busy in the early morning, was empty. The gunner, Aaron Deshay, was fretting while he scanned the bushes. Empty streets were a bad sign, he told me, because the insurgents tend to warn the locals—sometimes by writing with chalk on the road—whenever ambushes are planned. Not knowing the language, the troops miss these signs. While two children peered at us from behind one wall, soldiers threw candy on the road ahead, gesturing at kids to run and pick up the sweets. With children around, the attackers would think twice before setting off the explosives, the soldiers reckoned. The kids, however, stayed away. In places like Ramadi, Iraqi parents, not too sure that insurgents would be so scrupulous, usually barred their children from coming anywhere near American troops.

This patrol was organized together with the American-trained Iraqi police, "hajji cops" in soldier parlance. Skinny and dressed in light-blue shirts, without any body armor, the Iraqis were sent ahead to investigate suspicious mounds of garbage. The Americans, dressed in Kevlar helmets and bulletproof vests, hung back. There was little solidarity between the two groups. "I don't understand why we're training them—cuz now they're just gonna turn around and use it against us," one soldier muttered, reading the loyalties of these Iraqis far more presciently than official spokesmen in Baghdad ever did. Hundreds if not thousands of these policemen joined the insurgency in the following months, including the Ramadi chief of police with whom Mirabile and I feasted on lamb at a tribal reception.

As we quietly rolled along the riverside, Deshay noticed an old Iraqi man who was peering at us from behind a parked minibus, his curiosity getting the best of him. Rolling in his seat, Deshay trained the gun on the man. "Look at that hajji. Now, how stupid can you get?" he exclaimed. "Little does he know that he's our first target if something happens now."

Mirabile's battalion was one of a handful that returned from Iraq without losing a single member to insurgents (although one soldier deserted and many troopers were injured, some very seriously.) In a story about its homecoming that ran in the *Miami Herald* in May 2004, the colonel's driver praised his commander this way: "Mirabile's philosophy is shoot first, ask questions later."

✦ ✦ ✦

Less than a week after the Ramadi patrol, I was being bled upon in the back of another armored Humvee, in Balad. In June, I sat at the wakes of local villagers killed by American fire in the area, in Dhuluiya and Yathrib. Now, in October, the whole region was a blazing war zone.

The Balad air base, where I inquired about the villagers' bodies in June, had become a miniature American city. Color-coded buses ferried soldiers between their barracks, recreation facilities, and a gleaming dining hall that occasionally featured lobster tails on the menu. Almost every night the base's neighbors fired mortars and rockets into the perimeter, occasionally killing or wounding American personnel—including, once, a soldier waiting in the chow line on his last day in Iraq.

I was at the base to visit a tent hospital and to report on the stream of American casualties caused by the insurgents' rapidly improving combat skills. Barely a minute after I walked into the tent, the radio crackled with news of the latest attack. With two medics, I rushed in ambulance Humvees to pick up two wounded soldiers at the medevac helicopter's landing zone. The third man in the blown-up Humvee was already dead.

The soldier in my ambulance had pieces of flesh scooped out of his face and blood drizzling from his right arm and leg, which was peppered by chunks of shrapnel from a roadside bomb. Powered by morphine, he kept talking: "We've driven that road hundreds of times—and nothing ever happened to us. Damn . . ." A reservist from Kansas working on a master's degree in Russian studies, he later told me he had planned to join the State Department's diplomatic security branch. He would no longer be able to do that: half an hour after landing, military surgeons amputated his arm. His captain, killed by the same bomb, had filled in for the usual commander, absent on family leave. That leave ended the same morning, with the regular captain landing in Balad only to learn that a man died in his place.

After the surgery I sat down to talk with orthopedic surgeon Lieutenant Colonel Kim Keslung, who had a brief moment of respite before a new wave of casualties from another attack was flown in. Tired after months of nonstop horror, she was sitting on the floor, drinking a Kool-Aid mix from a plastic water bottle. Her desert-camouflage pants were stained with blood. "His nerves and blood vessels were just shredded. There wasn't anything left to fix," she said about the Kansas reservist. "Unfortunately, these are typical injuries." Like most of the doctors and nurses at this hospital, normally based at Fort Hood, Texas, she had grown inured to the daily gore—and, knowing full well what was happening outside the wire, refused whenever possible to leave the base. I asked her what she thought of the Iraqi resistance, which had become so efficient in killing and maiming young American women and men. Some of the wounded Iraqi attackers, she responded, actually ended up on her operating table as patients. "What they did outside the berm does not matter here. But I don't make friends with them. I don't know their names," Keslung said. "A lot of them are just stupid kids. But some are not very nice people."

Sometimes the wounded American soldiers had to lie next to the Iraqis who had attacked them. Sometimes the surgeons were more successful with the Iraqis, and the insurgents survived while the Americans didn't.

Keslung took another gulp of the Kool-Aid and sighed. "I didn't think it would last this long. I should have. If someone invaded Texas, we'd be doing the same thing."

✦ ✦ ✦

In November 2003, I came up for air and went home. While I was catching up with my family in Rome, a suicide bomber drove his truck into an Italian base in the Iraqi city of Nassiriya, killing nineteen Italians—soldiers, carabinieri guardsmen, and a film crew. The toll wasn't exceptionally high for the new Iraq—just a few days earlier, an insurgent rocket downed a U.S. Chinook chopper near Fallujah, killing sixteen soldiers aboard. But for the Italian military, it was the biggest loss of life since 1945. Italy, which didn't participate in the Iraqi invasion and in which a large majority of the population opposed the war, now suddenly felt that it, too, was being dragged into a conflict spinning out of control. Mourning, and shock, were intense.

In contrast to the United States, where Pentagon regulations barred the media from taking pictures of coffins returning from Iraq, Italy threw a high-profile ceremony for its fallen. The entire political class, from the president and prime minister down, attended a funeral service that was broadcast live on TV. Hundreds of thousands of ordinary citizens lined up all night to pay their respects on Rome's central Piazza Venezia. I felt bizarrely reassured: at least here at home, human life still seemed to have a proper value.

✦ ✦ ✦

In January, I had to return to Iraq. I promised my wife that this would be the last time. Her nerves were frayed from daily reports on TV, and she had made a habit of preventing our children—ages seven and four at the time—from watching the news.

The policies of "shoot first, ask questions later" were failing to contain the insurgency's spread. The advent of 2004 was marked by an attack on Nabil, a Baghdad restaurant where I used to eat almost every night. A car bomb killed several New Year's revelers inside and wounded scores of others, including reporters for the *Los Angeles Times*. In January, insurgents expanded their target list. While initially focusing on the Green Zone and military bases, guerrillas would now often fire rockets into hotels inhabited by Western civilians, including the Palestine—where guests tried to stay on the safer side of the building that faced the Tigris.

In Baghdad, I was cloistered in a discrete villa that the *Wall Street Journal* would share with *Newsweek* until the fall of 2004, when a car bomb nearby blew out its windows. Our landlord was one of numerous Western security companies lured to Iraq by a bonanza of American tax dollars. The landlord's armed guards were arrayed outside, and a collection of pistols somehow often ended up casually displayed on the desk in the reception area. Across the street was a European ambassador's residence; it featured mounted machine-gun nests on the building's sides, one of them facing straight into my bedroom. Embassy security had also blocked off street entrances with barriers, sandbags, and concrete blocks, thoroughly searching all cars trying to enter. A local grocery store was caught on our side of these walls of fear—a barrier that the hapless shopkeeper's usual customers understandably refused to cross.

Going to restaurants was now considered too much of a risk, so food was concocted in our kitchen by an Iraqi cook whose gastronomical acumen seemed on a par with that of an Iraqi Army mess hall. Home entertainment consisted of bootleg DVDs bought on the streets, and visits to similar fortresses inhabited by other Westerners. On the rare occasion when I mustered the courage to dine out—always choosing a table with my back to the wall and as far as possible from the window—a perceptible chill descended once I appeared. Iraqi restaurant patrons immediately realized that my very presence made them a target.

Westerners in Iraq, men and women alike, now wore the Arab headdress when riding in cars. Men tried to grow beards to blend in, and my own stubble soon reached Taliban proportions. At first it felt like a cheat to be masquerading this way. But, with time, it was reassuring to notice that people on the street were looking right past me, instead of staring intensely, as they had done in the past.

That January, Iraqi gunmen attacked a CNN crew on a road I had taken days earlier. The assailants killed two Iraqi staff members before being driven away by response fire from a CNN bodyguard. Shocked by these killings, Western reporters gathered in the Palestine Hotel's large ballroom with a CNN executive flown in from Atlanta.

Until then, Western journalists in Iraq believed themselves to be safer than other foreigners. Sure enough, some two dozen of our colleagues had been killed by that time—in several cases, by American fire. But the insurgents, who specifically targeted the U.S. military, the UN, aid workers, and reconstruction contractors, had at that point been known to spare reporters. After all, what was the purpose of spectacular attacks if CNN and Al Jazeera weren't there to film them? Now the mayhem had started to engulf all of us. The insurgents figured out that they'd get more mileage for their propaganda by killing a Westerner, reporter or not, on camera—and then e-mailing their snuff videos to eager satellite TV networks.

At the gathering in the Palestine, someone asked for an informal poll of colleagues' precautions. It turned out that most news-organization crews either traveled with armed guards, allowed their drivers to pack weapons, or carried firearms themselves. So proud of our impartiality, so used to imagining that we stood above warring parties, we were now rendered just another militia. I wondered how many Iraqis had been shot by media outlets.

✦ ✦ ✦

The sad, elderly clock master's son I met by the leaning Abu Hanifa tower the previous year stuck in my mind, and so, in early 2004, I made an effort to track him down in what was now one of the city's most violent neighborhoods. On the way to Abu Hanifa, I saw a bright billboard featuring a U.S.-produced poster urging Iraqis to turn in "terrorists." Set up on a traffic roundabout, the poster sported a larger-than-life photograph of an American soldier, his boot resting on the neck of a bound, middle-age Iraqi man in a traditional robe. Someone had thrown a firebomb at the billboard, and its corners were charred.

I was stunned by the insensitivity of the photograph—especially considering how many men in this neighborhood must have experienced just such treatment themselves during frequent roundups and house searches. My new fixer, Haaqi, couldn't hold back a chuckle. "Why did these guys bother to burn down the poster?" he wondered. "In truth, it's an advertising for the resistance."

Abu Saa, the clock master's son, agreed to meet us on a square outside the mosque. All around us, the anti-American graffiti had gotten thicker and more threatening. The old man arrived on time; he looked unchanged from April, his spotless shirt just as impeccably pressed. He came with his son, Saad, an electrical engineer. Since I last saw him, a wealthy Iraqi businessman had agreed to finance the clock tower's reconstruction. Laborers were already busy at work in the mosque's courtyard.

Luckily, the clock's mechanism had not been attached to the tower's walls. When the rocket hit the tower, the mechanism was simply propelled up the shaft and could be repaired. Abu Saa, the only man in Baghdad who really knew how the complicated clock worked, supervised the restoration. But the man was already eighty-four years old, his son quietly reminded me. "We're always in fear that my father won't be able to finish the work," he sighed. "It's immense."

Despite his personal pain, Saad wouldn't be drawn into politics. "Some people didn't want to repair the tower because they wanted to leave it as a symbol of what the Americans have done to us," he told me. "But we said, no, let's rebuild. This should be a symbol of how we can succeed."

✦ ✦ ✦

After partaking of honey-drenched sweets under the Abu Hanifa clock tower, I drove up the road to the ugly, sprawling al-Nidaa Sunni mosque, a fine example of kitschy Saddam-era architecture. The imam there, Sheikh Qutaiba Ammash, was one of the main Sunni religious leaders in Iraq. It was Friday morning, just before the noon prayer.

The courtyard of the mosque was patrolled by young men who covered their faces, guerrilla-style, with checkered scarves. Kalashnikov guns were casually slung over their shoulders and olive ammunition pouches bristled with spare banana-shaped clips. In contrast to a few months earlier, these gunmen felt no need to hide from American troops. A peddler sat by the gate, selling calendars depicting the cracked Abu Hanifa clock tower, with grinning GIs in the foreground. A black-and-white photograph of a bruised man hung on the gate itself. According to an accompanying notice, the man in the picture had been tortured to death, on suspicion of supporting the resistance, by U.S.-supervised police. His funeral was scheduled for later that day.

The imam saw me for a few minutes in his back office, exchanging polite conversation. I asked him what he thought about America's promises to instill democracy in Iraq. "America?" he laughed. "We only believe in American technology. We don't believe in American democracy, because the Americans themselves don't have any."

Chuckling, Ammash excused himself: it was time for a sermon. An Al Jazeera crew was on hand to transmit his words across the Arab world. I was allowed to stay in the courtyard and listen.

He started out by praising anti-American insurgents, including the man who would be buried after the prayer. "The brave men of Mohammed's nation are protecting our sanctities. They will earn a place in the books of the great, with their names written in gold, because they didn't live like traitors and hypocrites. Their blood is our gift to God, and we hope Prophet Mohammed will enjoy how it smells."

After that, the sheikh focused his invective on the "traitors"—who, in his definition, included all Iraqis on the Governing Council and in other U.S.-sponsored bodies. "They dared to proclaim a national holiday on April 9, to celebrate Baghdad's rape by the invaders," Ammash shrieked. "God bless our martyrs and protect our prisoners. Let God destroy the people who support the Americans and America itself."

✦　✦　✦

The gold-domed Kadhimiye shrine, one of the main Shiite pilgrimage centers in the world, stands just across the Tigris from Sheikh Ammash's mosque. In the past, a deep divide separated the Sunnis, the backbone of Saddam's regime, from the long-oppressed Shiites. But by early 2004, the anti-American rhetoric on both sides of the river had become almost identical—a prelude to the insurgency spreading all over Iraq.

In the maze of muddy, refuse-strewn streets around Kadhimiye, I looked for the Khalisi Madrasa, a Shiite academy that played a key role in the nation's modern history and was now fermenting with political activism once again. It was in this unremarkable-looking building that Sunnis and Shiites agreed to fight together against British occupation in the 1920s. I was invited to have a look at the hall where the first flag of an independent Iraq had been drawn up. Scattered on a desk inside were photocopies of a joint memorandum just signed by top Sunni and Shiite religious leaders, pledging to unite against a common foe—America and the West.

Sitting by the desk, I spent more than an hour chatting with Sheikh Majid al Saadi. Dressed in a white turban and brown frock, Saadi was one of the prayer leaders at the Kadhimiye shrine. I made the mistake of starting our conversation with an observation that Iraqi Shiites should at least be grateful to the Americans for removing Saddam. "Grateful?" he mocked. Wasn't it the Americans who supported Saddam in the first place during the worst horrors of the 1980s? And wasn't it Washington that betrayed a U.S.-inspired Shiite uprising in 1991? "That was our first experience with American promises of democracy. We realized it's a democracy of mass graves," Saadi said, prompting his disciples to break out in laughter. "The Americans say they have come to liberate us?" he sniggered. "Sure, they've come to liberate Iraqis from their bodies. Everyone who shakes a hand with these invaders should have his hand cut off. Everyone who smiles at the oppressors should enter hell."

As Saadi went on talking, I noticed that his worldview went beyond the familiar vision of Islam clashing with the infidel West. The way he saw it, human civilization was now subjected to an attack of uncouth, uncivilized, Coke-guzzling barbarians. America was not just the enemy of Islam: it was the enemy of mankind.

"Look at the three countries that are occupied—Palestine, Afghanistan, Iraq. Why them?" he wondered. "In Iraq, seven thousand years ago, we invented mathematics, geography, law. We taught civilization. In Palestine, the Christian Messiah was born. And in Afghanistan, the Buddhist religion was rooted, and it is one of the oldest religions in the world. Because of their deep history, all these people have a deep faith—and this angers America, which wants the entire world to become like it."

To the sheikh, this was a doomed enterprise. "America? They don't have any history longer than two hundred years. They're ignorant. They have no idea how to manage countries. There, the people come from many nations and have many religions, but they have no relationship with the land and with their faith." These words, I noticed, sounded disconcertingly similar to the 1930s bashing of "mongrel America" by the Nazi and Italian Fascist propaganda.

In his hatred, however, the sheikh was not bothered with consistency; within minutes he switched to a wholly different tack. "American rulers are not just the enemies of Muslims or Arabs. They are the enemies of the American people," he continued. "They will do anything for their benefit, sending their boys to the hell of Iraq or Afghanistan now, and Lebanon yesterday," he intoned. Then, with an air of sharing secret truths, he leaned toward me: "You know why? This is all planned by the Zionist lobby. The Jews are responsible for it all, from killing Jesus Christ to killing John Kennedy."

It was disheartening to see how America was reduced, in the minds of these clerics, and the mobs who hang on their every word at packed sermons, to a confused caricature of a soul-less vampire state. But I could see why such paranoia was flourishing. The only Americans most Iraqis have met were young, nervous soldiers in full battle rattle who usually expressed themselves with gestures and expletives and, above all, shot without paperwork. It would become even harder to argue about Western values of freedom once the iconic photos of naked Iraqis tortured by American soldiers at Abu Ghraib prison became, for many, the most memorable symbol of America's effort to spread democracy in the lands of Islam.

✦ ✦ ✦

Returning from Kadhimiye to our isolated compound in Baghdad's once-prosperous Mansur neighborhood, I passed by the new blast barrier walls that sheltered what had been a pleasant building crowned with a white stucco dome. Iraqi employees at our house told me that the building was a former art gallery, run by Widad Orfali, one of the country's best-known artists.

The gallery's leafy garden and crowded jazz concerts were still remembered in the city as a rare refuge from the country's overall nastiness before the war. Orfali, now a sullen woman of seventy-four, had been the darling of Baghdad's social set, charming local intellectuals and foreign diplomats alike at well-watered parties that often lasted until the morning.

Inside the Green Zone, I called on my old acquaintance Colonel Rice, the mayor from Colorado who now supervised Baghdad's democracy programs. In his office I met an Iraqi-American defense contractor who helped run the new self-governance institutions. The man's headquarters were inside the Orfali gallery, and I made sure he invited me to visit.

The sad irony turned out to be that the contractor, Adel al Hillawi, was also a professional painter. His personal Web site displayed a collection of cubist-style tableaus that he crafted back home in Princeton, New Jersey, to sell to the families of Ivy League kids.

Instead of brushes and sketchbooks, Hillawi, whose graying cropped beard gave him the appearance of a nineteenth-century whaler, kept an Austrian-made MP-5 submachine gun on his desk. The gallery was now ugly and bare, with all the charm of a police station. A board behind Hillawi's chair outlined his immediate aims, as written by an American colleague: "Stop giving himself haircuts. Quit asking for $. Get laid to reduce stress."

I asked him what happened to the gallery's previous owner. "I feel for Widad. She comes here every day, crying that she wants her gallery back," Hillawi answered. "But she will not get it."

I found Orfali in her crumbling home across Baghdad the following day. In 1983, Orfali, who had exhibited her Moorish-style paintings of imaginary Islamic landscapes in New York, London, and across the Arab world, created Iraq's first private art gallery. Happy to have a guest, she showed me newspaper clippings and brochures from her exhibitions. She didn't even know that Hillawi, the intruder, was a painter, too.

By the time Orfali had become famous in her homeland, Hillawi was living half a world away, studying at California State University and enjoying the artistic freedom he had been denied in Iraq. "In Iraq, they were asking me to go and paint all these murals for any occasion, and I felt I was going to just kill myself if I stay in Iraq," he told me. "I cut my rope, and thought: Bye-bye, Iraq, this is it."

Then, in 1999, tragedy broke his American idyll. Saddam's sex-obsessed son Uday ordered Hillawi's younger brother killed— essentially for refusing to share his new wife. Furious, Hillawi embraced the American-backed Iraqi exile opposition groups, including the one led by Chalabi.

The same year, Orfali signed a build-and-operate deal with the Iraqi Hunting Club, a Baghdad hangout where Uday often held parties and in whose management he was actively involved. Orfali insisted she never actually met with Uday. Her deal was common for Iraq. She agreed to build the gallery on the hunting club's land, operate the gallery for ten years for a symbolic rent of some $50 a month, and then turn the building over to the club.

After a year of busy construction that has kept Orfali $15,000 in debt, she opened the gallery in the summer of 2000. A frail but tireless woman with jet-black hair and carefully groomed eyebrows, she transformed the space into a magnet for the Iraqi cultured classes, organizing concerts and lectures on subjects that ranged from Old Baghdad architecture to parapsychology. "We had nothing to see on television except Saddam and songs about him," she recalled. "I wanted to discover talented people. I wanted to make people happy."

Then came the war. The gallery was unscathed by the bombing and by the looting that followed the regime's collapse on April 9, 2003. But when Orfali made her way to the gallery several days later, thinking about when to reopen it, she found Chalabi's American-backed militia, the Free Iraqi Forces that had just arrived in Baghdad from Nassiriya, where I had last seen them.

The militiamen had already broken the door into the gallery. "This belongs to Uday," she recalled them explaining to her.

"No, this is mine. You are doing the same thing as Saddam. You are no better than him," she responded, on the verge of tears. She tried to clarify that she had a legal lease with the hunting club.

"There is no club. We are the government now," Chalabi's aide replied.

"No, you are not government. You are nothing," she argued back.

Eventually, Orfali had to give in. She sat on a street near the gallery, crying and waiting with her piano, her paintings, and her power generator for a moving truck. After that, she went into a deep depression and stayed in bed for two months. A month later, Chalabi's representative knocked on her door, offering a check for $3,000 as rent. Orfali, aware that her agreement with the hunting club barred subletting the gallery, initially refused the money. The offer was repeated the following day, as a gift. Calculating that Chalabi's men had been using her air conditioners and furniture, Orfali accepted the cash. She wrote on the receipt that she considered the money a present.

By late 2003, the occupation authority disbanded Chalabi's militia and began looking for real estate to house a district council for Mansur, as part of Colonel Rice's local self-government program. Hillawi told me that the Americans initially wanted to seize the entire complex on the grounds that, according to property deeds, it belonged to Saddam's household.

"I told them you can't do that. Even if the hunting club belonged to Saddam, it was a social place used by many Iraqis. I lived here. I know that," he said. Instead, Hillawi lobbied for a compromise solution that called for the seizure of only Orfali's gallery, on the pretext that, by accepting the $3,000 from Chalabi, she had violated her commitment not to sublet.

I couldn't help feeling for Orfali, bewildered and summarily discarded, just like everything else from the ancien régime. An effusive host, she used a rare moment of working electricity to perform for me, on a synthesizer, a catchy pop tune she had composed. "I don't want to make a fuss about the Americans," she insisted. But after our third cup of tea, she changed her mind: "The Iraqis don't like the Americans," she confided. "Of course they don't. If somebody comes to your home with a gun, do you say thank you?"

The next time I passed by her former gallery, a crowd of Iraqis milled around the blast barriers, kept at bay by gun-toting security guards. Who are these people? I asked. Distraught relatives of local men detained by American forces were mobbing the building. Months after the detainees had vanished into the black hole of Abu Ghraib and other facilities, the families figured that U.S.-appointed district council officials could find out what happened and help speed up release. On the outer wall, a large baby-blue banner placed by Hillawi flapped in the wind. It proclaimed: "No to dictatorship!"

✦   ✦   ✦

Before leaving Iraq, I wanted to travel once again to the Sunni belt north and west of Baghdad—the heart of the insurgency, which was becoming more and more successful in derailing American reconstruction plans.

I had spent plenty of time in places like Ramadi and Fallujah, and so, in early 2004, I picked Tikrit, Saddam's hometown and the provincial capital of a strip of central Iraq that stretched from the outskirts of Baghdad to Kurdish areas in the north. Under Saddam, Tikrit's old downtown on a cliff overlooking the Tigris was bulldozed and replaced with a walled-off compound of presidential palaces. Just as inaccessible to mere mortals as before, this palatial city—as tasteless as it is monumental—now housed American soldiers and occupation officials in a miniature version of Baghdad's Green Zone. The Army gave me an "embed" slot in the palace, and a cot under a ceiling that was at least four floors high.

On my first day in Tikrit, I patrolled the town with soldiers, taking a back seat in a Humvee that, in case of attack, had been stripped of its doors to make jumping out easier. A tall pole was welded above the radiator, to break decapitation wires strung between buildings at the level of the gunner's neck. Looking out for roadside bombs, the patrol didn't let any Iraqis overtake our Humvees—causing a giant traffic jam behind us. It took just a slight wave from the soldiers for civilian drivers to hit the brakes and hang behind. Having been on the other side of such patrols, I felt, not without guilt, a certain sense of empowerment, of being part of a force that can crush and disembowel a country. That sentiment turned to shame when our patrol caused the first traffic accident of the day: an Iraqi driver, seeing us too late and afraid of being shot for getting too close, swerved into the wrong lane, colliding with another vehicle. The second car carried a large family, including a baby that flew into the windshield. The baby survived, and soldiers complained, half sincerely, that the parents had not strapped the baby into a child seat. Of course, there were no child seat laws— and, as far as I knew, no child seats—in Iraq.

A few hours later, we were responsible for another accident. Abruptly, the patrol U-turned across the median and plowed into traffic. Because an Iraqi truck, which carried a tractor in the back, couldn't brake in time, it flew across the divider and crash-landed on the other side of the road. The patrol just drove off; I never found out how badly the truck driver was hurt (or whether he even survived).

Tired of talking guns and riding in Humvees, I sought out the American civilian administrator for the Tikrit province, the man who tried to co-opt local notables into the American-sponsored political process. Bob Silverman, a career State Department diplomat, spoke perfect Arabic and was well informed about the country and the Middle East in general. He had once translated an Egyptian writer's book about visiting Israel into English and, in the process, weakened his eyesight to the point of having to wear bifocals.

I appreciated the difference between Silverman and most other occupation officials I'd met. Those always upbeat and often ignorant bureaucrats, frequently borrowed from the staffs of Republican members of Congress, never let the facts stand in the way of political spin and, during three-month assignments in Iraq, seldom ventured outside Baghdad's Green Zone. Their Arabic vocabulary rarely extended beyond "hello" and "thank you."

Silverman offered me a tiny room of my own in his part of the palace, and took me around the province. After a few days I was impressed by how he smooth-talked local tribal leaders, exchanging pleasantries at endless rice, lamb, and tea sessions. It crossed my mind that, with competent people like him, the occupation effort wasn't doomed after all; Iraq could still be transformed for the better. Prominent Tikritis, too, seemed ready to work with "Mister Bob."

Then we drove to Baiji, a major industrial center and a flashpoint of anti-American attacks. Silverman had brought several former Iraqi generals into the provincial administration, including Thamer Sultan, a man from Saddam's tribe who commanded wide respect in Baiji. The meeting with Baiji's tribal leaders was meant to stop the insurgency in the town—and Silverman planned to woo local support by announcing a large influx of funding for infrastructure projects. Sultan's role, he told me before the trip, would be "to read the locals the riot act."

Scanning Baiji's rooftops for snipers, Silverman drove me in his bullet-scarred SUV, with a Nepalese Gurkha bodyguard riding in the back and a spare Kalashnikov, just in case, hemmed in at the gearshift. We stopped at an oil company club. There, more than one hundred local elders, dressed in traditional robes and checkered headscarves, packed the hall. The local American military commander was absent because the sheikhs refused to be in the same room with soldiers. Soon it was Silverman, not the sheikhs, receiving the riot act. One man stood up, wiping off tears, and recounted how the military had raided his house and killed his brother and two children. Another man, Adel Turki Majid, a sheep trader, complained that soldiers had ransacked his home and confiscated $8,000 in cash and his daughter's gold jewelry, dowry for a wedding already planned. The soldiers, he said, claimed that this was money for terrorism. Because the cash and the jewelry were never returned, the wedding had to be called off.

"When you came here, you destroyed factories and homes, and burned cars with people inside them. What do you expect us to say—thank you, America?" shrieked Sheikh Rafeh Hamed Majid.

As the crowd became bigger and more hostile, Silverman tried to keep tensions at bay. "I know we have made some mistakes, but we know that your people have made mistakes, too," he told the sheikhs with a disarming smile, as he tried to steer the discussion toward reconstruction: he listed the new projects the United States was going to finance.

Talk of money was met with defiant pride. Ramadhan Toaman al Qaissi, another tribal chief, stood up to reply. "Even if you turn this country into heaven, we don't want it from you," he said, in a crisp, cool voice. "Just go away from Iraq and leave us alone. We've had enough of you and can't stand it no more." Suddenly, the hall erupted in thunderous applause that lasted minutes. Silverman's face was locked in an uncomfortable smile.

With things getting out of hand, we had to beat a retreat. Embarrassed, Sultan tried to explain what had just happened. "Our people have seen Americans in Hollywood movies and were impressed by how educated and polite the Americans are on-screen," he told Silverman once we reached relative safety. "But now these people have seen your soldiers in real life. And they are very surprised that the Americans have turned out to be so rough and so rude."

10

AFGHANISTAN

The Brandy of Kabul

In theory, President Hamid Karzai's new and improved Islamic State of Afghanistan is just as thoroughly faithful to Islam as the Taliban's Islamic Emirate had been. The new constitution, adopted under U.S. supervision after American bombs ousted the Taliban theocracy in late 2001, specifies that no law can contradict the Sharia. Just like Saudi Arabia and Kuwait, Afghanistan officially is a strictly dry country. When I disembarked at the Kabul airport in the summer of 2004, a stern notice at the arrivals hall warned that all alcohol (and pork) products are illegal and will be confiscated.

Threat of confiscation wasn't meant to be taken seriously, any more than the pretense that the Afghan government was fully independent from Washington. On my first night in Kabul, I was offered a pork chop and an ice cold beer. A stack of *Afghan Scene* magazines lay by the reception desk of my guesthouse, with bar and restaurant reviews inside, alongside ads for Kabul's new (and demined) golf course, a massage service, and designer clothing outlets. The only reminder that this wasn't yet a normal country came from a small line on the bottom of the magazine's cover: "Sold by children in the street who keep what you give them—$2."

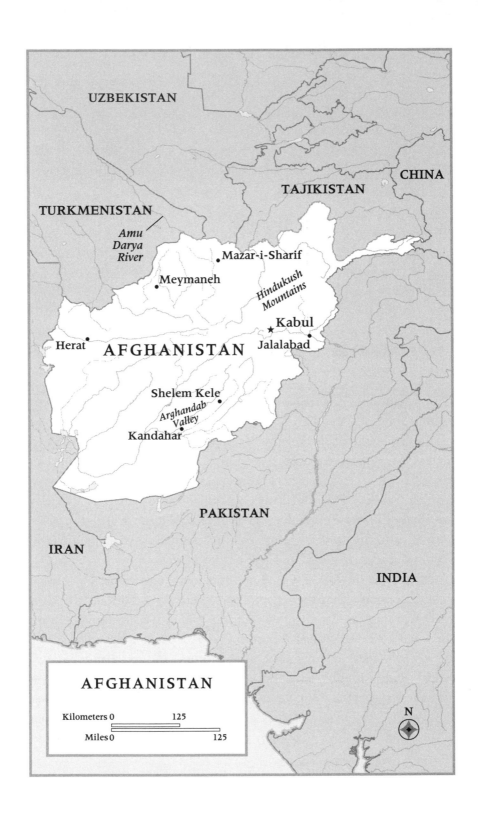

The night scene in Kabul had become lively thanks to the thousands of Western aid workers, UN employees, and other do-gooders who cruise in new SUVs and enjoy considerable disposable income; what they take home in a day can be more than most Afghans earn in a year.

Afghanistan, of course, remains a dangerous place, for Western civilians and soldiers alike. Western aid groups regularly come under attack, and the resurgent Taliban have transformed large parts of the country into no-go zones for foreigners and government officials. By mid-2004, the death toll among some 18,000 American soldiers and Marines deployed in Afghanistan had topped 100. As a percentage of troops, it was almost as bad as in Iraq. The Afghan dead were counted by the thousands, when counted at all.

Suicide bombings, rocket attacks, and roadside mines, so familiar to me from Iraq, became commonplace even in relatively safe Kabul, where a powerful car bomb devastated an expatriate residential area in front of the UN guesthouse shortly after my trip, and where UN workers had been kidnapped, Iraqi-style, and paraded in front of a video camera. But in stark contrast to Iraq, this war was one that the entire West supported; here, even France fought alongside the United States. So, unlike in Baghdad, Kabul's large expatriate community braved the violence and stayed put. Only a handful of aid groups, such as Médecins sans Frontières, pulled out after killings of staff members in mid-2004.

On my way from the airport, I noticed how, just as in Baghdad, bloodshed altered Kabul's streetscape. In both cities, countless blast barriers, miles of concertina wire, and walls of sand-filled Hesco boxes mushroomed after the Western takeovers, disfiguring entire neighborhoods. Containers piled one on top of another protected the more vulnerable buildings, the Western embassies and military units. At some points along the road into downtown Kabul, it seemed as though we were driving through frontline trenches.

The quality of these fortifications, more than the quality of food, made the difference between failure and success in Afghanistan's new restaurant scene. The UN mission in Kabul ran a special survey of restaurants to assess their vulnerability to attack. The result was an official list of venues where UN staff members, and employees of the many nongovernmental organizations that followed UN guidelines, were allowed to wine and dine. Getting on the approved list was Afghanistan's equivalent of receiving a Michelin star.

Kabul, I discovered soon, offered an embarrassment of choices. Two rival Thai restaurants served airlifted shrimp. Chinese, Indian, and Italian cuisine represented pleasant alternatives to the monotonous Afghan fare of mutton, rice, and green tea. Topping everything was a German beer hall with men in lederhosen, authentic wooden benches, foamy lager, grilled bratwurst, and checks tallied in euros. (Afghanistan, of course, now had its own American-era currency, the new afghani, which looked suspiciously similar in graphic design to the new Iraqi dinars, printed a few months apart. I never had a chance to spend my afghanis, bearing a Jamaican-sounding inscription of Da Afghanistan Bank: everyone wanted only hard cash.)

Dinner at Kabul's UN-approved restaurants usually cost in excess of an Afghan minister's monthly salary—a detail that explained why the customers who packed these outlets were almost exclusively Western. I wondered what proportion of international aid to Afghanistan went to pay wages and benefits for these expats. I couldn't blame the aid workers, who endured the risks and privations of the war-torn nation, for trying to replicate at least some comforts taken for granted at home. But for most Afghans, these watering holes seemed like mind-boggling, provocative luxuries, and a source of resentment deftly exploited by the Taliban.

There was another source of fast money in Kabul, of course. Afghanistan, after the Taliban, once again became the world's largest exporter of opium, with many of the American-backed militias actively involved in the lucrative heroin trade that the Taliban had tried to stamp out. Nowadays, business was done in the open. As I stopped for lunch at an Italian place, I noticed that the waiters paid exaggerated attention to the table right next to mine. At the head of it sat an obese man with long flowing hair and with the looks of a rock singer who had seen better days. The man, my fixer Qais interpreted in whispers, hailed from the former Soviet republic of Tajikistan. Next to him were two Russian men in bland clothes and with unremarkable appearances. They said little. The group was soon joined by two senior Afghan officers in neat U.S.-issue camouflage uniforms.

Without worrying about being overheard, the men discussed the timetable for a large shipment of Afghan heroin, first across the Tajikistan border and then on to Russia and Europe. The hairy Tajikistani didn't seem to trust his Afghan partners too much, and so the deal was complicated. "We can't give you money up front, so here's what we shall do," he told the officers. "I'm going to send you my brother as a guarantee, and you'll send the stuff our way. Once we get it, I'll return to Kabul with the money, and will get my brother back." The Afghans agreed, and the group sealed the deal with a loud toast and kebab, foregoing the restaurant's poor imitation of pizza.

✦ ✦ ✦

The Kabul guesthouse where I settled was called the Gandamack Lodge, in memory of the Afghan town where the last survivors of the routed British army were captured or killed in January 1842, in an ignominious end to the first Western attempt to rule the country. The lodge's owner, Peter Jouvenal, was an old Afghan hand. As a BBC cameraman, he was among the first Westerners to enter Kabul after the pro-American Afghan militias and the bombs I saw launched from the USS *Carl Vinson* had ousted the Taliban and Qaeda leaders from the capital.

Jouvenal decorated the place in the best colonial spirit, ordering glassware adorned with the likeness of Sir Harry Flashman, the womanizing hero of George Macdonald Frazer's novels, who survived the Gandamack rout in 1842 and gave his English country estate the name of Gandamack Lodge. On the walls hung an arsenal of century-old Lee Enfield rifles. In a country where rice is the main staple, Jouvenal's menu declared Gandamack Lodge to be a "rice-free zone." He had also perfected a system of fines to make sure that the Afghan peasants he recruited as waiters and outfitted with white shirts and bow ties didn't answer all clients' requests with a shrug and a "we don't have."

I wondered what the lodge's previous resident would have made of this. Under the Taliban, Osama Bin Laden's wife lived in this house, and the bearded Saudi himself was a frequent guest during his stays in the capital. I fantasized about what Bin Laden might have done in my second-floor suite, with its commanding view of mud houses climbing up the side of a brown hill that sprayed my belongings with its fine dust whenever the wind blew from that direction, which was most of the time.

Jouvenal disabused me of this fantasy, explaining that my part of the house was just a decoy, once inhabited by a modest Egyptian family. Bin Laden's actual home had been in the hidden, inner side of the compound. The Bin Ladens apparently weren't good tenants: that part of the mansion, found in utter disrepair after the war, had required major refurbishing.

Despite the official alcohol ban, nobody bothered the Gandamack Lodge, or other Kabul watering holes patronized by foreigners, about serving booze; the chief of police was a frequent guest himself. The NATO peacekeeping force in Kabul—which, unlike the U.S. Army in Muslim lands, allowed its soldiers to drink—had established a huge supermarket in Kabul called Supreme. The supermarket's entrance, decorated with a four-pointed NATO star, carried a warning that only foreign-passport holders could enter. The inner wall of the market was lined with a selection of duty-free liquors. Upon seeing me examine a bottle of wine, an attendant sprang up with a helpful query: "How many cartons will you take, sir?" For some of Kabul's expatriates, buying booze at the Supreme and reselling at mark-up to Afghan restaurant owners had become a major supplement to their income.

✦   ✦   ✦

During our breakfast banter about the contradictions of Afghanistan's new age, Jouvenal told me that the country once produced booze of its own. The sticky Afghan brandy, he said, used to be very popular among connoisseurs in neighboring Pakistan.

I decided to investigate what happened to it. Qais seemed to know where the old distillery was, so we headed toward the Jalalabad road that led east of the city. There it stood, just a short drive from the Supreme, a nondescript building with a sign that proclaimed: SUPPLE-MENTARY MEDICAL AND TECHNICAL MATERIALS INDUSTRY.

As we walked inside, the pungent smell of fermentation hit my nostrils. The place was clearly still in the alcohol business. The medical and technical materials made here turned out to be medical and industrial alcohol, brewed from mounds of red Kandahar raisins scattered in the courtyard, abuzz with fat flies.

The director, Said Anwary, wasn't in. I tracked him down on his cell phone, and he agreed to see me later that day in his apartment. He lived in the Soviet-constructed development called Mikrorayon, a cluster of bullet-marked concrete blocks that would look ugly anywhere else in the world but, in Kabul, gave the impression of positive luxury.

Anwary's living room was dominated by a huge poster of the holy shrine in Mecca. He constantly fingered worry beads, another outward sign of religious feelings. The room's Russian-style cupboard was, nonetheless, crammed with a dazzling collection of crystal wine, liquor, and champagne glasses. Kabul had gone from being one of the Islamic world's most assertively secular to one of its most rigorously religious cities in the span of just one generation, and traces of a different past continued to surface. Not long into the conversation, Anwary went to the kitchen and brought over a bottle of whiskey that he had concocted himself. Then he fetched a bottle of Jack Daniels and explained that his brother-in-law, who had purchased the real thing, couldn't distinguish, in a blind tasting, between the two beverages.

What I politely sipped from the glass didn't taste reassuring. Anwary, a man with a silver beard and ample gray hair, seemed upset that I didn't just down the drink. "Don't be afraid," he insisted. "This won't hurt you. If something happens to you, I'm responsible." I took another small sip.

I wanted to return to the distillery; we agreed to meet, again, in his office. There Anwary took out a folder with yellowed labels, which he spread out on his polished desk. "Whiskey, vodka, gin, rum, grappa, peach liquor, white wine, red wine—and, of course, brandy, the most famous of them all," he recited the distillery's former production lineup, his eyes lighting up. Gathering other employees in his office, Anwary then told me the distillery's story.

The state-owned factory, he said, was established with Italian help under the last Afghan king, Zahir Shah. The king, a tolerant man who wanted to open up the country, was eventually overthrown by a cousin and spent almost three decades in Roman exile before returning to Kabul in 2002. Back in 1968, Zahir Shah outflanked Islamic objections to brandy by saying that the booze would be sold only to diplomats and other non-Muslim expatriates. As one would expect, Muslim Afghans quickly became the main customers.

Anwary was appointed director in 1977, at a time when the deposed king's cousin, President Daoud, was flirting with Moscow. The distillery—called Afghan-Clemd—rapidly expanded to become one of the main revenue sources for the state, contributing as much as $60 million a year. Its zenith came after the Soviet invasion of 1979, as Kabul's Communist rulers were busy combating Islamic "prejudices" and American-backed Islamist guerrillas. Unlike the war zones in the countryside, Kabul was a relatively peaceful oasis, and the city's streets at the time were filled with unveiled women wearing high heels and heading to work.

The distillery shut down in 1992, when mujahedeen guerrilla commanders seized Kabul. Viewing Afghan-Clemd as a symbol of infidel corruption, the guerrillas wrecked the compound; the employees fled for their lives. Soon, the pockmarked distillery building became a frontline in the vicious war between rival mujahedeen warlords. Kabul, which had remained intact during the anti-Soviet jihad, was turned into rubble amidst the settling of scores between feuding commanders.

It was the ultrareligious Taliban who finally rebuilt the factory. The Taliban realized that it, too, needed alcohol for hospitals and industries. So, a black-turbaned Mullah Mohammed Omar—a namesake of the one-eyed Taliban leader—was dispatched to occupy Anwary's former office.

The irony of a Mullah Omar brewing booze was too much. I pressed the employees for details. "The Taliban were very strict, checking the machines all the time to make sure nothing is done on the side," recalled Abdulhay Hisari, a former captain in the Soviet-run Afghan Army who served as Mullah Omar's chief of staff at the distillery. Hisari now wore a clipped mustache, a T-shirt, and jeans. Under Mullah Omar, his beard reached his chest, he showed me with an upturned palm.

Before delivering the alcohol to pharmacies, the Taliban authorities mixed it with antiseptic substances, such as Dettol, that made it unfit for drinking. "But some Taliban would come here alone, with a plastic bag, and buy two or three liters of pure alcohol for themselves," Hisari chuckled. "They were afraid of each other, and were lying to us about why they need it. But of course we all knew it was for drinking!"

After September 11, 2001, as the United States started bombing Kabul, the Taliban evacuated the distillery's stocks—fearing a fire—and shut down production. Mullah Omar, the director who was still fondly remembered by employees as a "sweet, gentle man," returned to teaching Islam in a Pakistani madrassa. Weeks later, the U.S.-backed alliance of mujahedeen commanders marched into the city, looting and stripping the factory, again.

When one particularly unpleasant mujahedeen militia took over the premises, Hisari tracked down a former pro-Soviet Afghan Army buddy who was now a general in the anti-Taliban mujahedeen alliance—a commonplace switching of allegiances in Afghanistan. The general made sure that the intruders were quickly evicted, and the compound was briefly rented by NATO peacekeepers. The peacekeepers' rent, a whopping $25,000 for a few months, allowed the distillery workers to patch up surviving equipment with homemade spare parts and to restart production, using firewood instead of looted gas furnaces to boil the raisins.

In 2003, Anwary returned to Kabul after years of exile in Russia and Pakistan, and was promptly restored to the director's office. He made the distillery profitable again, and the government put it on a list of state properties that should be privatized. Seeing himself as an artisan winemaker rather than a simple bureaucrat, he told me he was anxious to regain Afghan-Clemd's past glory. "Authorities are keeping us handcuffed," he complained, "while imported liquors are available everywhere and there are at least two thousand moonshine makers in Kabul alone."

His lobbying wasn't successful so far. While Karzai's government was willing to tolerate foreigners drinking, it was a whole different matter to permit the making of booze at a government-owned distillery. Yet Anwary didn't seem deterred by the lack of official permissions. Over a watermelon snack, he volunteered that he had just sold an Afghan entrepreneur one hundred bottles of "sample" vodka he had distilled. He was vague about whether he produced the booze at the distillery or at home. Another businessman, aware that bottles of imitation Afghan-Clemd brandy still circulate in Pakistani bazaars, had offered Anwary a more lucrative deal. This entrepreneur wanted to bottle and market the real thing under the famous label if Anwary would agree to produce and smuggle the liquor to Pakistan's unruly northwest tribal areas in gasoline jerry cans. Anwary turned down the offer: "It's hard for me to make brandy now. I don't have the necessary essence."

With just dry, sweet Kandahar raisins now at its disposal, Anwary's factory, officially at least, made only 96-proof industrial and 75-proof medical alcohol. The sample products stood on Anwary's desk, with the medical alcohol in green brandy bottles topped with twenty-year-old Afghan-Clemd brandy caps, and the industrial one in bottles normally used for vodka. The price was $5 a bottle in Afghan bazaars. "While I must write on the labels that this alcohol is not fit for drinking, almost everyone who buys it does it to drink," Anwary chortled. "Actually, it is quite fit for drinking, and is very good for your health. It's made from the purest Afghan raisins!" An aide pitched in: "If you try our alcohol, you won't drink anything else."

In spite of such praises for the pure alcohol, it's the extinct Afghan-Clemd brandy that remained an object of fond reminiscence and fantasizing among the distillery's staff. After surveying the aged labels on the director's desk, Ali Shah, one of the distillery managers, closed his eyes, recalled the good old days, and sniffed the air. "Ah, our brandy," he murmured. "I can still feel the taste in my mouth."

Their memories were a secret affair. Alcohol remains such a sensitive issue in Afghanistan that the distillery's employees rarely admitted to neighbors and friends where exactly they worked. "If someone asks us, we just say we're working for the government," said Hisari. "Or at a food factory, making soup," another executive laughed.

A couple of days later, I went to see senior government members to gauge whether Anwary's dream of resurrecting the famed Afghan-Clemd brand might ever come true. Fazl Shinwari, Afghanistan's chief justice and most influential Islamic scholar, was surprised by the question. "In an Islamic country, it's simply against the Sharia—and in Afghanistan, also against the constitution—for anyone to be making alcohol drinks," the gaunt cleric told me, his wispy beard as pure white as his Pashtun turban.

Vice President Hedayat Amin Arsala, a former World Bank executive and a thoroughly liberal politician who is close to former king Zahir Shah, also thought that Afghan-Clemd was definitively dead. "I don't think this will come back," he said, with what I perceived was a tinge of regret. There are more important things than alcohol at stake in Afghanistan today, he explained, and it's crucial that "people are not provoked into a reaction that would affect all freedoms and not just these kinds of activities." Just look at what happened to the shah's Iran, he reminded me.

◆   ◆   ◆

It's hard to imagine it now, but back in the 1960s and 1970s, when Iran was a pro-Western, secular bulwark in the Middle East, neighboring Afghanistan was best known as a popular stop on the international hippie trail. Cheap accommodation and food, a ready supply of opium, and polite, friendly locals attracted thousands of American and European young people every year. This transit in the age of free love provided the average Afghans with their first massive exposure to Westerners since the ill-fated British invasion and occupation of the previous century.

The Afghans, of course, didn't like what they saw. The long-haired, unwashed, and permanently stoned backpackers who displayed little regard for local mores were taken to be representative of the entire West. Nobody wanted Afghanistan to end up like *these* people's home countries.

In the 1980s and early 1990s, two main ideologies battled it out in Afghanistan—Communism of various stripes and an increasingly radical Islamism, while pro-Western liberals remained a rare species. The Taliban—a product of obscurantist madrassas in Pakistani refugee camps—were as militant a breed of Islamists as one could find. They outdid even such fundamentalist warlords as Abdoul Rasoul Sayyaf, the patron of Arab jihadi volunteers who would later form Qaeda. (In one of the country's paradoxes, Sayyaf was now a senior member of Afghanistan's American-backed ruling establishment.)

In the bookshop of Kabul's Intercontinental Hotel, I found a treasure trove of publications, ranging from Soviet-style propaganda brochures of the 1980s regime to the latest photo albums trumpeting the successes of the Bush administration's Global War on Terror and Operation Enduring Freedom. I also came across a December 2000 copy of the Taliban's English-language magazine, *The Islamic Emirate.*

The magazine, I found out later, had been edited in Kandahar by an American convert to Islam who joined Qaeda—a fact that explained the perfect English inside. With today's Taliban inaccessible to Western reporters, I pored over the magazine's pages to understand the militia's lingering appeal. An article explained the fundamentalists' credo: "Any study beside that of the Quran is a distraction, except the Hadith (sayings of the Prophet) and jurisprudence in the religion. Knowledge is that He narrated to us, and anything other than that is the whispering of the Satan."

Both inside covers were dedicated to the messages of Mullah Omar, or, as the official signature went, "Servant of Islam and Muslims, Amir al-Mumineen (Commander of the Faithful), Mullah Muhammad Umar Mujahid."

In the first message, the mullah pledged "not to be dissuaded from my firm resolve by the strength of any arrogant Taghoot." This word is a traditional term for idol worshippers that, in the Islamists' political jargon, has come to refer to the West and its supporters. The second message was called "Forbidding the Mujahideen from Killing Women and Children." In addition to this privileged group, the text barred Taliban fighters from slaying captured "combatants and elderly men . . . without permission." The reason for the ban was explicit: "We know that taking a Muslim's life is a cause of defeat." This belief, presumably, made it okay to kill non-Muslim women and children after all.

An article on America predicted a U.S. invasion, which, in fact, would occur ten months later. The United States, it explained poetically, "wants to change this country—possessed of a unique geographical position and a tremendous wealth in raw materials—into a base for corruption and control of the region that extends from the Arabian Gulf to the China Sea and from the Indian Ocean to the frigid waters of the Siberian Seas." America, the article went on, is "isolated from and despised by every Muslim—nay, every honorable human."

What the magazine couldn't predict is that the top American in Afghanistan would be an Afghan.

✦ ✦ ✦

Unlike his counterparts in postwar Iraq—Jay Garner and then Paul Bremer, both of whom were little versed in Iraqi or Arab affairs—the American ambassador in Kabul had intimate knowledge of Afghanistan that only someone born in the country could possess. A native of the northern city of Mazar-i-Sharif, Zalmay Khalilzad first came to the United States as a high school exchange student. Probably the most senior Muslim in the American government, Khalilzad chaired the Bush-Cheney administration's transition team at the Pentagon and used to head the Islamic affairs desk at the National Security Council. In Kabul he was a living advertisement for America, the Land of Opportunity.

It was Khalilzad who orchestrated the Bonn conference of anti-Taliban Afghan leaders in December 2001, putting together the country's new political system. That conference brought into the American-sponsored government's fold most warlords and enthroned Karzai, a suave pro-American Pashtun of noble lineage who had once served as the nation's deputy foreign minister. Like Khalilzad, Karzai initially sympathized with the Taliban. (Khalilzad's attempt to unify the Iraqi opposition at a London conference a year later met considerably less success.)

The combination of one Afghan occupying the presidential palace and another Afghan holding the reins of real power at the American embassy allowed the United States to avoid in Afghanistan many of the mistakes that scuttled its effort to transform Iraq. In both places, national pride is almost pathologically acute; but while Afghan faces at the top saved appearances in Kabul, the naked foreign rule in Iraq in 2003–2004 made many Iraqis resent even those changes, however few, that improved their lives.

Rather than trying to transplant the appearance of Jeffersonian democracy on clearly unsuitable soil, Khalilzad, at least in the initial years, propped up traditional tribal and clan leaders and sought accommodation with the warlords. American soldiers wisely stayed away from the streets of Kabul, to avoid any inflammatory symbolism. Instead, the capital was patrolled by a fruit-salad-like NATO force, cobbled together by countries from Canada to Norway to Bulgaria. Nobody feared Bulgarian imperialism.

When I arrived for my meeting with Khalilzad, the American embassy was a giant construction site, with a special underpass in front of the building. Long-term ambitions were discernible from the sheer size of the work site. Across the street a huge billboard urged "our Afghan friends" in English and three Afghan languages to come to the embassy at specified hours with information about potential attacks. As I waited to be picked up, ordinary Afghans knocked on the metal outer gate, giving a bored Marine handwritten letters marked TOP SECRET and addressed to the ambassador.

Khalilzad still worked out of the old embassy building. The hallway had a persistent smell of mildew and rot—an inevitable consequence of the fact that the old embassy had stayed shuttered for much of the previous two decades. In the secured, and stench-less, part of the building, Khalilzad occupied a soft chair, under a black-and-white picture of him as a young man in front of a U.S. Air Force jet. Military officers in fatigues huddled in the antechamber. The ambassador still spoke with a perceptible accent and wore a dark business suit, rubbing his hands every few moments. He emitted a frequent, guttural laugh, and a drawling "sure" as he listened. I asked him about the resurgence of the Taliban and other anti-American guerrillas and about the increasingly frequent attacks on foreigners and government targets. As one would expect from a diplomat, he countered with a positive spin.

"There are some good things besides the problems that one has to take account of," he said. "There is a sort of uneven progress, but there is progress compared to where they were two and a half years ago."

He smiled: "We have to learn to crawl, walk, and run here at the same time." I noticed the shifting grammar, with Khalilzad interchangeably using the "we" and the "they" to describe the actions of the Afghan government.

We spoke about the presidential elections that would take place in October 2004, after several delays. Elections for Parliament were also supposed to occur at that time. But widespread attacks against election workers, especially in pro-Taliban parts of the south, prompted the joint UN–Afghan electoral commission to postpone the Parliament vote until May 2005 at the earliest. The decision left the Afghan president free to rule, for now, without the checks and balances of a separate legislative branch. Khalilzad told me he backed the postponement of the parliamentary poll in part out of concern that Afghan warlords, who stubbornly refused to disarm and acknowledge central authority, might hijack that election. "We want to make sure these things are not decided by the power of the gun and by intimidation," Khalilzad said.

I told him that most Afghans I'd met believed that the United States was stacking the deck in favor of Karzai, making sure that the president—until then unelected and viewed by critics as an American puppet—won the ballot and obtained badly needed legitimacy. Raising his eyebrows, Khalilzad replied that it was no secret that Karzai was the only "formidable" candidate. Going back into a diplomatic mode, he added quickly that Washington would work with whoever is chosen by the people.

The October election proved messy. While the feared Taliban onslaught failed to materialize, the legitimacy of the election was quickly thrown into doubt. Because of violence, either promised or delivered, only a tiny minority of polling stations, mostly in Kabul and other big cities, had foreign observers. Since most Afghans possessed no identity documents, the UN issued voter cards on the spot, based on trust; the card featured whatever name and address an applicant provided. It wasn't uncommon for Afghans to hold several cards, under varying names, either because of political pressure by pro-government warlords eager to inflate voter registration rates in their zones, or simply because a card applicant received leftover Polaroid mug shots for free. The main safeguard against multiple voting consisted of special indelible ink that, the UN organizers promised, would be applied to every voter's thumb.

But as Afghans lined up at the polls, it emerged that many stations either had no ink or used the kind that could be easily washed off. Each of Karzai's fifteen challengers cried foul, claiming that the vote had been stolen; they called on their supporters to stay home and boy-cott the election. "Today was a very black day. Today was the occu-pation of Afghanistan by America through elections," one of these candidates, the poet Abdul Latif Padran, told reporters at the time.

It took a direct intervention by Ambassador Khalilzad to sort out the mess. After a series of intense closed-door meetings with the aggrieved candidates, who *could* oppose Karzai even if they couldn't say no to America, the ambassador worked out a compromise. After much American arm-twisting, the opposition candidates backed down and put their trust into an investigative commission formed by the UN, the organization that administered the disputed election in the first place. Karzai, the UN said, won 55 percent of the votes; irregu-larities on election day were not deemed sufficiently grave to cast his victory in doubt.

✦   ✦   ✦

Since the end of the Cold War, it has become commonplace to describe Afghanistan as the Soviets' Vietnam, a place where a superpower had been dealt a defeat. Even before I arrived in Kabul, curious friends asked me whether the city had a museum to anti-Soviet resistance, something akin to the American War Crimes Museum that Vietnamese Communists established in Hanoi in the 1970s. I couldn't find any such thing in Afghanistan, even though Soviet occupation had unques-tionably been brutal. I asked around, and some Afghans came up with an explanation: Kabul's decade under mujahedeen warlords and the Taliban, from 1992 to 2001, was even worse than the years under Soviet rule. Occupation was evil, but, again, even evil can be relative.

Until the final days of the Soviet-installed regime of President Najibullah, Kabul, a city far more cosmopolitan than the rest of the nation, was spared most fighting. Then, in 1992, as rival warlords occupied different sections of the city, their American-supplied mili-tary might was used exclusively to obliterate each other's neighbor-hoods. Shelling and bombardment turned vast stretches of the urban landscape, especially in western Kabul, into what Dresden, Germany, must have looked like at the end of the Second World War. An esti-mated 100,000 Kabuli civilians, trapped in the fighting, paid with their lives. The warlords responsible for this devastation now sat side by side in Karzai's administration, together with men who had supported the Soviets.

Wanting to talk to someone who had lived through this upheaval, I invited Professor Kazem Ahang, the longtime dean of Kabul University's School of Journalism, for dinner. Dressed in a carefully ironed suit, Ahang interspersed his speech with quaint 1950s slang words he had picked up while studying at Michigan State University. Dismissed from his job and confined to his home under the Taliban, Ahang was restored to the university after 2001. He had been a senior official preparing the *loya jirga,* the traditional gathering of elders that preceded Afghan elections, but was since sidelined by Karzai. As we sat down, Ahang whispered that he couldn't be seen ordering alcohol, because he's a Muslim, but that he would appreciate it if I procured him a can of beer. Once the waitress brought the beer, he swiped it from the table in a masterful stroke, hiding the can in the recesses of his briefcase. "It will help me sleep better at night," he said.

I asked him to compare the eras of Soviet and American domination. Reflecting for a moment, he said that the Soviets had made the mistake of attacking Islam, which doomed them in the end. The Americans were smarter about religion, and therefore more tolerated.

But the Soviets, he surprised me after another pause, were much friendlier, providing education to thousands of Afghan students and showering even the most remote villages with food, blankets, and other assistance. Unlike in the good old days, when Ahang himself went to an American college, now the United States, preoccupied with possible terrorist infiltration, was hardly welcoming potential Afghan students.

"The intellectuals feel now that America is colonizing Afghanistan, and the rest of the people don't know why the Americans are here. They only see that the more time goes by, the more the American presence is growing," Ahang said. "So far, nobody has seen where this American money is spent, whereas, with the Soviets, it was visible. The only thing we have seen from the Americans is their soldiers."

A harsh assessment—especially coming from someone who had lived in the United States. After dinner I mentioned it to Qais, my

Kabul fixer. His family used to own a shop in the Kabul bazaar, but after the Taliban takeover, they fled north to the Tajik countryside. In late 2001, desperate to get out of Afghanistan, Qais considered taking up a drug smuggler's offer of passage to Russia in exchange for transporting narcotics. September 11 ushered in an invasion of journalists who suddenly made Qais's knowledge of English immensely valuable; he could make an Afghan's average annual income for a day's work accompanying reporters like me. Now he could even afford to go to Europe as a tourist, by plane.

Qais, too, thought that the Soviets, all in all, had been nicer. He recalled his childhood days in the bazaar. "When the Russian soldiers came shopping, they'd leave their guns in the truck and then would go into a store," he said. "The Americans now, they come inside with weapons, surround the store, and scare everyone away."

I was treated to a vivid illustration of just this shortly thereafter, on Kabul's Chicken Street, a former poultry market that, since the hippie age, has turned into a succession of carpet and souvenir stores. As I walked inside one such store, gaping at carpets sewn with helicopter-gunship-and-Kalashnikov motifs, two gray Toyota Landcruisers without license plates pulled up. Burly Special Forces soldiers jumped out, wearing shades, keffiyehs, and unkempt beards. As two of them went inside to haggle about a rug, the others set up a defensive perimeter outside, assault rifles at the ready. I hastened to leave.

That month Afghan authorities arrested another group of Americans, led by a former Special Forces man known to journalists simply as Jack. Without any government oversight, Jack and a group of men under his command had run a private prison in Kabul for months, arresting and torturing Afghans at will. All that time, no local authority dared to challenge their credentials. In fact, NATO forces even offered cooperation. Apparently, simply being a Westerner gave one the right to be in charge.

On my final day in Kabul, I quizzed Qais about which recent Afghan leader he liked best. He picked Najibullah, the last Soviet-installed president, who, in the late 1980s, adopted a more Islamic approach and managed to retain power for three years after the Soviet military withdrawal. Najibullah hid in the UN compound following the mujahedeen takeover of 1992. After seizing Kabul in 1996, the Taliban dragged out the former president, castrated him, and then hanged him and his brother from a traffic police booth in front of the presidential palace. To mark their victim's corruption, Taliban executioners inserted a dollar bill and a cigarette in Najibullah's dead hands.

"Killing Najibullah was the worst thing that the Taliban did," Qais exclaimed. I had read that the Taliban officials used to show off the fateful police booth to visiting dignitaries. I wondered aloud where it was, and Qais drove me straight to the area. Like many sensitive Kabul neighborhoods, this one was sealed off with barbed wire and blast barriers—a precaution stemming in part from the presence of a heavily guarded CIA compound just in front of the palace. But the forbidden zones, of course, were only forbidden to Afghans.

I put on sunglasses and a baseball cap, and Qais hit the gas, shouting, "It's a foreigner, foreigner" at the guards. Instinctively they jumped back and raised the barrier. We rolled on and finally came to the roundabout. The place of Najibullah's death was still there, intact, an empty traffic booth presiding over a downtown thoroughfare that no longer accepted any traffic.

11

AFGHANISTAN

Why Are You Afraid of the Soldiers?

Dawn had yet to break and I was half asleep, squeezed between American soldiers, weapons, and rucksacks in a Chinook helicopter that nearly grazed the edges of a craggy mountain range. One of the gunners sat on a cushion atop an open back door, strapped by a wire in case he slipped off. A second chopper followed our zigzags a few dozen yards behind.

The front-window gunner, who kept staring into the barren landscape below, opened up with a rattle of fire that awoke me. Everyone else in the chopper continued to doze. Nobody shot back at us from the ground.

Once the black sky turned bright pink, an hour after we had left south Afghanistan's main city of Kandahar, the Chinook landed in a parched, terraced field. Instantly the rotor blades whipped up a swirling cloud of brown dust. Shrugging off backpacks, the American soldiers and American-commanded Afghan troops jumped out. Partly blinded and choking, I followed suit, trying my best not to inhale. The chopper lifted off right away. The valley became jarringly silent again. After Kandahar's searing heat, the mountain air felt deliciously cold, tinged with the smell of wild flowers and ripening wheat.

It took me a while to realize that I was the only man standing up. All the others had hit the ground, ignoring the spiky thorns that seemed to protrude everywhere, and were now pointing black assault rifles at imperceptible foes. I didn't have a rifle, or the soldiers' comforting rubber knee pads, but I dove to the ground as well.

✦ ✦ ✦

The field where we landed, in the summer of 2004, was in the northernmost corner of Afghanistan's Zabul province, an area that jutted from the Pakistani frontier and—two and a half years after the fall of Kabul—was still largely controlled by the Taliban. Like a cluster of nearby provinces, Zabul was a place where foreigners didn't venture alone. The only way to see this Taliban heartland and come back with a story, alive, was to embed with American troops. I had been invited to travel here with a company of soldiers from the Army's Twenty-Fifth Infantry Division. Together with subordinate Afghan troops, the GIs were to spend the next several days combing through a portion of the upper Arghandab Valley, going from village to village and looking for weapons and Taliban sympathizers. There would be no vehicles: everyone had to walk and carry his load.

The most obvious difference between the valley and Iraq, a flat country with relatively good roads, was that this part of Afghanistan was really, really remote. I couldn't see asphalt, electricity lines, or, indeed, any sign of modernity. Otherwise, similarities abounded, down to the pejorative nickname—the "hajjis"—that the soldiers used in referring to Afghans and Iraqis alike. Just like the "hajji cops" I had seen on a joint patrol in Iraq's Ramadi, the Afghan soldiers with us wore tin helmets and no body armor, while the Americans were dressed in full battle rattle. Even accompanying journalists like me were required to wear a Kevlar helmet and a ballistic vest.

Iraq, of course, was formally under American military occupation until late June 2004; I watched the handover of power to Prime Minister Eyad Allawi from Kabul. Afghanistan, by contrast, was supposedly a sovereign country; the Americans were here simply to assist the local authorities. But in the Arghandab Valley, it was clear who was in charge: Afghan soldiers meekly took orders from an American sergeant.

The mission was led by Captain Mike Berdy, a laconic, sinewy man with sunburned lips. Commander of the Charlie company, he carried a map of target villages—all assigned code names starting with Charlie—that his troops were supposed to cordon and search. Other companies dealt with other sections of the valley, too far for us to see, while dozens of Apache helicopters buzzed in the sky like angry insects, all day.

The first dazed Afghan who came up against the Charlie company wore a black turban—a color preferred by the Taliban—and drove a bicycle. He watched agape as a dozen Afghan and American troops descended on him, unwrapped the turban for inspection, and meticulously searched him and the bicycle. Nothing was found.

Down the dusty path was the first village. Although Americans had not entered here before, the peasants, after decades of wars, seemed used to the routine of cordon-and-search missions by invading armies. The elder, Abdullah Khan, came out to meet Captain Berdy. Since neither spoke the other's language, an interpreter flown in from Kandahar stepped in. Like other interpreters—"terps," in the soldiers' parlance—he wore dark shades and disguised his face with a scarf and a baseball cap. He didn't want to be recognized even such a long way from home. "Do you have any weapons in here? Rifles, grenades, guns?" the captain asked. The elder emphatically shook his head: "Nothing, nothing here. We are poor farmers. We have nothing."

The captain nodded in response. "Okay, we'll search the village, and if any male refuses to come out and has a weapon, he can get hurt," Captain Berdy warned with understatement. "Hurt" most likely meant "shot on the spot."

The elder smiled obsequiously and sent an aide to fetch the village's men. Soon several dozen piled out, wearing turbans or the gilded black skullcaps of the Pashtuns. The Afghan soldiers did the first cursory check, lifting the turbans and patting the villagers' sides. Then American soldiers thoroughly rifled through every fold of the peasants' gowns. Once they were done, they motioned the villagers to sit on the ground, at gunpoint, one next to another. The sun was barely out, but I was already beginning to burn.

I walked into the village, a fortified compound of haphazard mud dwellings with simple wooden doors and an occasional window frame. Everything seemed abandoned in a rush. Half-eaten breakfast was scattered on the coal-fired stoves; flies hovered around small cups of undrunk tea on the straw mats. The Pashtuns, Afghanistan's largest ethnic group and the one that inhabited this valley, live by a strict ancient code, the Pashtunwali. It holds honor, or *nang,* above everything else, and the womenfolk are that honor's repository. One's home is considered inviolable, and exposing one's private quarters to outsiders a disgrace. Because the mere suspicion that a woman had violated the family's honor was punishable by death, most Pashtun families never let females outside the home. Now, I thought, we have forced an entire village to expose its women to unceremonious outsiders who proceeded to scrutinize the most intimate corners of their homes. I wondered how many potential recruits the Taliban had acquired in the village over the past fifteen minutes.

"When you see blankets, turn them upside down. Make sure everything gets pulled apart," shouted Staff Sergeant Brad Bricker, one of the squad commanders. Soldiers went into bedrooms, looked under mats and in stove pits, probing the ground with metal detectors and tearing down mud walls if the detector started beeping with a loud, whining noise. Afghan troopers, usually eager to break everything apart, were strangely shy this time around, prompting Captain Berdy to complain. I learned later that, elsewhere in the valley the same week, Afghan soldiers and an interpreter who became separated from their American unit in a similar village had been caught and beheaded by insurgents. The Afghan troopers didn't want to earn too much enmity.

The Afghan villagers, listless and seemingly reconciled to their condition, sat motionless in the sun outside. The women, shrouded in black or purple cloth, and the children, frightened and sobbing, clustered in a circle on a rooftop, looking inside and turning their backs on the soldiers. An elderly man with a long white beard crouched some distance away, propping himself with a curved walking stick. Every few minutes he angrily yelled at the women to calm down and not to worry. Behind a corner, the soldiers relieved themselves against the wall of someone's home.

The houses in the village were bare and dark. Only one was

decorated, with a few faded photographs of the owner holding a Kalashnikov gun. I couldn't figure out during which of Afghanistan's many wars the picture was taken. Was the man fighting the Soviets? Other mujahedeen? The Taliban? Or was he simply posing with a weapon, a natural possession for a Pashtun tribesman?

Despite the thorough search, the soldiers found very little in the first village. Then Captain Berdy's radio came alive with news that one of the squads had discovered a mortar. Finding my way through the deserted village's labyrinth, I walked to the right compound. On closer inspection, the find turned out to be a decades-old artillery shell with all its explosives long gone. Eager to explain through terps who barely spoke English, the elder imitated hammering gestures. The shell was indeed used for mortar—but of a different kind. For the past several years, it had served as a pestle to crush wheat and beans. "It's not a weapon, not a weapon," the elder repeated.

I was impressed by the villagers' passivity and seeming acceptance of this intrusion. So were the soldiers—one muttered that even a local police force could never get away with such a cordon-and-search mission back home, let alone with confiscating all the guns it had discovered. Unlike the Iraqis, who showed open defiance and anger, the Afghans radiated compliance.

Captain Berdy, whose brother served in Iraq, wasn't fooled. "You never know with these people. They smile at you and say they are happy you're here," he mused. "They're not in your face. They don't try to confront you, but as soon as you make a mistake, they hit you."

Once the search was over and the men were let go, I commandeered one of the terps and tried to find out what the villagers thought of the Americans and the upcoming election in Afghanistan. In these highlands the concept of democracy was so remote as to be immaterial, causing the interpreter to struggle for the right words. Since there is no native term for *elections,* he first used the pidgin English *elekshn,* which is employed by Pashtuns across the border in Pakistan. Then he tried the Arabic term *intihabat,* used by the Dari-speaking elites in Kabul. Zar Wali, the old man who was guarding the women, shook his head. "Nobody told us about this thing. We're poor people, all we know is the sky and the earth," he said, extending his hand for money but graciously accepting a high-energy biscuit. Another villager, thirty-year-old Nur Ahmad, stared at me with open suspicion. "Elections? These big political issues are for the generals and the emirs to decide. We don't care. It's not something for us," he said, scurrying away.

✦ ✦ ✦

Dispersed throughout the field to minimize the possible toll from mortar attack or a mine, we walked to the next village, Shelem Kele. A bearded young man by the name of Arapat ran out to say that the Taliban had been there just three days earlier. Some sixty Islamist fighters had seized weapons and cash from the peasants, he said, and had taken a local official away in handcuffs.

"All the countryside here is under the control of the Taliban," he whispered. "We are all afraid and can't do anything. They are very powerful here." Arapat was clearly expecting to be treated differently after providing this information, but he was unceremoniously told to sit down in the sun with the others. I wondered what would happen to him in a few hours, once the soldiers departed. Unlike Arapat, most villagers clammed up at the mention of the Taliban. Some said the guerrillas had never been to the village. Others said the Taliban came only by night. Still others vaguely pointed at the mountains, saying that the insurgents were there, somewhere.

The company's first sergeant, Matthew Grucella, understood the villagers' reticence. "They're afraid. They know we're not going to provide them with any lasting security," he said. Still at the village's gates, Captain Berdy was looking for the local elder to accompany the troops inside Shelem Kele. Unable to find the man, he finally ordered the soldiers to move in.

In the outer building, the soldiers poked open a door and found a pile of documents and manifestos inside a cloth sack. One of the terps peered in and fished out a booklet with a picture of a bearded man on the back cover. Breathless, he decreed "Taliban propaganda" and handed it over to Captain Berdy. It didn't look right to me, and I read the name under the picture. It was of Pir Ahmad Gailani, one of the most pro-Western Afghan mujahedeen commanders—ironically, of distant Baghdadi origin. Gailani, head of a Sufi order, was a sworn enemy of the Taliban, who considered Sufis to be apostates. The posters and the booklets dated from the 1980s jihad against the Soviets, and, I told Captain Berdy, were probably printed with American money. I added that Gailani's faction was well represented in President Karzai's national government. The captain, who had never heard Gailani's name, shook his head incredulously: "But there are Taliban supporters in the government, right?"

Afghan soldiers would have instantly avoided such mistakes. But nobody thought of asking their advice. As we continued our search, the valley resonated with loud explosions. I listened to radio traffic: Apache helicopters had lobbed missiles into a hostile machine-gun emplacement on a rooftop several miles away. An hour later, a clarification arrived. The emplacement actually belonged to local Afghan security forces; it was yet another case of misdirected friendly fire.

✦   ✦   ✦

Shelem Kele turned out to be rife with weapons. At first, Captain Berdy's troops had to make do with seizing Lee Enfield rifles, the kind that adorned my Kabul lodge, and a handful of rusted Kalashnikovs. But then, in a compound whose owner was said to be away, they struck gold. Using a metal detector, the soldiers found a box with nine shiny green rocket-propelled grenades, another box with bullets marked Royal Air Force, and a package of plastic explosives.

As Captain Berdy examined the arsenal, soldiers brought in a suspicious Afghan who had been intercepted outside. Seeing the troops, he had thrown a small plastic pack, containing some $90 in Pakistani currency, into a ditch. The soldiers noticed, and picked up both the man and the cash.

"Why did you throw away the money?" Captain Berdy wanted to know.

"I was afraid," the man said.

"Afraid of what?"

"Afraid of the soldiers," the interpreter explained.

"Why would you be afraid of the soldiers? Do you have a reason to be afraid of the soldiers?"

"He says he never saw soldiers like you," the interpreter said. This was, after all, the first time that American troops had come to Shelem Kele.

"So why was he afraid?" Captain Berdy persisted.

The culture gap was in full display. Of course, if someone in the States throws money away at the sight of an officer and says he's afraid, the act would be highly suspicious. But this was Afghanistan. Countless militias had been through the area in the past twenty-five years. A simple farmer stood little chance of retaining $90, a small fortune here, once it was discovered by Afghan gunmen; throwing it into a ditch, to be recovered later, was the most natural thing under the circumstances.

"So why was he afraid?" Captain Berdy asked again.

The man contorted his face into an ingratiating smile. "He says he is very sorry he was afraid," the interpreter relayed.

An Afghan soldier covetously examined the Pakistani rupees and indicated his intention to keep the money. Captain Berdy took the cash away and gave it to one of his officers for safekeeping. "If these guys take it, this will be the end of it," he griped about the Afghan troops. He then ordered his men to escort the villager to the field where all other Shelem Kele males had been gathered, and to keep him detained.

✦ ✦ ✦

As the search wound up, the troops led a total of four detainees from the village. These men now sat on the ground in a cross-like formation, with their backs facing inward and their hands bound by plastic cuffs. The owner of the Pakistani rupees expectantly smiled at me, mistaking me for a person of authority. Captain Berdy was briefed on the others.

"They practically volunteered to be detained," one of the soldiers explained. The troops had stopped and searched an old man, finding nothing incriminating in his turban and gown. But as the soldiers were about to let him go, another villager panicked, yelling at the Americans: "Don't take my father. Arrest me instead." The old man, it turned out, was the missing village elder. The soldiers arrested both men, plus another sibling.

As the troops opened up their Meals Ready-to-Eat, I entered into a weird conversation with the waiting Afghans. With my helmet and flak vest, the villagers saw me as an appendage of the intruders, not as a journalist who just happened by. When I asked them how they felt about the military operations, they glanced nervously at their hand-cuffed neighbors and tried their best to guess what answers would please me. "We are really happy that you came here to help our country. We are happy you are coming and searching our homes. It's good that the government is establishing itself here," one villager, Bakhar Khan, told me. "We don't want the Taliban. We want Islam. We flee from the village when the Taliban come down here," another man, Mohammed Nazir, assured. "Welcome, welcome," a third man said.

After the MRE lunch in Shelem Kele, a transportation problem arose. Despite the villagers' insistence that no weapons were to be found, Captain Berdy's troops had amassed so many by midafternoon that they couldn't carry them all on their backs. The next resupply chopper wasn't due until the following day, so Sergeant Grucella stepped up in front of the villagers with a proposition. "You can make a lot of money," he dangled in front of them. The troops, he said, wanted to rent two donkeys. He promised that the donkeys would be returned to the village once the mission was over. Although the villagers didn't seem to trust him, they agreed to the deal for $200 in American cash—enough money to replace the animals. Colorful rags on their backs, the donkeys appeared a few minutes later. The villagers taught Grucella the indispensable Pashtun word for prodding: "*Wush, wush, wush,*" he repeated. "Let's see now who's the real jackass."

The donkeys—christened Chicken and Fish—were loaded with RPGs, ammunition boxes, and rifles. Compliant, they followed the troops across the fields to the next village, and to the one after that. On a short break, Captain Berdy shared with me his doubts about how much had been achieved. The hard-core Taliban, who had dispersed into the mountains at the first sight of American helicopters, certainly weren't sticking around by the time the soldiers showed up. Possible hideouts for weapons abounded, and new arms could easily be smuggled from Pakistan. "We found nine RPGs here today, and there will probably be nine others there tomorrow," the captain said. "These people are smart. They just wait it out. They know we'll leave."

After searching through one more village—to my eyes, almost identical to the previous ones—the company finally settled for the night on a thorny hilltop. For beds we had to carve out foxholes in the rocky ground deep enough to be safe from mortar shrapnel, in case we were attacked overnight. As I began to dig with a borrowed shovel, I listened to the soldiers' conversation one terrace level above. "I don't mean to be a bleeding heart, but the detainees are sitting on thorns and it's really a bad place for them," one said. "You are a bleeding heart," his sergeant answered, laughing.

"No, man. I'm just trying to respect the Geneva Convention."

"Actually, the Geneva Convention doesn't apply to them here."

"So this means I can beat them?" the soldier wondered.

"No, you can't beat them."

"Why can't I beat them if there is no Geneva Convention?"

"Because we're such good people that we can't treat them badly, that's why."

"Man, it's not fair I can't beat them," the soldier grunted.

Half an hour later, the prisoners, who had also walked through the valley the entire day, were moved to a more comfortable spot and given a blanket, some water, and food. At gunpoint, the old man bent in prayer. The other three sat upright, looking into the horizon.

Captain Berdy also worried about the detainees. On his previous mission he had brought back another batch to Kandahar; after a cursory interrogation by military intelligence, they were all freed. Before shipping these four to Kandahar, he wanted an interrogator flown in to debrief them in the field. An interrogator wasn't available right away, so the villagers would have to trek through the valley with the soldiers for at least one more day.

With no electricity for dozens of miles, the valley soon became pitch black. In the absolute darkness, unimaginable in any inhabited area in the West, the stars shone with a brilliant intensity. The remainder of water in my camelback pouch became ice cold, and I shuddered in my down sleeping bag. Chicken and Fish were having trouble standing up after eating a sizable portion of the village's wheat crop, probably their best meal ever. Before falling asleep, I overheard soldiers talking about the two donkeys' future.

"We'll take them back to Kandahar and roast them," a sergeant said. The men started arguing over who would have the right to shoot the donkeys dead.

✦ ✦ ✦

In Kandahar, I was the sole resident of a baking-hot tent big enough to accommodate a platoon.

The American bombing I had seen launched from the USS *Carl Vinson* in October 2001 pierced a fort-like compound in the Kandahar airfield, dubbed the "Taliban Last Stand"; one part of the building that survived the bomb now housed a U.S. Mail office and an air-conditioned room where public-affairs reservists watched American football on Armed Forces TV. An espresso bar, trying its best to emulate Starbucks, sat next door. Just as at Balad in Iraq, the Kandahar base's dining facility seemed particularly fond of serving lobster tails and crab legs.

Every morning I woke up at dawn to meet my local driver and interpreter outside the main gate. Calculating the time was a challenge because the base lived on Greenwich Mean Time, known as Zulu Time in the military; Afghanistan's local time, in one of the country's many peculiarities, was four hours and a confusing 30 minutes ahead.

From the base we would drive in my interpreter's battered car into the city through a moonscape desert on a road that, I couldn't stop recalling, had been used hundreds of times by Bin Laden. In 1994, Kandahar was the first major Afghan city to fall to the Taliban. Pashtun to the core, it also remained Afghanistan's power center until the Taliban's ouster, in late 2001. Mullah Mohammed Omar, the reclusive Taliban leader, hailed from these parts, as did much of the Taliban leadership. Bin Laden—who was initially welcomed to Afghanistan by non-Taliban warlords—later settled on a farm near the Kandahar airport and was a frequent guest of Mullah Omar's in the city. The mullah escaped the American advance on a motorcycle, his Kandahar home already flattened by a U.S. bomb. But the unfinished concrete hulks of two giant mosques he had begun building in Kandahar continued to dominate the city. To me, these concrete shells looked just like the two giant unfinished mosques that Saddam Hussein left behind in Baghdad.

Kandahar was still very much an austere, ultrareligious city, little touched by the creeping Westernization that affected Kabul. The rare women I saw on the streets were enveloped in pale-blue burkas; Taliban supporters lurked in the mud-brick alleyways, launching regular attacks on foreigners and government targets. The few UN workers in town had begun wearing Pakistani-style *shalwar kameez*, the cream-colored traditional outfit, to present a less obvious target.

But within seconds of entering the city, I noticed that one Taliban legacy, the ban on graven images, was now very visibly gone. Motorized three-wheel rickshaws, encrusted with mirrors, fake gems, and ornamental hubcaps, displayed bright tableaux on their backs, the only streaks of color on Kandahar streets. In a Dali-esque juxtaposition, thousands of these smoke-belching chariots beamed with wild lions, Rambos blasting at foes, helicopters and horse-riding princesses, often crammed into the same scene.

Showcased with impunity nowadays, this art had been forbidden under the Taliban. I wanted to track down the painters and spent several hours looking for the Kandahar Rickshaw Market, an unmarked cement-floored compound on the city's edge. The market's courtyard was packed with several dozen rickshaws in various states of repair. The artists, recognizable by their paint-streaked gowns, doubled as mechanics. At least half the workers seemed younger than twelve.

I walked into the nearest workshop and introduced myself to one artist, Saleh Mohammed. Giggling at the unexpected attention, he fished a metal panel from a tall stack and exhibited an intense acrylic picture he had just created: a long-haired woman raising a pistol, her naked body obscured by a lion roaring in the foreground. A perfect example of this genre's aesthetic.

"If the Taliban ever caught me painting what I paint now, like this, they'd beat me and throw me in jail," Mohammed chuckled. "Under the Taliban, we could only paint in hiding—not for the rickshaws," echoed another back-panel artist, Mohibullah.

After the Taliban takeover, in 1994, hundreds of Kandahar rickshaws had to be painted over to remove imagery suddenly deemed illicit. The vehicles had been coated with plain colors, or decorated with imaginary landscapes that featured green mountains, crystal waterfalls, and Swiss chalets. Such landscapes were definitely out of fashion nowadays. "People are no longer interested in trees. They want beautiful things that are full of life," Mohammed said. As a crowd of several dozen surrounded us, Jumaa Khan, owner of a rival workshop, jumped in: "Now we're free, and the clients only want the designs that used to be prohibited in the past."

I walked around to inspect the rickshaws parked nearby. One displayed a larger-than-life painting of an Indian movie star, shades protecting his eyes and a cigarette stuck in his mouth. Another rickshaw featured a long-haired knight climbing a mountain on horseback, a bow in hand. The third depicted a soaring eagle with a snake in its mouth. But after two and a half decades of nonstop warfare in Afghanistan, most rickshaw owners clearly preferred bloodier scenes, Mohammed told me: "They think war and violence are beautiful."

The drivers, who charge a few cents for a city ride, told me they considered this art essential for business. "People watch the rickshaws and hail the one with the most beautiful pictures. Beauty is a necessity for us," said Said Ahmad, the driver whose rickshaw sported the Indian film star. A fellow driver, Mirza Khan, agreed. He proudly pointed at the new painting of stylized, fairy-tale fish on the back of his vehicle. "Beauty is not against Islam," he said, "and this fish is very beautiful."

✦ ✦ ✦

The Taliban's control of Kandahar—and with it the ban on rickshaw art, music, kite flying, and education for women—ended, thanks to American-backed warlords. These warlords now remained in charge, keeping their militias. Even soldiers in the supposedly national Afghan Army that I saw in action in Zabul, under American command, retained old allegiances.

When I asked these soldiers, as we rested in Shelem Kele, whom they considered their commander, they named a Pashtun warlord from Kandahar, Gul Agha Sherzai—and not the ethnic Tajik warlord who served as Afghanistan's minister of defense at the time. When I mentioned the name of a rival Kandahar warlord and the regional militia corps commander, Mohammed Khan, they spat on the ground with disgust and made a gesture imitating a knife slashing a throat.

Mohammed Khan occupied vast military barracks on Kandahar's edge. As we drove in, his militiamen leaned into the car and grinned. I noticed that they wore Russian-issue helmets and trophy Red Army belts, probably seized from dead Soviet soldiers. The warlord, who commanded some four thousand troops across south Afghanistan, including the Zabul province, was in a foul mood. He offered me green tea and complained about the Taliban beheading his soldiers' family members the previous week. "The Taliban are strong and the people are afraid," he said. "They come and go from Pakistan. They have no problem with money or weapons. They have everything they need—and we don't."

The Americans had no chance of defeating the Taliban on their own, he explained. "We know where the Taliban are, and who is a Taliban and who is a simple villager, who is a civilian. The Americans have no idea," he said. In fact, U.S. forces in Zabul might have killed Mohammed Khan's own men by mistake had he not warned the military just in time.

I asked Mohammed Khan how widespread the backing for the Taliban was. Could a distinction be drawn between the Taliban and simple civilians? "Some of the civilians, of course, are also with the Taliban," Mohammed Khan acknowledged. "They are relatives. They come from the same tribes." I pressed him to estimate the kind of support the insurgents enjoyed in the Pashtun heartland. Was it a majority or a minority? The warlord reflected for a minute and declined to provide a number.

As I rose to leave, he offered to share his lunch with me. I made my excuses, saying that I was supposed to meet the new regional governor sent in from Kabul. "Ah, that dog," the warlord scowled. "All he does is take money from Kabul and put it in his pockets."

I recalled, then, how the Taliban—a group of Pakistan-backed religious students with no political record—had seized power in much of Afghanistan. After deposing the Soviet-installed regime in 1992, rival mujahedeen commanders plunged the country into a free-for-all orgy of killing and looting that made the Taliban, with all its excesses, appear to many Afghans as a lesser evil. According to the Taliban's own founding myth—which had some ground in reality—the Islamist movement was launched after two warlords near Kandahar began an artillery duel over who would be the first to sodomize a handsome young boy. Pashtun men are known for such tastes, and a joke often told in Kabul says that crows fly above Kandahar with only one wing, using the other to protect their rears. The Taliban hanged both commanders, freed the boy, and seized Kandahar a few days later. Only slightly more presentable warlords who had escaped the Taliban's wrath now governed Afghanistan, sharing power with Karzai's administration under an American patronage.

✦ ✦ ✦

Before leaving the city, I stopped by for chilled watermelon with Abdul Qader Noorzai. An engineer by training, he headed the Kandahar office of the Afghan Independent Human Rights Commission, and was one of south Afghanistan's most prominent men. The wall of his spacious office was decorated with a fresco that depicted invading Soviet troops crossing the Amu Darya River into Afghanistan before being pulverized as they pressed farther down.

Noorzai told me he had encountered the Taliban founder Mullah Omar several times, and considered the man unimpressive. "He had no experience, no knowledge. He didn't do anything," he scoffed. "The Taliban did not want to work with the Afghan people. They wanted to work with the foreigners, the Arabs."

I chewed on the watermelon and wondered about the current warlords, about whom Noorzai was even more scathing. "The people here are not free. The mujahedeen commanders have all the power here, and they use this power to get what they want," he said. Karzai's government in Kabul had little authority here, and when faced with a choice between the Taliban and the warlords, many Afghans preferred the former. "The war is going on not because the Taliban are strong, but because the government is so weak," Noorzai said.

He offered an uncomfortable smile when I asked him whether American forces are still welcome in Afghanistan, especially after well-publicized cases of mistaken bombings that had wiped out entire villages. "We are discussing these mistakes with American leaders here," he said, "but so far we have not achieved any success."

He thought for a moment and tried again to couch his dismay in diplomatic terms. "We all know that the Afghans need the help of friendly countries, but also that the Afghans are culturally and religiously different from these countries," he said. "The conflicts spring from these differences."

SYRIA

LEBANON

Mediterranean Sea

★ Beirut

Khiam

Nabatiye

• Ayn al Arab

• — Metullah

Qana •

Kiryat Shmona

GOLAN
HEIGHTS
(occupied by Israel)

• Haifa

*WEST
BANK*

Tel Aviv •

Ramallah

Jerusalem ★

GAZA

ISRAEL

JORDAN

EGYPT

SAUDI ARABIA

N

LEBANON AND ISRAEL

Kilometers 0   125

Miles 0   125

12

LEBANON

Even the Goats Come from Hezbollah

Years before I encountered my first Hezbollah cadre, in late 2001, I was almost killed by the Lebanese militia. It was April 1996, and I was living as a reporter in Israel, which then occupied a swath of South Lebanon that it optimistically called a "security zone."

The security zone was not secure at all. Unlike occupied Palestinian territories and land seized from Syria, South Lebanon was off-limits to Israeli civilians. Israeli military convoys there were regularly targeted with rockets and remote-detonated roadside bombs—just as the American troops would be, later, in Iraq and Afghanistan.

Hezbollah, a Shiite group generously backed by Iran, was responsible for most of this fighting and usually videotaped each attack, sending members of its Office of War Information to accompany the ambush teams. Hezbollah's clips of Israeli vehicles going up in a puff of white smoke often made it to satellite TV newscasts just a few hours after the bombings themselves—a recruitment technique that Iraqi insurgents, and jihadis worldwide, would try hard to emulate.

The Israelis, unlike Americans in Iraq seven years later but like the Soviets in 1980s Afghanistan, had the disadvantage of geography. For them, the battlefield was, literally, too close to home. Iran had supplied Hezbollah with Russian-designed Katyusha missiles that could fly across the so-called security zone and slam northern Israeli cities such as Kiryat Shmona and Metullah. An organization born in response to the bloody Israeli invasion of Lebanon in 1982, Hezbollah made it a habit to lob its Katyushas into Israeli populated areas whenever the Israeli army killed Lebanese civilians. (Afghan mujahedeen, too, often fired U.S.-supplied missiles across the Soviet border.)

That week in April 1996, after fighting got out of hand and Hezbollah's Katyushas exploded in Kiryat Shmona, the Israeli military retaliated with massive air strikes. All-out war was imminent. Leaving my pregnant wife in Jerusalem, I jumped into a car and, together with Philippe Gelie, my French colleague from the newspaper *Le Figaro,* headed north. Another friend and colleague, Georges Malbrunot, joined us there.

By the time we arrived at dusk, Kiryat Shmona was a ghost town. Expecting the full might of Hezbollah's firepower, most residents chose to wait it out beyond the Katyushas' range. I noticed that some of the rare cars still on the streets were pierced by shards. All evening a foreboding silence hung in the air, interrupted every few minutes by the military patrol's loudspeaker messages. In a looped nasal-pitched recording, the broadcasts urged all residents to go to bomb shelters. We picked one and settled for the night on yellow bunk beds underground. The shelter was empty, except for the three of us, a forty-four-year-old construction contractor named Haim Arbeli, and his seven-year-old son, Yakir, who passed time underground by mimicking the sound of explosions. "I don't think peace is possible while Hezbollah exists," Arbeli mused before dozing off.

Nothing happened all night. At dawn we walked out, scanned the skies, and drove to the local command center in the municipality's bunker. The city fathers were furious. "We must bomb Beirut and other Lebanese cities. If we are not able to sleep here at night, there is no reason why they should in Beirut," one of the officials, Meir Marciano, told us. "The Hezbollah doesn't want just to destroy our homes. What they desire is human flesh," said another official, Gilbert Dray.

By lunchtime, tired of waiting for a barrage that still hadn't come, we returned to the car and started driving out, around an open plaza across from the bunker. That's when the whooshing sound of missiles prompted Philippe to hit the brakes and jump out of the vehicle.

All of a sudden, after spending several hours in a shelter, we were now in the open, in one of the town's most vulnerable places, just as the big-time shelling began. Philippe, his instincts honed by covering wars in Bosnia and the Caucasus, sprinted under the roof of a shopping arcade nearby. As I followed him, he shook his head: the roof was too thin to protect us. In a lull we darted across the plaza and back into the municipal bunker. Another round of missiles perforated the air with a whistle just above us. Then, halfway through, I noticed a different sound: my cell phone was ringing. I responded, breathing heavily, still running. It was my wife: she just heard on the radio that Kiryat Shmona had been shelled. "Do you know there's bombing? Are you okay?" she asked. I was okay. A woman who had driven ahead of us, and didn't seek cover, was not so lucky. Her car had just taken a direct hit.

Israel's response to the barrage of Katyushas on Kiryat Shmona was a massive escalation in hostilities. Just as the town officials had wanted, the Israeli military began bombardments across Lebanon, including Beirut, in an operation dubbed Grapes of Wrath. The grapes quickly turned sour, however. The following week an Israeli artillery salvo hit civilians sheltered at a base of UN troops from Fiji near the Lebanese village of Qana. Over one hundred people were killed, many of them women and children. Hezbollah was partly responsible for drawing this fire: its fighters had launched missiles from the immediate vicinity of the base. But amid international outcry, Israel was forced to stop the offensive. The United States—which had long classified Hezbollah as a terrorist organization—imposed a diplomatic understanding that, in effect, provided the Lebanese militia with international recognition of its right to combat Israeli troops. Qana took a place of pride in Bin Laden's speeches justifying jihad against Crusaders and Jews.

✦ ✦ ✦

When I first came to Beirut, in the final weeks of 2001, it was to see Hezbollah up close. The United States had just seized Afghanistan, and most people I knew in the Middle East considered the invasion of

Iraq inevitable. By looking at Hezbollah, I hoped to understand what the future might hold in the event that American incursions in the region bogged down—exactly what had happened with Israel's Lebanese adventure.

Israel's drive to the heart of Beirut in June 1982 was, after all, the most recent attempt by a non-Muslim power to refashion an Arab or a Muslim country to its advantage. Like the Soviet invasion of Afghanistan two and a half years earlier, the Israeli incursion backfired—and Hezbollah was its nightmarish, unforeseen consequence. Would Hezbollah soon become a model for those resisting foreign rule in America's new Muslim dominions?

The record was sobering. In May 2000, bled by Hezbollah's guerrilla attacks, Israel withdrew from the security zone, abandoning its Lebanese allies to their fate. The shelling of Kiryat Shmona stopped after that, and while skirmishes continued along some sections of the frontier, Israeli military casualties there declined dramatically. But the pullout turned Hezbollah into a model to be emulated across the Muslim world—and Israel had a steep price to pay even closer to home.

Hezbollah, which had already succeeded in expelling Western forces from Lebanon by truck-bombing American and French military barracks in 1983, now claimed the Muslims' first military victory over the Jewish state. The militia had just forced Israel into an unconditional withdrawal from occupied land—a feat that the combined efforts of Arab armies failed to achieve in previous wars. The lesson learned across the region was that only a maximalist, no-negotiations strategy could pay off.

A few months after Hezbollah's triumph, Palestinian leader Yasser Arafat refused to compromise with Israel at peace negotiations sponsored by President Bill Clinton in Camp David, Maryland. Then, electrified by Hezbollah's success, Palestinian gunmen launched a bloody uprising that killed thousands on both sides and wrecked hopes for establishing a Palestinian state. As control over the Palestinian struggle slipped from his hands and the initiative was seized by Hezbollah-inspired militias, Arafat died a broken and isolated man in November 2004.

Hezbollah, which opposes the very existence of Israel, didn't stop its own direct combat, either—although now it concentrated mostly on the so-called Shebaa Farms, a patch of Israeli-held mountainous land that the militia claimed was Lebanese and that, according to Israel and the UN, was part of the Golan Heights seized from Syria. On my first day in Beirut, I went for a walk on the central Hamra Avenue, flanked by Parisian-style outdoor cafés. The victorious face of Hezbollah leader Hassan Nasrallah beamed at me from an oversize billboard. Behind him was a picture of the al Aqsa mosque, the image of a Kalashnikov rifle, and the promise: OUR JERUSALEM, WE ARE COMING.

Focused on Israel, Hezbollah had ceased targeting the United States beginning in the early 1990s. But it continued to embolden Iraqi and Afghan insurgents by the sheer force of its example. Such was Hezbollah's appeal that, once Iraq's Shiite leader Muqtada al Sadr had launched the uprising against American forces, in April 2004, he declared his militia to be an Iraqi extension of the Lebanese group. Just like the Israelis in Lebanon, the U.S. forces in Iraq soon discovered that they had no easy answers to the ruthless but supremely efficient guerrilla strategies pioneered by Hezbollah—from kidnappings of foreign civilians to suicide truck bombings to remote-detonated mines.

✦　✦　✦

Getting to meet Hezbollah leaders nowadays isn't especially complicated. The militia, which in its early days kidnapped Western journalists such as Terry Anderson of the Associated Press, who was held captive for six years until December 1991, now employed a new attention-getting strategy. It had a press office.

Beirut journalists knew where to find it, and so, armed with directions received from one of them, I headed from my ritzy hotel on the downtown waterfront to the city's southern Shiite slums. The borders of Beirut's Hezbollah-land were easy to spot. Soon after the Kuwaiti embassy roundabout on the airport road, Western-style advertising billboards for lingerie, cigarettes, and soft drinks disappeared from sight. Instead, every lamppost was decorated with a mug shot of a Hezbollah "martyr" who had died fighting Israel, often in a suicide bombing—a string of fuzzy, blown-up photos of intense, wiry young men. The streets were also awash with Khomeini portraits and banners of Hezbollah—the Arabic equivalent of the letter *o* in the middle topped by a fist clutching a Kalashnikov rifle.

The press office was on the second floor of a bakery in a residential building—a location that, presumably, would make the Israeli Air Force think twice about bombing the place. As I climbed the stairs, I came across some of the building's inhabitants and wondered what they thought of the neighbors. I didn't dare ask.

Inside the Hezbollah-occupied apartment, bare except for a few desks and portraits of Khomeini and Iran's current "supreme leader," Ayatollah Ali Khamenei, I was greeted by a man named Hussein Naboulsi. All smiles, he kept addressing me as "My friend"—but wanted to start out by checking my credentials. After Naboulsi carefully photocopied my passport and my press card, I explained that I wanted to meet as many Hezbollah officials as I could, both in Beirut and in Israel's former security zone in the south—to understand how the group works and what made it so popular.

True to its reputation, Hezbollah proved the most efficient organization I have come across in the Middle East. A day later, Naboulsi called me back with a schedule of days of interviews; each would happen exactly as planned. In my dealings with the U.S. military, I never saw such precision.

✦   ✦   ✦

I started out my Hezbollah journey in the Lebanese Parliament, in Beirut's downtown. The once-elegant area had been turned to ruin during the Lebanese civil war and was being rebuilt to its old glory by the country's billionaire prime minister at the time, Rafik Hariri. Unlike every other Lebanese militia, Hezbollah retained its weapons after the civil war ended in 1990—using its duty to fight Israel as the excuse. But now Hezbollah also participated in peaceful politics, with twelve deputies, about 10 percent of the total, in its parliamentary bloc. To make sure that this embrace of democracy wasn't seen as a sign of going soft, the bloc was called Faithfulness to the Resistance.

The Hezbollah lawmaker I was meeting, Abdullah Kassir, was a member of the militia's inner circle and headed its executive bureau in 1992–1997. As a militant since Hezbollah's first days, he was no doubt involved one way or another in the terror of the 1980s.

Kassir, who had been trained as a sociologist, wore an unassuming gray suit and, in Iranian fashion, an open-collared shirt. These days

Kassir belonged to the legislature's Agriculture Committee. A colorful leaflet on the desk of his tiny Parliament office assured "From Lebanon—the Quality Label" under pictures of ripe apples, cherries, and grapes. Kassir was also a member of a committee that focused on luring Western, including American, tourists to the country, a remarkable position for a man who used to see all Westerners as targets.

Kassir's ideology, however, was little changed. He squirmed when I asked him about the September 11 attacks and whether he thought Bin Laden was responsible. As Shiites, the men of Hezbollah have little affinity with Qaeda, a Sunni movement whose ideology deems Shiites to be apostates. But after the Israeli pullout, Hezbollah sought to broaden its appeal well beyond the Muslim world's Shiite minority, positioning itself as a global paladin of Islamic honor and pride. So despite my repeated prodding, Kassir just wouldn't condemn the Saudi exile.

"The information we have about Bin Laden is only from the media, and the media does not give all the truth," he said. "But we know that what the Americans are doing in Afghanistan, targeting the entire Afghan people, is a form of organized terrorism." From Lebanon's own experience, he thought that American efforts to revamp the Muslim world are doomed: "History and the nature of life show that aggression cannot last a long time."

I asked him to tell me about Hezbollah's beginnings, after the Iranian revolution and the 1982 Israeli invasion. At first the Shiites, Lebanon's largest and poorest sect, were often well disposed toward Israelis, seeing them as liberators from Yasser Arafat's thuggish Palestinian militiamen. Yet, like most military occupations by alien powers ill versed in the local ways, Israeli rule soon transformed Shiite sympathy into outright hatred. In addition to the daily humiliations of foreign control, the Lebanese Muslims—Shiite and Sunni alike—were outraged by Ariel Sharon's grand project of installing, in Beirut, a client Christian regime that would perpetuate their second-class status. A pro-Israeli Christian president, Bachir Gemayel, was duly blown up. And after Sharon had succeeded in driving Arafat and the PLO from Lebanon in 1982, a new radical group that would become Hezbollah—Arabic for "Party of God"—sprang up, with massive Iranian help, to lead the battle against Israeli invaders.

"There used to be massacres taking place, and no one did anything to support the Lebanese people," Kassir reminisced. "So we were just a bunch of guys who were angry with what's going on, and we organized ourselves and formed Hezbollah—whose main goal was to resist the Israeli terrorism."

But, I asked, what about Hezbollah's actions that have earned the movement a place on America's list of terrorist groups? How did they square with the group's claim of solely resisting Israel? The record was long: blowing up American and French barracks and the U.S. embassy in Beirut, hijacking a TWA jet in 1985, kidnapping and sometimes killing scores of Western civilians, and, as recently as 1994, murdering at least eighty-five people at a Jewish cultural center in Argentina. All these attacks were almost universally ascribed to Hezbollah. While the militia officially denied responsibility, Nasrallah's senior aides, like Hussein Mussawi, even now publicly praised the perpetrators as "noble and courageous people."

Flushing with anger at my question, Kassir stuck to the official denials. "The Hezbollah that I know are honorable people who have resisted the Israelis—and Hezbollah can't be classified as terrorists because they are actually victims of terrorism themselves," he said, flustered. As for the Argentine Jewish center's bombing, Kassir added: "I myself accuse the Americans. Maybe they themselves bombed to have an excuse for supporting Israel. Or maybe Mossad did it."

Probing again, I asked Kassir whether he knew Imad Mughniyeh, the secretive Hezbollah military commander believed to have masterminded many of these attacks. Mughniyeh, who has a $5 million American bounty on his head, one-fifth the reward for Bin Laden, hadn't been seen in public for years and is believed to be living in Iran under a false identity. Kassir flashed a blistering look and responded curtly, "I have no answer."

He seemed unconcerned that the United States might take action against Hezbollah for such links and openly mocked American threats: "For the U.S. to attack us is like for an elephant to step on an ant. Maybe the elephant will find out that its step is not as strong as it thinks."

A few minutes later, Kassir added that he himself could have become a U.S. citizen. Like many Lebanese, he had relatives in the United States, and in 1978 an uncle offered him a way of immigrating to America. Kassir told me he had refused: "We don't believe that the U.S. is something to look up to."

Unlike the United States, most European nations don't classify Hezbollah as a terrorist organization, taking at face value its denials of responsibility for attacks against non-Israeli targets. So at the same time that he refused to meet American officials, Kassir was being courted by some of America's closest allies. As a member of Parliament, he was given red-carpet treatment on recent visits to Italy, Germany, and Brazil, meeting Cabinet ministers and other senior officials. His smile broadened as he recalled a speech he gave at a Brazilian state legislature in 2000: "Everyone there supported Hezbollah, considering us a group that promotes freedom and international law."

Despite this new respectability, it looked to me as though Kassir missed the good old days of his youth. As we were parting, he blurted out that he wished Israel would invade Lebanon again. "To clash with Israelis is our climax of pleasure," he grinned, making sure the sexual connotation was preserved in translation.

On the way out, Kassir lingered for a minute with my fixer. The lawmaker didn't like the interview one bit, she told me later. "The reporter has been asking suspicious questions. Maybe I should refer him to our security bureau," he had told her. I didn't know whether to take Kassir's remark as a threat or as a joke.

✦　✦　✦

I returned to Shiite South Beirut the following day, accompanied by a Lebanese friend. Born into a privileged Christian family, she had lived in Europe for several years, spoke better English than Arabic, and enjoyed the privileges of a European passport. Yet in spite of traveling halfway around the world, she had never set foot in the Hezbollah part of town, just a ten-minute taxi ride away. "I never thought I'd be walking here, with a Westerner!" she mused, looking with surprise at the lingerie displayed in a shop window. "And I never thought these people also wear bras."

The culture gap between Hezbollah-land and the easygoing play-grounds of central Beirut, a city where chic neighborhoods could be mistaken for Greek or Italian towns, was stunning. But Hezbollah, in contrast to its earlier practice of smashing up bars in Beirut's luxury hotels, no longer tried to convert the rest of Lebanon to its creed. It was content to merely hold power of veto over key national issues while retaining the ability to start or stop a war on the Israeli frontier.

Kassir's words about the climax of pleasure expressed a fundamental fact: Hezbollah, born out of war, could maintain its strength only as long as violence with Israel continued. In the parts of Lebanon under its control, the group had created a parallel state, a separate resistance society, that would come unglued without an enemy to resist. That's why the organization disputed the UN certification of the Israeli withdrawal from Lebanon as complete, continuing the battle over uninhabited Shebaa Farms. Syria, which effectively controls the Lebanese government, was all too happy: Hezbollah's attacks at Shebaa keep alive Syrian demands for the return of the Golan Heights, without exposing Damascus itself to direct retaliation. While non-Hezbollah Lebanese politicians have no choice but to second this policy in public, many bristle in private. "You know what Hezbollah will do once Israel leaves the Shebaa Farms?" went one joke that I heard from an associate of Hariri. "It will say it will continue the fight until Israel returns all the Lebanese fish that had swum down the coast."

✦ ✦ ✦

The next stop on my Hezbollah itinerary was a South Beirut complex known as Beit al Jarrah, or the House of the Wounded.

The official who greeted me there, Abu Hassan Yassin, had the calm gaze of a true believer. "These Hezbollah men, they all have the same look in their eyes. Scary," my uneasy fixer whispered. Yassin took me through the airy halls where men, some without limbs, listened to lectures on computing, wove baskets, or carved out wooden trinkets with Hezbollah's logo. Beit al Jarrah cared for some three thousand disabled Hezbollah war veterans, providing them with medical help, counseling, and education. Yassin proudly showed off pictures of another rehabilitation center, including a hotel, education facility, and soccer field, that Beit al Jarrah was building in the south.

Funded by Iran and by the Shiites' charity tax, the *khoms,* Beit al Jarrah also constructed access ramps in the houses of wheelchair-bound former guerrillas, paid for household help, and even funded costly medical treatment in Europe. It also gave stipends for injured militants' college study, in Lebanon and abroad. "Our people have become architects and lawyers," Yassin said with pride. A similar Hezbollah foundation helped the families of "martyrs"—guerrillas killed in battle.

Yassin introduced me to Beit al Jarrah's head of cultural programs, a veteran who went by the name Hajj Imad. The man, who lost his leg in a clash with Israelis in 1986, now worked full-time bolstering fellow disabled veterans' morale. "We have a special ideology here from the beginning, and this helps to cope," Imad said. "The people who get wounded because of the war are stronger than normal people. We are the sons of the resistance and this is a resistance society. This makes us much tougher than people with other ideologies."

Such sacrifice wasn't expected only from men. Beit al Jarrah easily matched willing brides with disabled guerrillas, even those unable to move and needing round-the-clock care. "It's not that difficult. Here, many women would consider marrying the war-wounded, those who are really sick," Yassin said. "They see it as their personal contribution to the jihad."

✦　✦　✦

Another subsidiary of Hezbollah's jihad was run by a soft-spoken agronomist by the name of Ibrahim Ismail. He was the general manager of Jihad al Binaa, or "Construction Jihad"—Hezbollah's business arm.

I met Ismail in his cluttered South Beirut office, just a short walk from the PR headquarters. On his desk I spotted sheets of correspondence outlining aid projects on the letterhead of the Iranian Ministry of Agriculture Jihad, Lebanese Section. Hezbollah's strength, I heard often, was that—unlike other Lebanese parties—it wasn't corrupt. Indeed, it didn't clamor for a slice of the state's resources and lucrative government contracts and jobs. Hezbollah could afford to maintain the image of cleanness and purity because, also unlike the other parties, it had an alternative source of financing: oil-rich Iran. The Iranian letters on Ismail's desk showed this money link, usually denied by Hezbollah's spokespeople.

Jihad al Binaa was created in 1988, initially to rebuild the homes of Hezbollah sympathizers or members that had been destroyed by Israel. "We know that the Israelis wanted our people to leave their villages. They wanted to create a gap between the people and the Islamic resistance," Ismail said. "So once they stopped bombing, we started building. Within three months we reconstructed the houses, for free, and the villagers returned."

Now that Israeli soldiers had withdrawn behind the frontier and no longer destroyed Lebanese homes, Jihad al Binaa was expanding into new areas. Ismail ticked off his priorities: providing fertilizers to Lebanese farmers, building Islamic schools, establishing beehives, and raising trout in the Bekaa Valley. Altogether, some three thousand farmers in the Bekaa Valley and one thousand in southern Lebanon were served by Jihad al Binaa, he said. Hezbollah also ran a meteorological station and a veterinarian service, and tried to teach its militants how to cultivate champignons. Ismail saw this rural development aid in military terms, as securing the battlefield: "Whenever the area is empty of people, it means that the Israelis can reoccupy it without resistance."

When I asked Ismail about Jihad al Binaa's budget, he gave me a figure of $6 million to $8 million a year. It seemed awfully small, considering the organization's scope. Ismail explained that such an amount, when spent by Hezbollah, produced the same effect as $60 million to $80 million disbursed by conventional aid organizations. There was some truth in this explanation: unlike Western NGOs, Hezbollah surely didn't spend cash on flashy SUVs and expatriate benefits packages.

"People listen to what we have to say. They know we are different from the private-sector engineers and agronomists," Ismail said. He was just as scathing about the state's development programs: "The Lebanese government's budget is for salaries, not for projects."

Gesturing at the busy street outside his window, Ismail said that even the drinking water in South Beirut came from Hezbollah, not from the state water utility. The seven-story concrete apartment blocks here, erected haphazardly during the civil war, had no plumbing that worked. So Jihad al Binaa purchased fresh water from a Lebanese government company and distributed it for free through 120 tanks, usually emblazoned with the Iranian flag and positioned on street corners. "We used to do the garbage collection, too, but now the state takes care of it here," he said. "People trust us. They know we're not in it for the money."

✦　✦　✦

After meeting Ismail, I hoped to see the beneficiaries of Jihad al Binaa's largesse in the former Israeli security zone, in the south. Hezbollah arranged a tour. I left from Beirut early in the morning and headed, with a Palestinian fixer, to the Shiite town of Nabatiye, just north of the former frontline.

Nabatiye had long been a battlefield between Israeli troops and Hezbollah guerrillas, and its streets were bedecked with the militia's banners and posters. The former Israeli forward post towered on a hilltop just above town. I remembered watching a news report on Israeli TV about soldiers shooting into town from that post, with footage of Nabatiye's streets as seen through a sniper's scope.

My Palestinian fixer and I had to meet up with one of the local Hezbollah commanders—our assigned escort in the south. The militia didn't like unsupervised foreigners wandering through the territory it had wrested from Israel, and its roadblocks and checkpoints dotted the southern roads. We picked up our guide, a man with a leather jacket whose name I never learned, in an unmarked house on Nabatiye's edge, after spending half an hour in a waiting room decorated with images of bearded Shiite ayatollahs against intense blue-violet backgrounds.

I wasn't prepared for the transformation of the former security zone, a green, hilly area that, because of the violence, had been spared the uncontrolled construction boom that disfigured much of Lebanon.

Now, a huge advertising billboard towered on every spot where Hezbollah had carried out a successful attack against Israeli troops. The boards advertised Hezbollah's kind of warfare and were signed by the militia's Office of War Information. Each one, in gaudy Islamic-kitsch style, was written in Arabic and in English, and carried the "martyr" bombers' names and mug shots. It also displayed the details of the attack, as well as clippings from Israeli newspapers showing the incident's victims and their weeping families at funeral wakes. In the two decades of Israeli presence, there had been plenty of attacks in this area, so a new billboard appeared after every twist of the road. The pictures of destruction stood out, almost surreal, among the verdant countryside.

✦   ✦   ✦

After traversing the whole south of Lebanon, we finally arrived at the Israeli frontier, at a border gate facing the town of Metullah. Kiryat Shmona, where I had been ducking under Hezbollah rockets, was a couple of miles farther south. In the past, this site was the main crossing point between Israel proper and the security zone. Now it was shut down, and heavy Israeli fortifications loomed across the fence.

In the first months after the Israeli withdrawal, Hezbollah turned the gate into a tourist attraction, busing thousands of Lebanese, Palestinian refugees, and sympathetic Western visitors to throw rocks at an Israeli position across the frontier. This anti-Zionist sport proved highly popular, and the Lebanese border village did a brisk trade in the rocks. The rocks, of course, could be recycled, because only the most athletic of participants managed to launch the projectiles above the tall fence and into Israeli territory.

But by the time I arrived, there were no tourists, and no rock merchants. My Hezbollah escort, about whose past I could only guess, was visibly uncomfortable lingering just a few feet away from Israeli cameras and from the muzzles of Israeli machine guns permanently aimed at the Lebanese side. He rushed us to leave, taking me, instead, to an abandoned Israeli position on an escarpment just above Metullah.

I had been to Metullah before, a prosperous town of red-roofed cottages that even boasted an ice rink—much favored by its sizable population of North American immigrants—and, at least until the withdrawal from the security zone, Israel's best Lebanese restaurants. Looking from war-wrecked South Lebanon, Metullah, with its straight roads, manicured lawns, and other signs of obvious affluence, seemed utterly alien to the chaotic Middle East. From where we stood, the nearest Israeli homes—spacious white villas—were just a few hundred yards away. In fact, I could make out Israeli license plates. My immediate thought was that, to kill Israelis, Hezbollah no longer needed to launch missiles: if it wished, it could now shoot into Israeli bedrooms with one of the simple Kalashnikovs so proudly displayed on its logo; with Katyushas, it could strike as far south as the outskirts of Haifa.

My Palestinian fixer, who had never visited the land her parents fled in 1948, looked at Metullah enthralled. Our Hezbollah escort finally broke the silence. "God willing, next year you'll get rid of the Jews in your land as we did in ours, and it will all be yours," he told her. She smiled at the thought and responded "*Inshalla*—God willing." I wondered what would happen if any of my Israeli acquaintances chanced to see me, from the other side of the fence, and shouted or waved.

✦ ✦ ✦

We headed inland from the border, and after an hour of roads spiked with hairpin turns, arrived at a fort perched high on a mountain. A billboard atop the parking lot showed the faces of three Israeli soldiers recently seized by Hezbollah on the border, in Shebaa Farms, and a promise to capture more. The pictures had been taken from Israeli newspapers.

Another poster showed a Hezbollah-marked boot stomping on a negotiating table and sweeping away frightened-looking Israelis and Americans. We had arrived, my escort told me, at the notorious Khiam prison where the Israeli-sponsored South Lebanese Army militia used to hold and torture its detainees.

The prison, initially a fort built by the country's French colonial masters, was now yet another Hezbollah-run tourist attraction—complete with a souvenir shop hawking AK-47-branded trinkets manufactured by wounded war veterans in South Beirut. Former Hezbollah prisoners of Khiam were back at the prison, as tour guides. Hezbollah insisted on bringing visiting journalists here. Our guide was a bearded young man in a blue Adidas track suit named Ali Darwish, who, he said, had spent three years behind bars at Khiam, after being arrested in 1993, at the age of fifteen. According to the young man, he had indeed belonged to a Hezbollah unit at the time of the arrest and had been released only because of a serious neck injury resulting from the torture.

Standing in a small courtyard where even the sky was fenced off, he relished ticking off the prison's horrors. "There were dogs, there was shit, and we had black bags on our heads for two, three days," he said. At the time, I took his description with some skepticism. It evaporated a couple of years later, when I saw the pictures of U.S. Army dogs attacking hooded, naked Iraqi prisoners at the Abu Ghraib prison, near Baghdad.

Inside Khiam, the cells were helpfully marked in English for visitors' convenience. A ROOM OF THE BOSS OF WHIPPERS, said one sign. ROOM WITH INVESTIGATORS WITH THE HELP OF TRAITORS, explained another. PLEASE KEEP CLEAN, incongruously added the third.

Darwish and my Hezbollah escort urged me to try the prisoner's experience for myself by entering a tiny, windowless cell and having a door locked behind me. I peered inside the dank darkness but didn't quite feel like going for the full immersion. Hezbollah, after all, had been in the imprisonment business itself, just ten years earlier—with Western journalists as its captives of choice.

✦ ✦ ✦

As we continued our drive through a village near Khiam, I remembered that I wanted to see a recipient of Jihad al Binaa's aid. When I mentioned this to my Hezbollah escort, he pulled over, shouted through the window and, a couple of minutes later, appeared with a sheepish thirty-three-year-old man named Ali Alout.

On the way to Alout's farm in a hamlet known as Ayn al Arab, the man recounted his family story. The family abandoned the farm shortly after the 1982 Israeli invasion and eked out a living in the grim slums of South Beirut, taking no part in anti-Israeli resistance. In 2000, a few months after the Israelis departed, Alout decided to return—to what had become a wasteland.

We got to the end of a dirt road and had to walk uphill to see Alout's land. The disputed Shebaa Farms—still an active war zone—were just a mountain away. I asked my Hezbollah escort whether the area was mined. He shook his head, but I noticed that, as he followed the farmer, he took care to step only in Alout's footprints, without touching undisturbed ground. I didn't know whether this was an old guerrilla's habit or a necessary precaution, but I followed his example anyway.

Alout's farm was of breathtaking beauty. Olive trees sprouted among white limestone boulders. Goats grazed on an intense emerald hillside. It had just rained, and the air smelled of a crisp, mountain freshness that, I thought, must be intoxicating after the smog-filled shantytown where Alout had to spend most of his life. The farmer proudly showed me a new field of olive saplings. These came from Hezbollah, he said. The militia had also sent a bulldozer to clear the field, provided the nine goats grazing nearby, and regularly dispatched a veterinarian to check up on the animals' health.

"On my own, I couldn't even afford to rebuild our house," Alout said. "Hezbollah did all this. Without them, it'd be impossible."

Characteristically inscrutable, my escort showed no emotion as he heard all this praise for his organization. We returned to the car and drove back to Nabatiye, without speaking. Then, along the way, we had to make a bathroom stop for my Palestinian fixer. As we waited for her, the Hezbollah man looked out the window and took in a breathful of country air. Birds sang from an age-old tree nearby. He smiled and addressed me for the first time. "This nature, isn't it nice?" he said.

✦　✦　✦

Back in dusty South Beirut, the last item on my itinerary was the gleaming headquarters of Hezbollah's TV network, Al Manar—the one that topped the channel listing in my Tunisian hotel. The new white building, packed with state-of-the art equipment, seemed far better endowed than the tiny studios of the best-known Arab satellite network, Al Jazeera, based in Qatar. Al Manar—Arabic for "beacon"—now even sent reporters to cover press conferences at the American embassy, which Hezbollah blew up, twice, in the 1980s.

The man in charge of Al Manar, Nayef Krayem, greeted us in an oversize office, a sleek TV screen facing his desk. A longtime Hezbollah militant, Krayem had the facile smile and polished manners of a media executive. He told me his network's story. At its founding, in 1991, he said, Al Manar's purpose was to help the guerrillas and preach Islamic values to Lebanese society. Since 1995, the station—

then using terrestrial broadcasting—also started beaming Hebrew-language psychological warfare messages at Israeli soldiers and civilians. "Mothers of soldiers, do not let your sons come to Lebanon, because they will return home dead," went one typical spot.

After the Israelis withdrew, in 2000, Hezbollah's ambitions went global, and Al Manar began satellite transmissions worldwide, lending hours of daily airtime to programming in support of Palestinian Sunni groups such as Hamas and its suicide-bombing campaign. Krayem estimated that Al Manar now had between 10 million and 20 million regular viewers across the region, most of them Sunnis rather than Shiites. "We are pushing for the Palestinian resistance to free Palestine the way we have freed Lebanon," he explained.

The psy ops continued, too—now aimed at persuading Israeli Jews that their "Zionist entity" was doomed and would soon be wiped out by victorious Arabs. One ad showed a blown-up Israeli bus in flames, with this voice-over: "O Zionists, there is no safety in Tel Aviv, so we advise you to go back to Europe, America, and other states from which you came." Krayem chuckled as he watched the spot: "Bin Laden spoiled everything for us." A few months after September 11, America didn't seem all that much safer than Tel Aviv, he conceded: "Next time we'll have to be more creative."

At Al Manar, everything was subordinate to fertilizing the region with Hezbollah's uncompromising ethos. Even the network's quiz show, *The Witness Witnesses*, focused on Israel. I watched one installment, during which an actor, with a mandatory beaky nose, was dressed up to represent a prominent Israeli leader—this time Prime Minister Yitzhak Rabin, gunned down by a Jewish extremist six years earlier, in late 1995. Previous subjects included Moshe Dayan and Ariel Sharon.

"Your history is quite bloody!" the moderator thundered from his *Jeopardy*-like set, introducing the personage.

"Yes, I know, this is Rabin the murderer," one of the participants yelled in recognition.

"No, I don't agree with your characterization of me," the Rabin character answered pompously.

The moderator cut him off: "We're here to tell the truth, not to listen to your lies. Your history is bloody indeed."

At this point, a child character floated into the scene. He was supposed to represent Mohammed al Dura, a twelve-year-old Palestinian whose killing in Gaza was filmed, in a piece of footage that has since been broadcast nonstop across the Arab world and especially on Al Manar, by a French TV crew in the first days of the new intifada in September 2000. "This is what you did to my life," the child character sang, pointing an accusatory finger at the Rabin personage. For the quiz show writers, obviously, it didn't matter that Rabin had died five years before the young Mohammed al Dura.

The moderator proceeded to quiz the participants about the details of Rabin's biography. One question—where was Rabin born?—offered three possible answers: Russia, Poland, or Palestine. I knew that Rabin was the first Israeli prime minister born in the Holy Land; so did the participant who answered correctly: "Palestine." But that response didn't jibe with Hezbollah's ideology, which considered all Jews to be alien invaders who could be expelled from what was now Israel just as easily as they had been forced from Lebanon. "Wrong answer," the moderator shouted. The participant lost.

Game shows weren't the only form of Hezbollah entertainment. Al Manar also aired its own soap operas. The first two, *Ashoura* and *Stories of Prophets,* focused on Hezbollah's core Shiite audiences. The third, and newest, show airing while I was in Beirut, *Izzeddin al Qassam,* spoke to Arab nationalist pride across sectarian lines. In graphic detail, it dramatized the life of a Sunni Arab nationalist guerrilla who fought French colonialists in Syria and Lebanon before dying in battle against British troops in Mandate Palestine, where he had inspired an uprising against Jewish settlement. Every episode of the series began with rousing martial music, and the theme, in most viewers' minds, was inextricably linked to current affairs. Izzedin al Qassam's name, after all, had been adopted by the military wing of Hamas and was used in signing suicide-bombing press releases.

I asked Krayem whether he employed Hezbollah's own actors for this soap opera. He laughed at my question. "Of course not. We hire just regular Lebanese actors," he replied. Then he grew serious. "Hezbollah doesn't have actors," he said. "When it does something, it's for real."

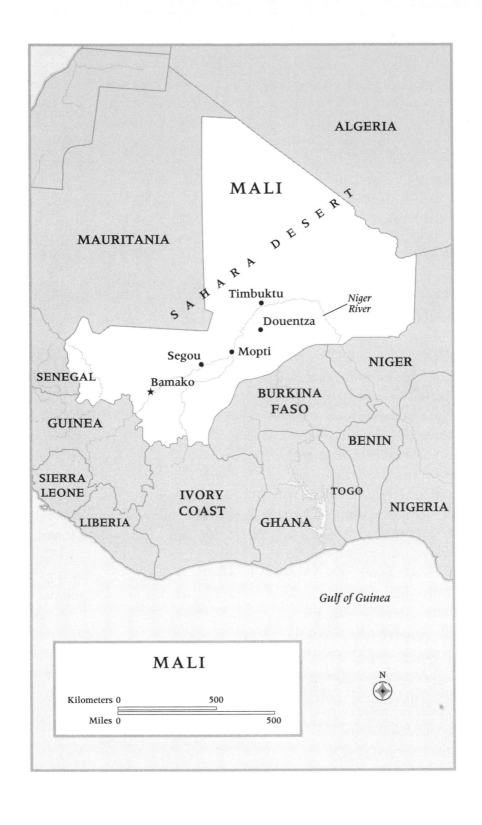

ALGERIA

MALI

MAURITANIA

S A H A R A   D E S E R T

Timbuktu

Niger
River

Douentza

Segou

Mopti

NIGER

SENEGAL

Bamako

BURKINA
FASO

GUINEA

BENIN

SIERRA
LEONE

IVORY
COAST

TOGO

NIGERIA

LIBERIA

GHANA

Gulf of Guinea

MALI

Kilometers 0   500

Miles 0   500

N

13

MALI

A Ballot Box in Timbuktu

As I settled in the Landcruiser's back seat, exhausted by the Sahara sun, a monotonous landscape of sand, rock, and shrubs stretched out to the horizon. There was no road—only a backbreaking desert track across scorching northern Mali, with at least four more hours to go until asphalt and the first town. We had left the last inhabited hamlet more than an hour ago, at the Timbuktu ferry crossing on the banks of the meandering, brown-hued Niger. Since then, no other vehicle had crossed our path.

Just as I began to doze off, my fixer, Sadio, screamed in horror. With a bump and a clunk, the car suddenly lost steering and veered off track, spinning like a top in a cloud of sand. Knocked off the back seat, I found myself lying on the car floor, my brain registering the accident in meticulous slow motion. When the spinning ended, I stepped out of the car, shaking, into the blazing heat.

The damage was clear. All the bolts that connected the front wheel axis with the Landcruiser's steering mechanism were gone, lost one by one in the desert sand. The SUV now rested on diagonally inclined front tires, pointing back to Timbuktu on the wrong side of the path. It was a painful sight, like the unnatural angle of a broken limb.

Badra, my driver, hadn't thought of bringing a tool box. Sadio tried to improvise by tearing a blue Tuareg turban she had purchased in Timbuktu into narrow strips and then weaving the strips into a cord that, she hoped, could hold the broken parts together. Realizing this couldn't work, she gave up and sought shelter from the sun inside the car. The air-conditioning system gasped, and stopped working, too.

It sank in: we were now marooned in the Sahara. Initially, I took comfort in the fact that we weren't completely alone. A Tuareg nomad, his face hidden behind a black scarf, witnessed our misadventure and approached the Landcruiser without saying a word or even acknowledging our presence. For an hour he crouched by the car, silently, looking at our increasingly desperate efforts to patch the vehicle together. Like a ghost, he then picked up, mounted his camel, and vanished into the desert haze.

Things could have been much worse if, before leaving Timbuktu, I hadn't insisted on buying two boxes of bottled water and a bagload of food. I also carried a GPS device to pinpoint our exact position, and an Iridium satellite phone that provided communications with the outside world even from the middle of the Sahara.

In Timbuktu, where I had spent the previous week talking to local notables and politicians, I had met the regional governor and the city's mayor and jotted down their cell phone numbers. These men had the power to dispatch a rescue mission that could arrive within a couple of hours, and so I tried to call them. My satphone stubbornly refused to connect with Mali's telephone system; I called the *Wall Street Journal*'s Paris bureau, asking a French-speaking colleague to beg the Malian authorities for help. She couldn't get through, either, and left desperate-sounding voice mail messages in Timbuktu.

Then we noticed a Malian military patrol. The soldiers had spotted us, too. They stopped, inspected our Landcruiser, and promised to send a mechanic later in the day. The heat had become unbearable, and the plastic water bottles in the car too hot to touch. An hour went by, then another. Sadio sat listlessly, too tired to speak or move. Trying not to dehydrate, I drank the hot water that now smelled of melting plastic, and cursed myself for coming to Mali in the first place.

✦ ✦ ✦

I had traveled to this West African country, not often visited by Western reporters, because of a think-tank report.

Authored by the Freedom House, a New York organization that has ranked political freedoms and civil liberties worldwide since 1973, the report landed on my desk in the spring of 2004, when the insurgency in Iraq had just expanded into an all-out war and America's post–September 11 promise of spreading democracy in the Muslim world rang increasingly hollow.

While democracy flourished in formerly dictatorial regions after the end of the Cold War, from eastern Europe to South America, the lands of Islam proved stubbornly resistant to the global march toward freedom. Virtually no Muslim dictatorship crumbled from within. Younger monarchs succeeded their fathers in kingdoms such as Morocco or Jordan. Presidents' sons took the helm in republics like Syria and Azerbaijan.

The bloody outcomes of American invasions in Afghanistan and Iraq did little to improve democracy's appeal in the region. By 2004 the very word "democratization" had become something of a slur in Arab political discourse, denoting obedience to Washington's agenda and a betrayal of the nationalist cause. Islamists, of course, long held that Western-style democracy, rule according to man-made laws adopted by the people, is inherently incompatible with an Islamic society, which should be ruled by the God-given, immutable Sharia.

It was no surprise that, among the forty-nine nations that the Freedom House report ranked as "not free" in 2004, more than half were Muslim. (They included both Iraq and Afghanistan, not quite a ringing endorsement of American-controlled governments there.)

Among the forty-seven Muslim-majority states in the survey, only two—the same number as in 1973—qualified as fully "free," the lowest proportion for any regional group. They were not, as I had expected, the industrialized societies of Malaysia and Turkey, or European states such as Albania and Bosnia-Herzegovina. Those four ranked merely "partly free." Instead, the broadest political and social freedoms in the Muslim world were enjoyed by the citizens of two impoverished West African nations few Americans or Europeans can find on the map—Mali and Senegal. The poorer of the two, Mali, was the first to earn the rating.

I was eager to understand how a landlocked African country—sandwiched between the twin horrors of Algeria and the Ivory Coast—could build a stable democracy, and what lessons the rest of the Muslim world could draw from Mali. Had Mali somehow discovered a miraculous recipe that reconciled Islam and democracy and that could be applied elsewhere? Or was Mali just an exception that confirmed the rule, a democracy that flourished because Islam in Mali, while age-old, was also only skin deep?

✦ ✦ ✦

It was the peak of the hot, dry season when I landed in Bamako, the low-rise Malian capital that's spread on both banks of the Niger like a giant smoky village. The next morning I met my fixer, Sadio, a radio journalist who grew up in freewheeling (and Christian) Brazzaville, on the banks of another great African river, the Congo. She wore a Charlie Chaplin–style bowler hat and a sleeveless top, utterly unconcerned with Islamic mores.

Unmarried, she was raising her son and a couple of adopted boys, plus a bull that had been given to her as a gift by the Malian president. Over breakfast she filled me in on the intricacies of Mali's history and politics.

A largely desert nation the size of Texas and California combined, Mali is traversed by a strip of cultivated land that follows the Niger, a geography similar to Egypt's. Medieval Arab traders believed this stretch of the Niger to be the upper Nile, and, accordingly, gave the name of Nile Gate to the riverside exit from ancient Timbuktu. Like Egypt, Mali is a land steeped in millennial history, at the heart of regional empires that have succeeded each other for centuries.

Islam reached these parts at about the same time as Christianity penetrated Scandinavia and Russia. But, unlike East Africa's Swahili coast, where the Arabs of Zanzibar maintained control until the arrival of British colonialists, it was the native black Africans who created Mali's distinctive Islamic civilization. The most famous of them,

Emperor Kankan Moussa, shocked the Arab world, around 1324, with his display of ostentatious wealth while making the hajj, or pilgrimage to Mecca. Kankan Moussa reportedly brought so much gold in his caravan that his extravagant spending depressed Cairo's currency rates for twelve years.

Mali's society is built on the tradition of "cousinage," which places a taboo on violence within an interlocking network of tribes and castes. The tradition stems from imperial history: whenever one Malian empire replaced another, the winners and the losers usually became "cousins" to prevent their conflict from carrying over into new generations. This seemed like a good lesson to learn, in Africa, in the West, and in those parts of the Islamic world where rage over the Crusades and the loss of Spain still burns raw.

✦ ✦ ✦

Sadio moved around Bamako in a dented stick-shift car that, I realized by noon of my first day in Mali, she didn't quite know how to handle. We were pulled over by the police a couple of times for running red lights and creating near-accidents. Just as quickly, we were let go once Sadio flashed her press card. "This is a democracy, and so they all want to be on the good side of the journalists," she said triumphantly after yet another conversation with a suddenly forgiving police officer.

A monument in front of my hotel, a sculpture of a bereaved mother holding up a dead child, commemorated the price Mali paid for its freedom. Street protests broke out on that spot in March 1991, against the country's longtime dictator, Moussa Traoré. As any African dictator would do, Traoré responded by ordering the Army to shoot into the crowd.

From there, a succession of unlikely events occurred. After more than one hundred protesters were killed, a young lieutenant colonel in charge of Mali's elite paratroopers' battalion led a coup d'état, deposing Traoré. But unlike virtually all such coup leaders in Africa, the officer, Amadou Toumani Touré, didn't cling to power. Instead, he called for free elections, in which he himself refused to stand.

An intellectual who had led the pro-democracy protests, Alpha Oumar Konaré, won that election. In an unusual move for Africa,

Konaré didn't change the constitution so he could run again once his two terms had expired, in 2002. Touré—now a retired general—returned to the fray. He defeated Konaré's ruling party, Adema, and reclaimed the presidential palace—leading the nation thanks to ballots rather than bullets this time around.

As I arrived in Mali, yet another election, for the country's municipal councils and mayors, was in the works. I was eager to witness the campaign, and to measure the degree to which Islamic clerics—key political actors in many other Muslim lands—held sway over the country's democratic process.

✦　✦　✦

To meet one of the most influential men of Islam in Mali, Sadio drove us away from Bamako's center, which is dominated by modern Saudi- and Libyan-built mosques, and into the capital's semirural outskirts. There, among trash-blanketed streets that double as pastures for unhealthy-looking goats, towers the palatial villa of a cleric named Ousmane Madani Haidara. Believed to be a holy man with a reputation for miracles, Haidara draws million-strong crowds and fills stadiums with his sermons, drawing adepts from all over West Africa. His organization carries the threatening name of Ansar ed-Din, or Protectors of Faith. To my ear, it sounded all too similar to Ansar al-Islam, or Protectors of Islam, the deadly Qaeda affiliate operating in Iraq; I didn't expect to like Haidara.

On the street, vendors peddled key chains made of the cleric's laminated photographs. Inside, I saw hundreds of people reclining on straw mats in the vast courtyard, under a roof made of plastic sheeting. Mothers comforted shrieking babies; old men snored under dirty blankets; sullen-eyed teenagers sat upright as if entranced. It was like coming into an African railway station, minus the trains. Food was boiling in industrial-size vats, and spicy vapor floated in the air. We asked to meet the holy man and settled down on a free stretch of the mats. For half an hour only the moist, hungry flies paid attention to us. Angry and hot, Sadio decided that the aides were probably too afraid to disturb Haidara with the news that he had visitors. Within minutes, after arguing loudly, we were ushered upstairs, to the cleric's suite.

Haidara, who claimed descent from Prophet Mohammed, was barefoot and shrouded in a purple robe, occupying an expensive curved sofa in the middle of sheer chaos. With a fox-like face and long, slender fingers, he effusively welcomed me and Sadio. His loud laugh surprised me; it had none of the somber, deliberate demeanor I expected from a senior cleric. The room was cluttered with a cacophony of objects, like a shopping mall after an earthquake—VCRs, cameras, jugs of oil, flashlights, books, cell phones. Next to Haidara on the sofa lay a brand-new laptop computer. Speaking in Bambara, Mali's lingua franca, the cleric apologized that he knew little French. His inability to speak Arabic, either, indicated that he had probably never gone to school. Sadio kept wondering afterward what exactly an illiterate man was doing with a pricey laptop.

My antennae went up as I saw, under Haidara's sofa, a stack of campaign posters for the upcoming elections. Was the cleric endorsing a particular candidate? I asked. "Ah, all these politicians, they all come here, asking me for a blessing. I bless them, of course, but in my role I can't support one against the other," he answered dismissively. "I myself, I don't know much about politics, but Islam and politics are two very distinct things. We, in religion, we need to be clean. And it's not so easy to find a politician who isn't corrupted."

This was a sweeping indictment, but I appreciated his belief in the separation between religion and state—not something I heard often from Islamic scholars. I asked Haidara where his own money came from. Ansar ed-Din, he replied, collected about $2 in CFA francs, a currency used in French-speaking West Africa, every month from its members. The sect's membership was now over one million in Mali alone, and at least as much in the neighboring countries. As representatives from the Ivory Coast and Burkina Faso joined our discussion, I made a quick mental calculation: Haidara was collecting almost $50 million a year. If his figures were true, he was the country's biggest enterprise.

Haidara's outfit focused on preaching Islam and good morals at its stadium sermons, while taking care not to undermine the old African rituals, still ingrained in Mali's way of life. Despite its militant name, Ansar ed-Din, unlike Islamists in charge of northern Nigerian states, didn't endorse the imposition of Sharia law. "The Sharia cuts off hands of thieves. But if you preach the right way, the thief will not steal," the cleric laughed. "Here it is a secular country. If you like to drink, you can drink. It doesn't matter to me." Women, he added, do not have to wear the veil as long as they keep their breasts covered: "You have to be worthy—do not steal, do not kill, do not commit adultery. It doesn't matter what you wear." I warmed up to the man.

But he wasn't the only face of Mali's Islam. Throughout our meeting, Haidara kept carping about the Arab-funded Wahhabi proselytizers who prowled his turf. "Our relations with them are very bad," he said. "Wahhabis say that all those who wear *gris-gris* charms are infidels, and this is clearly false."

✦   ✦   ✦

I was interested in hearing what Mali's Wahhabis had to say on the subject, so I headed the same afternoon to Bamako's Saudi mosque, a not-too-refined structure of concrete minarets that soars up from the sea of humanity swirling in the city's main market.

I noticed some curious items on sale by the mosque. Spread on the asphalt were mounds of severed monkey hands and heads, half-dried mice that attracted swarms of insistent insects, antelope horns and assorted bones, potions, and minerals. The young men selling the stuff, dressed in sneakers and fake Nike T-shirts, didn't like being photographed.

This was the sorcery market, Sadio explained: all those items were the ingredients for traditional African magic. In Saudi Arabia the vendors would have long ago been beheaded; witchcraft, after all, was a capital crime. But nobody seemed to mind in the shade of Bamako's *mosquée saoudite*.

The mosque complex also housed the Malian Association for the Progress and Unity of Islam, the country's main Muslim body, and the city's Islamic radio station, the Voice of the Quran and the Hadith. The man who ran both organizations, Mahmoud Dicko, also happened to be Mali's top Wahhabi preacher.

Laughing, Dicko greeted Sadio as an old friend, joking that he would find her a bearded husband and turn her into a model Muslim housewife. I soon realized that, despite Haidara's complaints, Mali's Wahhabism had little to do with the harsh Saudi creed. The last thing Dicko, educated in the Saudi holy city of Medina, appeared to want for his country was a Saudi-style theocracy.

"Mali was always a particular place. It's for everyone's advantage for the country to stay secular," he told me. "This is our tradition. The religions always coexisted here. When the ancient emperors of Mali held court, they had a Muslim marabout on one hand, and a fetish doctor on the other." I tried to probe Dicko more deeply, enumerating the violations of Islamic law I had already seen: ubiquitous beer, women bathing bare-chested in full view in the Niger, and of course the ever-present *gris-gris*. Wouldn't he want all this to end?

Dicko responded with a good-humored shrug. "If Mali today changes and starts to respect the norms of Islam, this will make me happy. But I'm not for imposing my vision." He reminded me of bloodshed in places like Nigeria after the introduction of Sharia law: "We have no interest in plunging our country into something like this."

Like most Malians I've met, Dicko didn't consider his own country's traditions to be inferior. But unlike many people I had encountered on the Muslim world's periphery, he saw no need to imitate the Arabs— the original Muslims in whose tongue the Quran had been revealed. "We're not Arabs here. We're Africans. I never dress up as if I were from the Gulf," he said. "When I invite the people of my village, we eat together, men and women. I can't close a door on them just because I studied in Saudi Arabia. We are Malians. We have our own culture."

As I listened to Dicko asserting his rejection of fundamentalist Islam's segregation of sexes, I remembered a passage penned by Ibn Battuta, the fourteenth-century Moroccan traveler who visited Mali as part of a world journey that took him as far away as China: "Their women have no shame before men, and do not veil themselves, yet they are punctilious about their prayers," Ibn Battuta wrote reproachfully about Mali's inhabitants. "Women there have friends and companions among men outside the prohibited degrees of marriage, and in the same way men have women friends in the same category. A man goes into his house, finds his wife with her man friend, and does not disapprove," the Moroccan traveler added, amazed.

"The companionship of women and men among us is a good thing and an agreeable practice, which causes no suspicion. They are not like women of your country," Ibn Battuta's Malian friend had tried to explain, to no avail. "I was astonished at his silliness. I left him and did not visit him again," the angered Moroccan traveler noted. The Malians were probably astonished at the silliness of Arab critics like Ibn Battuta, I thought.

✦ ✦ ✦

I had braced myself for an accident from the moment I saw how Sadio drove—and, indeed, it duly occurred on the way back from our encounter with Dicko. The mishap wasn't, however, Sadio's fault. While idling at an intersection, we were rear-ended by a shiny SUV driven by a young woman in high heels and a designer dress.

Half an hour later, as Sadio and the woman were engaged in an escalating shouting match, a bored policeman ambled by. He filled out a form and collected both drivers' licenses and car registration papers, which Sadio was supposed to pick up at the precinct in the afternoon—and wouldn't for over a week. It turned out a few hours later that the woman driving the SUV was the young wife of a senior police officer who was a friend of Sadio's and, above all, a "cousin" from whom it was taboo to ask compensation.

During the altercation, I noticed that Sadio's driver's license came from Nigeria, a land where any document can be purchased for a small fee. As we drove off in the damaged car, I asked Sadio whether she had liked Nigeria. She told me she hadn't quite been to that country.

I didn't yet know what would happen to us in the Sahara, but I was already beginning to think that the gods of automobiles weren't happy.

✦ ✦ ✦

As the number of election posters on Bamako's walls increased, day after day, I had to decide on which race to focus. Unlike other Malian cities, Bamako is divided into several municipalities and doesn't have a single mayor. Writing about a borough election didn't seem that exciting.

Naturally, as I looked for the right city, my thoughts turned to Timbuktu—the one place in West Africa that every Westerner has heard of. Located in northern Mali, at the northernmost bend of the Niger, Timbuktu had an added advantage for me: it sat on the crossroads between black Africa and the more familiar Arabic-speaking world beyond the Sahara.

The cradle of Islam in West Africa, Timbuktu seduces any traveler by the sheer appeal of its name. Here, I thought, was a perfect opportunity to examine how Mali made democratic politics work in a spot famous as the City of 333 (Muslim) Saints.

Timbuktu, of course, is also known as the end of the world—and even from Bamako, not exactly the center of the universe, getting there isn't simple. In the cooler rainy season, when a trickle of tourists drops in on Mali, it's possible to sail to Timbuktu by a Niger riverboat. But as I plotted my trip, there was no rain, and temperatures topped 110 degrees every day. The Niger was too shallow for navigation, and the tourist traffic was dead. The occasional scheduled flight into Timbuktu was often canceled, too.

This left me one option: overland. Because there was no paved road to Timbuktu, we needed a sturdy, four-wheel drive. Sadio's friend introduced us to a driver, Badra, presenting him as an expert on sandy northern roads. Badra came with a Toyota Landcruiser that seemed to run smoothly on a test drive around Bamako.

We set off the next morning. For the whole first day, we rolled north on a narrow asphalt road, stopping at night in the city of Mopti. On the second day the asphalt ended; from there on, it was just sand and gravel. Having driven in Middle Eastern deserts, I noticed that Badra was doing everything wrong: while hitting a patch of sand, for instance, he'd slow down instead of riding it out at full speed. I became highly suspicious of his northern credentials, and so did Sadio.

Low bushes and boulders were scattered in the flat expanse of ochre-tinted nothingness as far as the eye could see. Halfway to Timbuktu, we encountered a broken-down truck by the side. The truck, manufactured in the early colonial era and of indeterminate color, transported several dozen people. Now they all sought refuge from the blistering sun underneath, packed like sardines in the tiny space between wheels. The driver, in a torn shirt soiled by motor oil, tried to tinker with the engine, in what looked to be the unlikely hope of fixing it with strings and coil wire. There was little we could do to help, so we just left behind water and cigarettes and drove off.

Using a map that indicated lakes where I could see only dry riverbeds, we managed to get to the bank of the Niger opposite Timbuktu by early afternoon. Another hour later, we crossed the river on a rusted old ferry and rolled into town, at the feet of the fourteenth-century Great Mosque, a towering structure made of raw mud and retopped with fresh dirt after every rainy season. It was Friday, and the main prayer of the week had just ended. Crowds of men flowed onto the streets from the mosque, a sea of blue-and-white gowns and turbans washing against the light-brown monochrome of the pavement, the buildings, and the desert. The faithful looked at me curiously: now, outside the tourism season, I was probably the only Westerner in town.

✦ ✦ ✦

In its glory days of centuries past, Timbuktu was a hub of international commerce, a Hong Kong of the Sahara. Slaves, ivory, and gold were ferried to its marketplace by Niger boats, to be exchanged for salt, Arab rugs, and Mediterranean goods transported on camelback across the desert. Mali's emperors had turned the city into a center of learning, spreading Islamic knowledge across the region. At the time, the city's Sankore University had little reason to envy rival academies like Zeitouna, in Tunisia, or Qaraween, in Morocco; nevertheless, as Malians like to mention, Sankore is older than the Sorbonne University, in Paris.

The families of Timbuktu still treasure old medieval manuscripts and other relics from that golden age. Almost every household seems to have some, passing the books from generation to generation. It's only in recent years that Mali's authorities started cracking down on antiquity smugglers and preserving the most valuable books. I went to see some of these in the house of Mohammed Alwangari, an Arab-educated collector who has preserved hundreds of manuscripts in a modest mud house that now doubles as a museum.

"It's only after the white people left that the families here started taking the manuscripts from their hiding places. Before that, the locals were afraid that the whites will take their books away," Alwangari explained. "This is the real heritage of Timbuktu." On his table were spread several yellowed, crumbling books, bound in aged leather and written by hand in fading ink. One was a medieval Arab treatise on health, another was a commentary on the Quran. In some cases, the ink had corroded the paper, and the written lines were falling off the brittle pages. I was too afraid to touch them. Alwangari didn't have a copier—and many of these texts only existed here, with no backup.

Timbuktu's glorious era that produced these books began to wane once Portuguese navigators discovered ways of circumventing the Arab monopoly on trade with the African interior. As Portuguese colonial forts dotted tropical African coasts all the way to Mombasa, the slave trade was redirected south and Timbuktu began its inexorable slide into irrelevance. In 1591 a Moroccan expeditionary force led by a renegade Spaniard and staffed by many European mercenaries, who had converted to Islam, seized, and sacked, the town.

As the real Timbuktu declined, its fame ballooned in Europe. The magical city at the end of the world was said to have streets literally paved with gold, and houses full of glittering treasures that inflamed the imaginations of countless adventurers. These legends were easy to peddle because, for centuries, no Christian traveler had actually seen Timbuktu.

In 1826, a British major, Alexander Gordon Laing, was the first Christian to enter Timbuktu, but he didn't live to tell the tale. Tuareg tribesmen murdered him shortly after he left the city, fearing, correctly, that letting one infidel across would encourage others to follow suit. The first explorer to survive his visit, a Frenchman named René Caille, made it to Timbuktu in 1828 by pretending to be a Muslim Egyptian. After a grueling journey that destroyed his health, Caille found himself thoroughly disappointed. Instead of a town of splendor and unfathomable wealth, he wrote, Timbuktu was merely "a mass of ill-looking houses, built of earth."

Having read of Caille's experience, I held my own expectations in check. We settled in the town's only half-decent hotel, and as its only guests, looked out from the roof. Timbuktu, which still perfectly matched the French explorer's description, was sinking in fine Sahara sand. People's living rooms, with straw mats used as beds, were nothing but oversize sandboxes. A thin coat of today's freshly blown sand covered my possessions. The bread, baked with dung fuel in a mud oven outdoors, was made of dough with so much sand inside that it scraped the teeth and gums, making screeching noises as I chewed my breakfast.

In the dry season, it is too hot for the Tuaregs to stay in the desert, so they camp in tents on Timbuktu's edge. Once word spread that a foreigner was in town, Tuareg youngsters swarmed to the hotel, extracting traditional jewelry and daggers from the deep folds of their robes and trying to sell them to me for ten times the going price in Bamako.

"Mister, this is ancient silver."

"Mister, this is really good deal."

"Mister, just look, no need to buy."

"Mister, here, here."

My image of the Tuaregs—the noble "blue men of the desert" lionized by romantic travel writers—was shattered in a second. These were the pushiest hawkers I had encountered in Africa. Sadio tried to defend me with the René Caille approach, telling them I was not a European to be bilked, but an Arab—an Iraqi, she decided. The peddlers had never seen a real Iraqi, and knew enough Arabic to realize that I spoke the language. Confused, they shied away. "Are things still really bad in your country?" one asked me in broken Arabic, concerned. "You bet," I replied. "God willing, it will be better," he said, looking at me with sympathy.

✦ ✦ ✦

On the town's edge, facing sand dunes that roll uninterrupted toward the Mediterranean shore, I saw a fleeting reminder of Timbuktu's glorious past as a caravan crossroads. The town remains an important trading center for one commodity: giant slabs of violet-brown rock salt mined deep in Mali's northern desert. Each camel transports two slabs, and it takes a caravan of dozens several weeks of rough desert marching to get to Timbuktu, from which the salt is distributed across West Africa.

Arab-speaking Moors organize these caravans, and one had just arrived. Wearing sleeveless blue tunics and turbans, the Moors, with goatees and burning eyes, looked as if they had come straight out of a yellowed medieval treatise, or from an Arab television soap opera about the life of Prophet Mohammed. As I looked at these hard men and imagined their life of sand, in which travel time is measured by weeks of monotonous marching and navigation is strictly by the stars, I felt farther from home than ever before. One slab of salt—the fruit of all this sacrifice in the desert—sold for just a couple of dollars.

Timbuktu, of course, wasn't completely bypassed by modern troubles. Algeria's Islamist rebels, who roamed along the salt caravan routes, used the vast north of Mali to hide kidnapped European hostages. Following the release of these hostages, in August 2003, after five months of captivity during which one German woman died, the United States sent Special Forces into Timbuktu to help patrol the desert badlands and train the Malian military. Western governments continued to advise their citizens against travel to the area.

By the time I arrived, the Special Forces had already gone. But the Americans left behind a fleet of expensive SUVs and a bad impression. The locals, I was told again and again, didn't appreciate the perceived disrespect that accompanied the Americans' apparent belief that everything could be purchased with money. (Most things probably could, in fact, be purchased with money here—but only after some appropriately respectful foreplay.)

Despite the travel warnings, I felt unusually serene in the languid maze of Timbuktu. It took me a couple of days to understand the sensation. In Timbuktu, Africa and the Arab world overlapped. The old town's adobe alleyways and Moor market stalls reminded me of the similarly desolate neighborhoods I had seen in Egypt, Yemen, and Iraq. But in those neighborhoods, Westerners weren't usually welcome, and I had become accustomed to staying alert, my skin burning from hostile glares and my eyes and ears attuned to ever-present dangers. After a couple of days in Timbuktu, I realized that, while the cityscape was profoundly familiar, this magnetic field of imminent violence was blessedly absent.

After I went to a couple of rallies in the unfolding election season, I felt even more comfortable. Eleven rival parties were campaigning for twenty-three seats on the Timbuktu municipal council. While elections in Africa are usually marred by violence, and in the Arab world frequently have preordained results, the race in Timbuktu went on without an incident, its outcome in suspense until the day of the vote. In the depths of Africa, the universal rules of democracy seemed to work—producing a political process that was easily recognizable to an American or a European.

✦ ✦ ✦

The first campaign rally I watched was held for Mali's former ruling party, Adema, which had controlled Timbuktu's municipality over the past decade. The ambience was of a village feast, with women in colorful boubous performing a traditional dance and voters sitting on mats spread across a sandy square. The ethnic diversity was striking. There were Songhais in blue gowns, Peul cattlemen in conical leather hats, Tuaregs hiding the only visible portion of their faces behind mirror sunglasses, and Arabs in pristine white robes.

The party's leader, and outgoing mayor, was a thoughtful man by the name of Mohammed Ibrahim Cissé. He belonged to the Bella community, the Tuaregs' former black-skinned slaves who share the Tuaregs' language, Tamashek, and parts of the Tuareg culture. "There are many countries that, with the development of democracy, have broken up or were ravaged by war—and this isn't the case here in Mali," Cissé told me as the rally was about to start. "We have managed to preserve peace and security. We are a poor country that just can't afford the price of conflict, and so we need a consensus—a consensus that, of course, doesn't mean unanimity."

At political rallies across the Middle East, I have been distressed by the ways in which the rhetoric of victimization and conspiracy theory seemed to stir the crowds. Here in Timbuktu, however, Cissé spoke as a hardheaded realist dealing with mature adults. "We can't promise to bring anything to the population from the outside. All we can do is to help the people codevelop with the resources at hand," he told me, and then continued with that message in the public speech.

"We're telling you the truth because we don't want to lower our heads when we meet you tomorrow. We're not promising you the impossible, such as building a highway to Bamako," he bellowed into the microphone. The crowds cheered nevertheless, and then an elderly Tuareg man in a green turban seized the microphone to scream at the top of his lungs: "Vote Adema. Vote for peace."

✦　✦　✦

The next day I sat at the rally of Cissé's main rival, a young NGO organizer by the name of Abdoul Hamid Maiga. Unlike Cissé, the challenger promised plenty: "We'll create many jobs, especially through new information technologies that will put an end to our isolation and establish links between our young people and the rest of the world," he said. Maiga, prematurely introduced to the crowds as "Monsieur le Maire," or "Mr. Mayor," blasted Cissé's record as an unmitigated disaster. As party militants sucked free berry juice and dropped empty plastic pouches all over the floor, a banner across the square urged: "Vote Abdoul Hamid Maiga for a cleaner city." I didn't risk tasting the juice: just that week, several people had died of cholera in Timbuktu, where human waste trickled from houses in open-air canals lining the streets before collecting in fetid puddles.

Teenage girls hired for Maiga's rally swung their hips in suggestive gyrations and crooned in mellifluous, high-pitched voices: "Vote for the party of the most honest." To reward the singing, the women of Timbuktu—in their traditional flowing, colorful dresses—ran up, in the interlude between songs, to stuff cash in the girls' clothes, strip-joint style. This was campaign financing, the Timbuktu way.

Timbuktu—where Christians had been unwelcome for centuries—was supposed to be one of Mali's most profoundly Islamic cities. And yet, I realized after a few days, there were no references to Islam and Islamic causes in the campaign. To understand this paradox, I knocked on the carved Moroccan-style door of Abdramane Ben Essayouti, the imam of Timbuktu's Great Mosque and the head of the region's council of Islamic clerics. Ben Essayouti wore gold-rimmed eyeglasses, and his black face was framed by a snow-white beard from below and a long white turban above. I noticed the pamphlet on his desk, *Leprosy Is Not a Fatality. Leprosy Can Be Cured.*

Like the clerics I met in Bamako, Ben Essayouti was blessing all the candidates but endorsing none. "When you are neutral, you have no fear. I side with no one and will vote for no one," he said. Even his blessings were deliberately ambiguous: "I tell them: if what you're looking for brings you happiness, then let God give it to you. If not, then let God steer you away from what you desire." Sadio asked for a blessing, too. The imam, taken aback, looked at her Charlie Chaplin hat, trying to decide whether she could be Muslim. Then he grabbed her hands, closed his eyes, and muttered a rapid-fire prayer. Another visitor knocked on the door. It was yet another mayoral candidate seeking divine intervention.

✦   ✦   ✦

Going from rally to rally, I discovered that there was even a feminist candidate for mayor to woo the Timbuktu electorate, a schoolteacher of German language named Dembele Aissatou Touré. A plump woman in a purple robe and matching headdress, she ran for a party called CNID. There was an irony in this affiliation: CNID's national leader, Mountaga Tall, was the direct descendant of Haj Omar Tall, a fiery Islamic warrior who carved out his empire in much of Mali in the 1850s and 1860s by declaring wars of jihad first against pagan African tribes and then against the encroaching French colonizers.

Now, instead of jihad, CNID in Timbuktu was preaching the gospel of women's lib. "Women want decisions to be made. It's only the women who know the problems both of the household and of the society," Madame Touré told me in her living room, dominated by pyramids of enameled cooking pots, obviously of non-African origin. "Nobody is suited better than us women. Even the men here want to be ruled by women. When a man here is sick, it's his wife that takes care of him. If children are sick, it's the wife who takes care. If the wife is sick, again, there is no one but her to take care of herself."

At CNID's campaign event—a late-night dance party in the open— two smiling women approached me. They were candidates for the municipal council, hammering home the same message. "We'll take the men's place. We have let the men do what they wanted for too long. We won't be taken in for a ride anymore," one of the women, a schoolteacher by the name of Arby Fraton, yelled into my ear, trying hard to outshout the music. The DJ announced to the crowd the presence of a distinguished guest—me—and I wasn't allowed to leave until I danced with the two candidates. With no choice but to accept, I looked on as a circle of excited teenagers gathered around us, clapping. The dance was a *takamba,* the traditional Tuareg emulation of a camel walk that involved wave-like arm movements: a lambada in slow-mo.

Sweating after one round, I wished all the best to the two women, who tried to have me for a repeat performance, and left, looking at the brilliant starry skies and thinking that this was my first post–September 11 dancing experience in the Muslim world.

Adema, the former ruling party, easily won the municipal elections in Timbuktu, even though it no longer controlled the national government. "This has shown that our people are mature and don't believe in irresponsible promises," Cissé crowed after the peaceful vote.

✦ ✦ ✦

While we were in Timbuktu, the Landcruiser's radiator blew up, and Badra spent a whole day with a mechanic. But as we set out for the return drive to Bamako via the desert, he assured me that the car was in perfect shape.

Now, as we waited for help in the middle of the Sahara, wheels detached from steering, Badra kept silent while betraying a guilty look, pacing around. I stayed inside: the skin on my neck was thoroughly blistered by the sun in the half-hour I had spent making satellite phone calls.

The Malian soldiers kept their word. In the afternoon a truck with three military engineers, men in tattered overalls, appeared on the horizon, visible by a contrail of sand rising into the sky. The soldiers found a few missing pieces on the ground and patched up the Landcruiser with wire, enough to make it to their base, about twenty kilometers away. There, a vat of rice with gravy of indeterminate nature was to be everyone's lunch. It was impolite to refuse, and—weighing the fear of cholera against the likelihood of remaining stuck in the Sahara—I tasted the meal, squeezing the rice into balls and letting the gravy trickle out of my hand and down my arms.

An hour later, the Landcruiser appeared to be fixed. The soldiers, however, were worried; they told me the axle was badly corroded and could give way at any time. As we were about to leave, the base had new visitors: a rescue car dispatched by Timbuktu officials who had received my Paris colleague's voice mail. The rescue car, which we no longer needed, came with a pricey invoice for services rendered. As I haggled, the Timbuktu municipality's Tuareg driver noticed the half-empty can of tinned pork that Sadio had bought in Bamako and that we had opened in the desert. Hungrily he dug in with his fingers, oblivious of Islamic prohibitions, and cleaned it out in a couple of minutes.

Barely outside the base, Badra managed to get stuck in a sand dune, first braking to lose traction and then sinking in by stepping on the gas. Neither he nor the soldiers had a tow chain, so the municipality's car tried to pull us out with a rope, which immediately snapped. Finally, a giant road-building bulldozer was brought in by the soldiers. The monster machine scooped up the back of our Landcruiser, as if it were a toy car, and gently pushed it out of the dune.

If we drove fast, I then calculated, we could make it to the paved road by nightfall. Looking at my GPS, I counted the distance remaining to civilization. With only about forty minutes of driving left, I began fantasizing about the cold bottle of Coke that I would buy at the first village stall—when the car skidded off the road and almost flipped, kicking up dust and throwing me out of the seat, again. Now the left front wheel had completely fallen off. There was no sense in even trying to fix it.

Sadio started laughing hysterically. Badra rolled the wheel and sat on it, motionless, in the glow of headlights. Pitch-black darkness had enveloped the desert, and I remembered the travel warnings about Tuareg raiders and bandits. "Do you feel safe?" Sadio asked me, shuddering at the animal sounds in the blackness around us. "No, not really," I answered.

Then I recalled that I had a *Lonely Planet* guide in my backpack, with a phone number for a hostel in Douentza, the nearest town. Miraculously, the satellite phone connected this time and Sadio managed to talk to the hostel's owner, who promised to send his brother with a car for the rescue.

The wait wasn't long. In the desert at night, a vehicle approaching from far away is first visible as an almost imperceptible glow on the horizon, then as a dot of light, and then, finally, as a pair of headlights. A young barefoot driver in another Landcruiser, which lacked air-conditioning or seat belts but did have all four wheels, helped us transfer the bags and slabs of salt. Abandoning the broken car in the desert, we headed to Douentza.

The town lies in the part of Mali populated by the Dogon, a fiercely animist people who sought refuge from Islam on the rocky escarpment and who worship traditional deities. We left Badra in Douentza, to deal with the car, and hired our barefoot rescuer, a Dogon, for the rest of the way. The next morning we stopped by a Dogon holy lake inhabited by magical crocodiles that, according to local belief, transform themselves into villagers by night. Supposedly, the crocodiles never attack local people and their livestock—indeed, goats pastured undisturbed just a few feet from the water. These crocodiles live off ritual offerings. We were urged to make one to appease the gods of automobile circulation, who had given us so much trouble.

Two potentially lethal accidents in the past twenty-four hours seemed too much, so I handed the guardian a 1,000-CFA-franc note, about $2. He promptly brought, to the lake's shore, a black-feathered rooster, tethering it to a stick by the water. The cock, which screamed and convulsed while in the man's hands, smelled the crocodiles' presence and suddenly went limp. The crocodiles sensed the bird, too, and raised their heads to the muddy surface. Nothing happened for minutes. Then the guardian threw a rock at the cock, making it move. In an instant, several crocodiles pounced at the bird, dragging it underwater and fighting each other for the meat. The lake's surface seemed to boil. I felt sick watching this. But the automobile gods appeared appeased: after that, our new Landcruiser worked without a hitch.

Halfway to Bamako we stopped for dinner at the house of Sadio's aunt, in the town of Segou. The aunt was a pious Muslim, who wore a black veil. But like most Malians, Sadio explained, she combined Islamic faith with traditional pagan beliefs. As I gobbled down her rice, topped by a fermented fish sauce, I recounted the tale of our rooster sacrifice. The aunt seemed to know what we were talking about. Sitting down, she started quizzing me with the precision of a connoisseur. "Was the cock black?" was her first question.

✦ ✦ ✦

After our return to Bamako, and with the elections pronounced a success, Sadio took me around to meet Mali's national politicians.

As I queried them about Mali's exceptional status as a free country
in the Islamic universe, these politicians repeated one mantra: Mali
was democratic because it was secular, and because, unlike most of the
Third World, it had a millennial history of statehood. The local tradition of consensus and tolerance had deeper roots than Islam. In short,
this Muslim country was a democracy because Islam had been kept
out of politics.

The nation's president and former coup organizer, Amadou
Toumani Touré, met me and Sadio in his hilltop palace a few hours
before my departure from Mali. He wore a Western suit and sat under
a large official portrait of himself in a traditional robe. He began to
chuckle once Sadio, who used the familiar *tu* instead of the respectful
vous, handed over a photograph of her bull as a way of boasting about
the good care the presidential gift was receiving.

The president stopped smiling once I started quizzing him. According to official statistics, Muslims make up at least 90 percent of Mali's
population. But Touré was surprised, and seemed displeased, that I
had phrased the question as one about Mali, an Islamic country.

"We never looked at the problem from this angle," he told me. "If
you look at our constitution, this is a secular state. It is clear. The state
never enmeshed itself with the affairs of religion, and that's what
allowed us to have a stable and peaceful country.

"We see nothing in our religion that's against democracy," he went
on. "It wouldn't even come to a Malian's mind to think that there is a
contradiction."

14

BOSNIA

All These Books,
I Got Them from the Arabs

Nermin Karačić didn't always have a large, shaggy beard. And the place where I met him wasn't always a mosque.

In the frosty winter of 2002, dirty snow blanketed Sarajevo's streets and hung from trees in small puffs, like cotton. The forlorn housing blocks around us looked identical to Communist-era developments, from Warsaw to Siberia. Except, that is, for the shrapnel and bullet marks that scooped out the concrete in tattoo-like zigzags that now distinguished every crippled building from its former twins nearby.

These were the scars of Europe's most vicious war since 1945, a conflict in which the predominantly Muslim Sarajevo was subjected to daily barrages by largely Christian, ethnic Serb forces. Back then, the Serbs liked to fashion themselves as defenders of Christendom against the rising threat of Islam. The Muslims said they were fighting for a tolerant, multiethnic, united Bosnia-Herzegovina.

The new mosque was a sign of life after the war. Gold letters above the gateway proclaimed that it was named after the Saudi king, Fahd bin Abdelaziz. Saudi money paid for this soul-less concrete-and-glass structure, smack in the middle of Sarajevo's Dobrinja neighborhood. The mosque's courtyard teemed with men in white, Arab-style gowns,

SLOVENIA

HUNGARY

CROATIA

ROMANIA

REPUBLIKA SRPSKA

● Banja Luka

● Bocinja

**BOSNIA-
HERZEGOVINA**

★ Belgrade

SERBIA

Srebrenica ●

*FEDERATION
OF BOSNIA-
HERZEGOVINA*   ★
              Sarajevo

Mostar ●

MONTENEGRO

Prishtina ●

KOSOVO
(Administered by
the United Nations)

BULGARIA

Adriatic Sea

MACEDONIA

ITALY

ALBANIA

GREECE

N

THE WESTERN BALKANS

Miles 0   100

Kilometers 0   100

cut short in *salafi* fashion. Veiled women who flocked to the area sometimes went as far as donning black burka-like attire that left not an inch of skin exposed. Walls nearby were daubed with the fading logos of Persian Gulf charities that demanded Islamic dress as a condition of aid.

Bosnia's Muslims, who make up about half of this country's population, these days prefer the more neutral term Bosniaks—not to be confused with Bosnians, a name that includes all of Bosnia's citizens. Under Yugoslavia's Communist rulers, Bosnia had one of the world's most secular Muslim communities. Intermarriage with Christian Croats and Serbs was commonplace, veils almost unheard of. Then the leaders of Bosnia's Serbs, drunk on nationalist delusions and abetted by Slobodan Milošević's regime in Belgrade, attempted a genocide of the Muslims in 1992–1995. As the West did precious little to stop the carnage, jihadis from the world over flocked to help the Muslim defense. Some 200,000 deaths later, it wasn't all that surprising that young Bosniak men like Nermin Karačić decided to grow a beard and turn to Islam—switching from atheism to a firebrand faith learned among these mujahedeen.

"Look at the world—Afghanistan, Chechnya, Palestine, Bosnia, Kashmir, the Philippines. In every place that has a war, the war is against Muslims," Karačić mused as we sat in the cemented courtyard of the King Fahd mosque, shuddering from the cold. "Why? I can't talk about other places, but I can certainly talk about Bosnia. Before the war, we were all living together in the neighborhood, and my friends were Serbs, Croats. Then, one day, they all started shooting bullets at me—just because I'm a Muslim."

Karačić stared at me. "I couldn't understand it at first," he shook his head. "Then I thought—well, if they want to kill me just because I'm a Muslim, then I should start behaving like one."

A Bosnian Army special forces soldier during the war, Karačić was impressed by the Arab jihadis he had seen in battle. Now he followed *salafi* rites and headed a fundamentalist youth organization named Furkan. In the months after September 11, the United States and the fragile Bosnian government began to take notice of such radical groups, fearing that the Balkans were becoming a springboard for international terrorism. Arab charities were shut down, many Arab expatriates expelled, and authorities started investigating Furkan's books for financial links with terrorist groups.

Karačić agreed to meet me because he was eager to explain that Furkan wasn't violent. "Muslims look at America as an enemy of Islam," he told me, in between taking Arabic-language calls on his sleek cell phone. "But what's the way to fight America? Killing surely isn't. The goal is not to kill the American people," he grinned.

I had come to now-peaceful Sarajevo between trips to Saudi Arabia and the Gulf—just as Danny Pearl went missing in Pakistan—and I noticed myself growing apprehensive as I listened to Karačić's vision of the world. The September 11 attacks, he expounded, must have been the work of a ghastly Jewish conspiracy. Muslims just couldn't do something like that. Osama Bin Laden must be innocent, too, Karačić thought—and the war in Afghanistan, as a natural consequence, was an unforgivable aggression.

At the time, Bosnia's investigation found Furkan's books in order. In May 2004, the U.S. Treasury and the European Commission designated Karačić's organization a Qaeda affiliate, noting that some members had engaged in "multiple instances of suspicious activity," including the surveillance of the American embassy and the UN headquarters in Sarajevo.

I had listened to hours and hours of similar rants in Jeddah, Cairo, and Kuwait, places where opinions like Karačić's were commonplace. But it was especially unsettling to hear them parroted here, in the middle of Europe, by blue-eyed, blond natives who grew up drinking beer and eating pork chops.

✦ ✦ ✦

Postwar Bosnia, of course, is no Saudi Arabia. Walking the streets of downtown Sarajevo, you're likely to see at least ten miniskirts for every veil, and pictures of naked women on the back pages of newspapers. Sidewalk cafés are protected from the sun by umbrellas that advertise Heineken and the locally brewed Sarajevsko Pivo. Beach holidays in secular Tunisia, the rare country that allowed Bosnian citizens to enter without a visa, are all the rage.

But it is also a land where Islamic radicalism has taken root—embraced by a small minority that is, nonetheless, potentially dangerous. It's enough to give a close look at the bookstalls along the city's main pedestrian mall, a bustling street that begins with fin de siècle Hapsburg edifices, one of them occupied by the new Iranian cultural center, and that ends in the cobblestone Ottoman quarter of mosques. What the bearded vendors offer here isn't quite the kind of popular literature you'd find on the sidewalks of another European capital. There is usually a Bosniak edition of the writings of Ibn Taymiya, the fourteenth-century Iraqi cleric who is widely seen as the precursor of modern jihadi ideology. There are works by Hassan al Banna, the founder of the Muslim Brotherhood in Egypt, and by modern Islamist ideologues like Al Jazeera telepreacher Yousuf Qaradawi. There are Saudi-sponsored books that promote Wahhabi mores, and videodiscs that glorify jihad, from Chechnya to Palestine. And in the most prominent spots, there are volumes of writings by the man who led Bosnia's own Muslims into war, the late president Alija Izetbegović.

One of these works, a 1970 treatise called *The Islamic Declaration*, landed Izetbegović in a Yugoslav Communist jail in the 1980s, on charges of inciting ethnic violence. In 1990, as Izetbegović was elected Bosnia's president, the book was republished. And once Bosnia's real violence began, following a referendum of independence organized by Izetbegović in 1992, this book was often held up by the Serbs as an excuse for raining mortars and shells on besieged Sarajevo.

✦ ✦ ✦

In the 1990s, of course, Izetbegović and his Party of Democratic Action no longer pressed for an Islamist utopia; instead, he campaigned as a secular democrat, pledging to lead a multiethnic, tolerant Bosnia, in which all the religions would be respected. But the damage was done.

As Serb TV and newspapers incessantly reminded, Izetbegović's book drew from the Muslim Brotherhood and modern *salafi* thought, calling for a ban on dance halls and savaging Ataturk's secular reforms in Turkey. An oft-quoted passage from the book stipulates that "there can be neither peace nor coexistence between the Islamic religion and the non-Islamic social and political institutions" in a land with a Muslim majority. Muslims' political future, the book says, lies in a "great Islamic federation stretching from Morocco to Indonesia, from tropical Africa to Central Asia"—not exactly a land in which the Serbs, one-third of Bosnia's population at the time and a relative majority until the mid-1960s, wished to end up.

The radicalism of *The Islamic Declaration,* while shared by few Bosnian Muslims at the time, was deftly exploited by Serb nationalist demagogues like the Sarajevo psychiatrist Radovan Karadžić and President Milošević in Belgrade, both wedded to the dream of Greater Serbia that would incorporate much of Bosnia and large parts of Croatia. In the post-Communist confusion, many Bosnian Serbs, raised on bitter memories of Ottoman rule, which lasted until 1878, believed Karadžić's warnings that an independent Bosnia would reduce non-Muslims to second-class status, again. Amid the psychosis, Serb militias, seeking to capture as much of Bosnia as possible, slaughtered thousands upon thousands of Muslim civilians. The victims included much of the male population of the UN-protected Muslim "safe haven" of Srebrenica, gunned down in 1995 by Serbs, just as, in the words of Bosnia's top Muslim cleric, "Dutch soldiers who happened to be Christian" refused to fire a shot to protect their charges. Throughout the war, the Bosnian government, headed by Izetbegović, was subjected to a crippling UN arms embargo—while the Serbs enjoyed free access to the vast depots of the Yugoslav army.

After Srebrenica, the United States launched belated air strikes against Bosnian Serb positions. Later, peace talks sponsored by President Clinton in Dayton, Ohio, in December 1995, awarded 49 percent of Bosnia to a Serb entity, Republika Srpska, where Izetbegović held no power and from which almost all Muslims had been expelled. Even in the remainder of Bosnia, the Muslims were left without a statelet of their own. Instead, they were grouped with the Croats to create a decentralized, secular Federation of Bosnia-Herzegovina, an entity in which the president's job rotates yearly between a Muslim and a Catholic Croat. Above all, the Dayton arrangements gave indefinite, supreme authority, in both Republika Srpska and Bosnia-Herzegovina, to a Western proconsul, who can fire any official, amend the constitution, and promulgate any law. Even the new, post-Dayton, Bosnian flag, the ultimate symbol of sovereignty, was designed by a foreign bureaucrat after Muslims, Croats, and Serbs failed to agree on a common version.

Trying to woo public opinion in the Islamic world and to prove that the United States isn't hostile to Islam, American diplomats often cite Bosnia's peace as an example of America's intervention on behalf of Muslim causes. A senior Turkish diplomat, miffed by Izetbegović's criticism of Ataturk and Turkey's secularist reforms, saw things differently as we shared a high-calorie Balkan version of Turkish dolma in a Sarajevo restaurant in 2002. Dayton's chief virtue, the diplomat told me appreciatively, was that the agreement derailed a project to establish Europe's first Islamic republic. Of course, in the eyes of Islamists worldwide, and Bosniaks like Karačić, this was one of Dayton's, and by extension America's, chief flaws.

✦　✦　✦

In the years after Dayton, the West's attention remained focused on Bosnia's Serbs, unrepentant about the bloodshed they had caused and unwilling to cooperate in the return of Muslim refugees and the prosecution of war criminals. With America going to war against Serbia over the treatment of Kosovo Albanians in 1999, few people cared about what Muslim charities were doing on the friendly, supposedly pro-Western Muslim side of Bosnia.

The Dayton accords required the departure of all foreign fighters, including the thousands of mostly Arab mujahedeen, grouped in the special El Mudžahid brigade of the Muslim-led Army of Bosnia-Herzegovina. But Izetbegović, while still in charge of the entire Bosnian state apparatus, circumvented Dayton's repatriation requirement by granting Bosnian citizenship to the mujahedeen. In the following years, most of them ended up leaving Bosnia for the still-active fronts of global holy war: Chechnya, Kashmir, Algeria, and, inevitably, Taliban-ruled Afghanistan. According to the final report of the 9/11 Commission, two of the hijackers who crashed Flight 77 into the Pentagon, Nawaf al Hazmi and Khalid al Mihdhar, fought alongside the Bosnian Army in 1995. So, too, did the future chief of Qaeda's military operations, Khalid Sheikh Mohammed.

Unlike these men, hundreds of other mujahedeen decided to stay put after the peace accords, often marrying Bosnian women and taking jobs in Saudi- and Gulf-sponsored foundations that poured hundreds of millions of dollars into mosque construction, religious education, and other Islamic projects.

In an informal division of labor over the following years, "the Europeans and Americans were rebuilding houses, and the Saudis were rebuilding mosques," Wolfgang Petritsch, an Austrian diplomat who served as Bosnia's chief international administrator at the time, told me. "And any outside assistance transfers values. They did a disservice to this country and its culture by promoting the Wahhabi style."

Rebuilding in Bosnia, the Saudi way, turned out to be more like destruction. The austere Wahhabi ideology holds frescoes and paintings to be un-Islamic, and considers elaborate gravestones and Sufi *tekke,* prayer lodges, a common sight in the courtyards of Bosnian mosques, to be miscreant abominations. Saudi-financed rebuilding of mosques damaged in the war usually consisted of bulldozing the cemeteries and the *tekkes*—many dating back to the Middle Ages—and refashioning the ancient mosques in a graceless Saudi style. Even Sarajevo's Begova Džamija, the jewel of Balkan architecture, built in the sixteenth century and once famed as the largest European mosque west of Istanbul, wasn't spared by Saudi "aid." The mosque's rich murals and shining Ottoman-era tileworks, not always respectful of rigorous Islam's prohibition on depicting living creatures, testified to Sarajevo's long history as a crossroads of cultures. A few weeks after Saudi-funded renovation began, the tiles were scraped off, the ornaments stripped bare, and the walls covered with white plaster. It was as if someone decided to renovate the Sistine Chapel by giving Michelangelo's frescoes a coat of hospital-white paint.

The Islamist charities didn't just transform buildings. The Saudi-funded proselytizing machine also brought young Bosnians to study in Saudi universities, converted them to the Wahhabi creed, and financed radical organizations such as Furkan and the Active Muslim Youth. The old Bosnian Islamic establishment was aghast at the changes, especially after some of these Wahhabi activists physically assaulted

Sarajevo's mufti, disagreeing with his decision to replace an imam in one of the mosques.

"This Wahhabism, these long beards and short pants, it's all so different from what we Bosnians practice here," fumed Jusuf Ramić, the Egyptian-trained dean of Sarajevo's Islamic Studies Faculty, the main Muslim religious academy in the country. "These young people know nothing about Islam. All they have is superficial learning. Can you imagine? We spent our entire lives here practicing Islam, and now some guys come over from abroad and tell us that everything we have been doing is wrong!"

A clean-shaven man wearing a tie and a dark suit, Ramić met me in early 2002 in his elegant, Western-style office at the academy's shaded headquarters. His mouth widened in a bitter smile as he recounted a recent trip to Saudi Arabia, where he lunched with Bosnian students learning Islam in the kingdom. "There were forks and knives on the table," he said. "So I started eating, as we all do in Europe, with a fork in the left hand and the knife in the right. You can't imagine what outcry it all caused, with all these people accusing me of being un-Islamic!" Ramić didn't think of it much, but puritan Islam—which considers toilet paper an infidel innovation—mandates the use of the left hand for washing up after bodily functions and deems only the right hand sufficiently pure to handle food. By holding his fork in the left hand, Ramić violated a taboo that had long been forgotten by Bosnians.

"Maybe all this can pass in the Middle East, but here in Europe it is just too weird. Bosnia is a multireligious place, and these people are a thorn in the eye, causing damage to the image of all the Muslims who live here." He shook his head, sadly.

✦ ✦ ✦

Official tolerance for Wahhabi proselytizers ended soon after September 11. Once Bosnian passports were found on Afghan battlefields and intelligence agencies realized the crucial role that the Bosnian war had played in creating and sustaining global jihad, NATO forces in Bosnia sprang into action. They raided scores of Arab charities, finding what the United States said was evidence of impending terrorist plots, and took several Arab employees into custody.

A few weeks before my arrival, six of these detained Arabs—Algerian natives who, except for one, had adopted Bosnian citizenship—were brought before a Bosnian criminal court. The United States, citing confidential evidence, accused them of conspiring to attack the American embassy in Sarajevo and of communicating with a senior Qaeda planner, Abu Zubayda. One piece of evidence was the fact that Abu Zubayda's satellite phone number was allegedly stored in the cellphone memory of one of the detainees. Although only one of the six Algerians was a Bosnian war veteran, almost all of them had been employed at charities that were now designated as Qaeda fronts.

The crackdown suffered a rapid setback: Bosnian judges refused to take action without evidence, and the United States was unwilling to compromise intelligence sources. The Bosnian Human Rights Chamber, a state organ whose decisions are mandatory under the Dayton accords, ruled that the six Algerians should not be extradited from Bosnia until all legal avenues were exhausted. But Washington, whose peacekeeping troops still patrolled Bosnian streets and whose support for Bosnia's reconstruction was indispensable, became increasingly impatient. Desperate to please the United States and to dispel Bosnia's image as a terrorist haven, the Bosnian government took a risky step: it ignored the ruling of the Human Rights Chamber and handed over the six to FBI agents. Within hours, the Algerians were en route to Guantánamo Bay. President Bush hailed the Bosnian cooperation in the State of the Union address, in early 2002.

"Bosnia's statehood would have ended" and Bosnia would have been "treated like Afghanistan" if it had refused to comply with U.S. demands, argued Zlatko Lagumdžija, the Bosnian prime minister at the time. A Social Democrat, Lagumdžija headed a shaky coalition of nonnationalist parties that, for the first time since the war, had wrested government control away from Izetbegović's Party of Democratic Action and the monoethnic parties of Bosnian Croats and Serbs.

The Algerian extradition decision caused such a fury that one of Bosnia's main newsmagazines, usually unsympathetic to the Islamists, ran a cover that showed Uncle Sam urinating on the Bosnian constitution. Secular human rights groups condemned the deportation as violating basic rules of democracy. In part because of the controversy, nine months later the Party of Democratic Action was voted back into power, Lagumdžija was out of a job, and the nonnationalist coalition was in tatters.

By then, Izetbegović, weakened by an illness that would cause his death in 2003, was already on the margins of politics. His job as the Muslim member of the three-person Bosnian presidency and the chairman of the Party of Democratic Action was taken by Sulejman Tihić. A relative moderate seeking to dispel the party's Islamist aura, Tihić famously said that he also sought "the beer-drinkers'" votes. Yet he exploited to the hilt public fury over compliance with U.S. demands. "Our public feels a bitter taste," Tihić told me about the Algerians' extradition. "There is a certain anger among the Bosnian Muslims— not at the U.S. but against our own authorities. We cannot accept that people are being disturbed or arrested just because they are Muslims."

The 9/11 Commission had not yet revealed the direct link between wartime mujahedeen sponsored by Izetbegović and the September 11 perpetrators; Tihić insisted that Western security fears about these fighters—a touchy subject for his party—were downright exaggerated. "It's nothing but propaganda—propaganda that's now exploited by Croat and Serb politicians who were fighting Bosnia," he assured me. "It's a very small number. We didn't invite the mujahedeen to come here. We had enough people to fight. What we needed was the weapons. These people's influence on Bosnian Islam is not significant at all."

Instead of shutting down Muslim charities, Tihić suggested, the NATO-led Stabilization Force (SFOR) should be hunting for Karadžić and the wartime military commander of the Bosnian Serbs, General Ratko Mladić. Both were indicted by the international war-crimes tribunal in the Hague, where Milošević already sat in the dock, and both remained uncaptured. "It's popular to speak about Muslim terrorists nowadays and not to mention the others," Tihić complained. "But we have been fighting terrorism here for ten years. And the biggest terrorists, Karadžić and Mladić, are still free even though we have tens of thousands of SFOR troops in the country."

Bosnia's radical young Islamists, sensing this kind of tacit support from parts of the establishment, went beyond words to back the

Algerian suspects. Spurred by the country's new Islamist radio station, Radio Naba, the militants clashed with the police and tried to block the path of the vehicles that were transferring Algerian detainees to American custody. Arab TV broadcast images of the protesters lying in the snow and bleeding after truncheon blows from the police. "On that day I was ready to die for the name of Allah," one of the protesters, a starry-eyed university student named Ali Ihsan, told me with a sweet smile.

✦ ✦ ✦

I met Ihsan at the offices of the Young Muslims, Bosnia's oldest Islamist organization, which was formed under the influence of the Muslim Brotherhood in 1941 and which Izetbegović had joined in his youth. The Young Muslims occupied the inner courtyard terrace of an Ottoman-era compound in Sarajevo's cobblestoned old quarter, above souvenir shops full of Turkish-style carpets and copperware. The walls were lined with posters calling for solidarity with Islamic causes around the world: Kashmir, Palestine, Iraq.

On that trip to Sarajevo, my fixer was a young woman, Jasmina, who was born to a Muslim father and a Catholic mother. Only after Serb and Croat classmates—in the runup to the war—started teasing Jasmina for her Muslim surname did she ask her nonreligious parents about her faith. The parents now lived apart, with Jasmina's father working in Saudi Arabia. A new mosque stood by her Sarajevo apartment, and a new Catholic church by her beach house on the Croatian coast. In neither place, Jasmina joked, was she able to sleep—because of the muezzin's predawn call to prayer and the church's early-morning bell-ringing.

Ihsan, Jasmina's college friend, had been just as secular before the war. Now she called herself by a newly adopted Arabic name and donned a black *abaya* and a bright-red veil—the new fashion among the hip and politically active in downtown Sarajevo.

Jasmina set up a series of appointments for me in Sarajevo's elegant coffee shops, where I queried young Islamists over Bosnian *kahva,* a variant of Turkish coffee, and honey-soaked sweets that sometimes retained Arabic names. One of the more outspoken activists was a twenty-two-year-old named Faruk Višća. He ran the IslamBosna.com

Web site, where wired Bosnian Islamists exchanged acerbic commentary about the sufferings of the *ummah*—in posts occasionally graced by portraits of Bin Laden, or of the Arab emir of the Chechen jihadis, Abu Khattab. Višća, too, protested against the extradition of Algerian detainees. Earlier he had been detained for putting up posters that questioned Bosnia's decision to hold a minute of silence for the victims of September 11 but not for Muslims dying in conflicts elsewhere. American agents, he said, helped interrogate him while in detention.

"It's horrible that American lives are considered much more worthy than the lives of others. A victim is a victim," Višća said. "And the American government is the enemy of Islam and Muslims all around the world."

But, I interrupted him, what about Bosnia? Didn't the American air strikes help Bosnian Muslims launch a successful offensive in late 1995, regaining lost land and frightening the Bosnian Serbs so much that they signed on to President Clinton's peace deal at Dayton?

And what about Kosovo, another predominantly Muslim part of former Yugoslavia? After all, the streets of Belgrade these days are still splattered with graffiti such as *Columbus, You Curious Motherfucker*—a reaction to the 1999 American bombing of Serbia that convinced Milošević to withdraw troops from Kosovo and to let it become a UN-supervised international protectorate.

Such quick intervention ensured that the Kosovars, unlike the Bosnians and the once secular Chechen guerrillas still battling for independence from Russia, didn't have to turn to help from the global network of Islamist mujahedeen, and retained strong pro-American sympathies.

Kosovo's Prishtina, alone among Muslim capitals, even named its main thoroughfare after a recent U.S. president: a gigantic likeness of the forty-second president of the United States smiles and waves a hand, with stars and stripes in the background, above the traffic on Bill Clinton Boulevard—the central road formerly known as Vladimir Lenin Street. The name of Madeleine Albright, Clinton's secretary of state during the 1999 war, graces a Prishtina high school.

Višća dismissed my argument with a chuckle: "If it is in America's interest, America may help Muslims sometimes, somewhere. If not, not." Bosnia, he argued like many Islamists, didn't fall in this category: "The West, under American leadership, tied our hands with the arms embargo, while the others had all the weapons they needed. For four years we were slaughtered and the Americans did nothing. Then, the minute the Americans saw that we are winning the war, they said: stop."

As he understood it, the U.S. intervention prevented Bosnia's Muslims from completely driving out the Serbs—something, he noted enviously, Catholic Croatia managed to do with a parallel offensive, at the same time, that routed centuries-old Serb communities.

The coarse grains of *kahva* stuck to my lips as thick cigarette smoke engulfed the coffee shop. Višća turned to the future. "America is maybe on the top of the world right now, but it is certainly not for long. Islam is God's way—and it will dominate the entire world, in Sarajevo just as in Washington, D.C." How did he propose to make this happen? I inquired. Višća said he believed that people in some parts of the Muslim world must take up arms for the cause. "In different countries, there are different tactics," he said. "But in Bosnia, violence is not the solution, now."

Višća was too young to have fought in the war, and so Jasmina took me to see an older neighbor of hers who had also demonstrated on behalf of deported Algerians. We walked to Ahmet Alibašić's cramped apartment across the small bridge where Austro-Hungary's Archduke Franz Ferdinand was killed by a Serb assassin in June 1914—the event that unleashed the First World War and, with it, from the Islamic standpoint, the most tragic outcome: the collapse of the Ottoman state and the fall of almost the entire Muslim *ummah* under colonial rule.

Alibašić's bookshelves were packed with Islamic literature. Mujahedeen fighting for Bosnia had made him see the light, he said. "All these books, I got them from the Arabs." He pointed to the shelves as his fully veiled wife brought us cookies. "The primary goal of all the Arabs here was first to teach us religion, then help with the war."

A former fighter with the Bosnian police special forces, Alibašić met his first jihadi on the frontlines. He grew dreamy recounting the details. "There was this guy coming to us, with a black bandana and a beard down to the stomach," he recalled. "God, he was scary. I was glad we were not on opposing sides." Then, in the summer of 1995 came the battle for the hamlet of Greda, on the strategic Vozuča elevation in north-central Bosnia. The capture of the highland by Muslim forces reversed the course of the war. Alibašić fought there alongside the Arab-staffed El Mudžahid brigade.

"The preparation among us, in the Army of Bosnia-Herzegovina, was normal: planning, reconnaissance, this kind of thing. But the Arab mujahedeen were just reading the Quran and cleaning their weapons all night, nothing else," Alibašić said. "In the morning, they went off to fight, with their commander going in first and their cameraman going in last, to film it all. They knew they could only capture the hill with lots of casualties, but they went ahead, and captured the hill." A cameraman, I noticed, was an indispensable part of jihad—in Bosnia, Lebanon, or Iraq.

Now, in 2002, Alibašić was still awed by those jihadis' idealism. "They were honest. I think none of these guys ever lied, not even on a small thing."

✦ ✦ ✦

Clearly, many Bosniaks shared Alibašić's emotional reminiscences about the jihadis. While not necessarily approving of the mujahedeen's Islamist ideology and religious ways, people here didn't forget that the Arabs were the only ones coming to fight on their side at a time when the West professed a neutrality that, objectively, helped the Serb genocide. To see more, I traveled to the Vozuča area myself.

Not far from the site of Alibašić's battle nestled the formerly Serb village of Bočinja, which, under the Dayton accords, was allotted to the Muslim-Croat part of Bosnia. After the offensive of 1995, the Serbs fled from their homes while the Arab and Bosniak soldiers of El Mudžahid, in an effort to Islamize the country, one village at a time, promptly established a rigorously Muslim community. The Bočinja mujahedeen tried to impose their version of Islam on nearby Maglaj, at gunpoint sometimes, and often prevented Western peacekeepers from entering the enclave.

In the late 1990s, Bosnia's international administrators pushed for a return of the refugees, and persistent Western scrutiny made many of these former mujahedeen uncomfortable in Bočinja. Some, however, managed to buy homes from the Serbs and were determined to stay on, even as the influx of returning refugees slowly gave the village a Christian majority.

As we drove to Bočinja through snow-covered mountains, I took in the sheer beauty of Bosnia, a land of clear rivers, Alpine meadows, and pristine forests that would be perfect hiking country if not for the omnipresent land mines. Marking the religious patchwork, tall minarets pierced the skies, and were matched by crosses atop the unusually tall bell towers in the Croat villages' Catholic churches. The final stretch of road to Bočinja ran in a quiet valley, alongside the slumbering Bosna River. The recent history of the area was obvious from graffiti on road signs. DŽIHAD, someone had written, in a Bosniak transliteration of *jihad*. MUDŽAHIDINIA—the land of the mujahedeen—was scribbled on another sign.

The mujahedeen themselves weren't numerous anymore, and, upon arrival, the place seemed anticlimactic. Of the 150 or so Muslim families inhabiting Bočinja in its jihadi glory days, only 7 remained in the village, all of them Bosnian natives converted to the *salafi* creed. Once the Serb refugees started returning in previous months, most mujahedeen had to leave. The few Arabs still here fled after September 11, fearing arrest and extradition to Guantánamo Bay.

The Muslim men who stayed behind were spending their days in a car repair workshop along the main road, where we rolled in just before prayer time. Hurrying into a makeshift mosque, the hosts sized me up and told me to return half an hour later. As powerful loudspeakers boomed "Allahu Akbar" across the valley, I glanced at the garbage that was heaped in a ditch nearby. The plastic bags bore the logos of the Haramain Foundation, a Saudi charity whose Bosnian branch had just been shut down for links with Qaeda.

Waiting for the prayers to finish, I talked to the Serb returnees. The house of one, seventy-one-year-old farmer Boško Jovanović, stood just across the road. "When these people came here, they expelled us. Now they've opened a mosque, they try to tell us what to do, they wake us up with their prayers five times a day!" Jovanović unleashed a torrent of complaints. A clash had occurred after Serb villagers barbecued a pig at a mourning ceremony for a local woman who had drowned. The mujahedeen, taking offense at the roasting, threw the pig into the Bosna River.

"These people should leave. They don't belong here. They are foreign here," Jovanović insisted. I pointed out that the Arabs had already departed and that all the remaining Muslims in Bočinja were native Bosnians. Jovanović peered outside his fence, watching his bearded neighbors emerge from the mosque, and grimaced. "Yes, the Arabs are gone from here," he said. "But they've left their seeds behind."

Five minutes later, the prayers ended and I recrossed the road, marveling at how this narrow stretch of asphalt had crystallized into such a palpable divide between the Christian and Muslim universes. The leader of Bočinja's Muslims was a bear-like beekeeper named Semin Rizvić, who had served as a lieutenant in the El Mudžahid brigade. Like many Bosnian Islamists, possessed with the enthusiasm of neophytes, Rizvić himself discovered Islam during the war, as a prisoner in a concentration camp.

"I was a child of the Communist system. And through the school, and the Yugoslav Army, I trusted the people with whom I was living," he recalled, echoing Karačić, the Furkan leader I had met at Sarajevo's King Fahd mosque. "With the war, all these rules were suddenly broken."

Rizvić's family, secular like most Bosniak households, lived in Novi Travnik, a predominantly Croat satellite of the mostly Muslim city of Travnik. In 1993, as fighting broke out between Croat and Muslim forces in the area, Rizvić, along with many other Muslim men of Novi Travnik, was interned by the Croat militia in a former Yugoslav Army jet-fuel depot. Accused of being a sniper, he shared a makeshift prison in an underground storage area with scores of fellow detainees.

"I thought I would be killed, and I started to think about what will happen once I die," Rizvić recalled. "I was lucky because I had a good example before my eyes. There was a Muslim prisoner in the camp who always prayed at prayer times even though the Croats beat him for that. He wasn't afraid like the rest of us. I saw that he had strength, and that the others didn't."

Twelve days later, a truce was arranged between the Croats and the

Muslims in Travnik, and Rizvić was released. He was already hooked on Islam: he stopped drinking and swearing and left his drug-infested neighborhood. Once the El Mudžahid brigade arrived in the area, Rizvić volunteered to join it. "The Arabs proved their faith by paying with their lives. They are the ones who taught us what Islam should really look like," he told me, his eyes misting up. "In action, Bosnian Army commanders would stay behind us—but among the mujahedeen, the commanders were first, and they weren't afraid of dying. In fact, they yearned to become martyrs themselves."

Now, Rizvić said ruefully, the Bosnian government betrayed the country's most faithful friends. "I never dreamed something like this could happen. These people came here and sacrificed to help this country, and now we're just throwing them out!" Not surprisingly for a former jihadi, Rizvić saw a devious Jewish hand everywhere: "The Jews caused this problem because they are afraid of Islam." To make the same point, posters put up in Sarajevo to protest the Algerian deportations featured a photograph of Prime Minister Lagumdžija, a Muslim, wearing a Jewish skullcap during a visit to the Western Wall in Jerusalem.

✦   ✦   ✦

On the way back from Bočinja, Jasmina was tense. Like many Bosniaks, she was suspicious of the motives of foreigners who brought attention to her community's Islamist fringe. For years during the war, the threat of Islamic fundamentalism was used as an alibi by the Serb genocide perpetrators. After September 11, the West, too, suddenly focused on extremism among Muslims—paying little attention to the probably stronger extremist currents among Catholic Croats and Orthodox Serbs.

I tried to explain to Jasmina that the West was acting out of natural self-interest. The Serb and Croat extremist fringes were, by and large, contained in the region. The jihadi sympathizers in Bosnia, by contrast, had tight ideological, and personal, connections with the people actually killing Westerners in the name of Islam around the world at that very moment.

I offered Jasmina the following afternoon off. It was Eid al Adha, one of the two main Muslim holidays during which Bosniak families gathered around the table for an evening feast. The holiday, marked by the slaughter of sheep, commemorates Abraham's willingness to sacrifice his son—according to Muslim tradition, Ishmael, the forefather of Arabs, rather than Isaac, the biblical ancestor of the Jews. In cold, windy Sarajevo, flocks of bleating gray sheep were being herded through the streets hours before their throats would be slit and their blood poured out in ritual.

Alone on that festive night, I returned to my hotel, a gaudy yellow cube of a Holiday Inn, its wartime damage repaired. In my room I watched the latest CNN updates about Danny Pearl, paraded by kidnappers in the macabre Pakistani track suit he had been forced to wear. Deep at night, the phone rang. It was one of the editors in New York. Relishing the spooky symbolism, Danny's kidnappers chose the night of Eid al Adha, the Feast of the Sacrifice, to release a tape showing how they had slit his throat and severed his head. That's the way we all learned that Danny was dead. I stayed awake until the morning, numbed and thinking about the grisly unfairness of it all.

Months later, I found out that the killing had a connection to Bosnia's mujahedeen, maybe even to those who had lived in Bočinja. The militant who set up Danny's kidnapping, a British-born Muslim of Pakistani descent named Omar Sheikh, traveled to Bosnia with a humanitarian aid convoy in May 1993. Along the way, he met hardened Arab veterans of Afghanistan's wars who were also heading to the Bosnian frontlines. They took Sheikh, then a nineteen-year-old first-year student at the London School of Economics, under their wing and inducted him into a Qaeda offshoot. Soon after, he traveled to Afghanistan and Pakistan, specializing in using his accent-less English and pleasant demeanor to kidnap unsuspecting Westerners.

✦　✦　✦

Two and a half years later, with the six Algerians still detained at Guantánamo Bay without trial, I returned to Bosnia—and drove to Bočinja, again. In the steamy August of 2004, Rizvić was still there, sitting in the car repair shop that was now flanked by a pale-green, three-story building—the largest in the village—that served as the Muslim community center and mosque. A white banner with the Arabic words of the Islamic profession of faith, THERE IS NO GOD BUT ALLAH, AND MOHAMMED IS HIS PROPHET, fluttered from the roof, directly facing a Serb Orthodox church up the road. The number of Muslim families in Bočinja had doubled, to fifteen, but the Serbs still refused contact; they went so far as to exclude the former mujahedeen from the village council. The only place where the two communities mixed was at the elementary school, where Muslim and Serb children were educated by two secular Muslim teachers from a nearby town. Rizvić's car had just been burned, and he complained about the lack of support from Bosnian authorities. "The government turned their back on us, and nobody wants to be in a close relationship with us. Some people are frightened by us because they don't understand Islam," he grumbled.

To show support for the mujahedeen enclave, hundreds of Islamists from all over the area made sure to converge on the Bočinja mosque for the Friday noon prayer. While I was there, a Muslim wedding procession took a detour to drive through Bočinja, honking and waving green flags, with the Islamic crescent, at the dazed Serb peasants. I asked Rizvić whether he had any news about his Arab comrades from El Mudžahid days—men now being tracked by all the main Western counterterrorism agencies. "Many ended up in prison when they returned to their own countries—Egypt, North Africa," he responded grudgingly. "Others stayed in Europe. But we still hear from them sometimes."

✦　✦　✦

By then, everybody in Bosnia was talking about a different war. Just as countries from Spain to Honduras to the Philippines abandoned the American-led coalition in Iraq, burned by their exposure to the ruthless insurgency there, war-ravaged little Bosnia, where bullet-scarred facades were only now beginning to undergo repairs, decided, in the summer of 2004, to send a military unit of its own to Iraq.

That such a decision was possible at all was a sign of how far the reconciliation had progressed. Many among Bosnia's "ethnically cleansed" refugees had now returned to their former homes. The borders between Republika Srpska and the Muslim-Croat federation became all but invisible as Bosnians zipped right across, their town of origin disguised by new numerical license plates. Nine years after the war, most Muslims here seemed utterly uninterested in Izetbegović's vision of a "great Islamic federation stretching from Morocco to Indonesia." Instead, everyone's aspiration was to get Bosnia into negotiations to join the European Union, a club seen as a guarantee of future peace and prosperity.

That summer, the formerly warring Serb, Muslim, and Croat armies came under the joint command of the nation's multiethnic presidency. The defense minister of Bosnia-Herzegovina happened to be an ethnic Serb—something unthinkable a few years before. The presidency, still dominated by the three monoethnic parties that had dragged the country into war in 1992, wanted to send the world a signal that old demons were truly dead.

Following Paul Wolfowitz's visit to Sarajevo, the three copresidents volunteered to deploy to Iraq some three dozen demining experts—a hot specialty, considering that a large proportion of U.S. casualties were caused by the insurgents' mines and roadside bombs. Although the Bosnian unit was small, politically this was a huge step. After all, it wasn't so long ago that Muslim Bosniaks had fought side by side with the same jihadis who now confronted Americans in Iraq—just as the Bosnian Serbs had, themselves, been bombed by U.S. forces.

Adnan Terzić, the prime minister of Bosnia-Herzegovina and the deputy head of the Party of Democratic Action, the movement founded by Izetbegović, explained to me the rationale behind the decision. To him, the Iraqi deployment was clearly a price for maintaining American friendship at a time when Bosnia's murky mujahedeen past kept popping up in intelligence reports. "Bosnia-Herzegovina's future lies in strong political ties with the U.S.," Terzić told me. "Bosnia has survived as a single state mainly, if not solely, thanks to the U.S. The European countries failed their test. It's only when the Americans said that enough is enough and put their planes in the air that the war ended here." The Iraq expedition, he went on, would certify Bosnia's new status. "This is our main message: we're such a stable country that we ourselves can assist the stabilization of other countries."

But Bosnia's public wasn't quite buying Terzić's argument. Polls published in Bosnian newspapers showed that the dispatch of soldiers was highly unpopular. Opposition leaders, including former prime minister Lagumdžija, who had paid a price for seconding American wishes in the Algerian affair, now built political campaigns on rejecting another entanglement on America's side. Many Muslims fretted that helping with the occupation of Iraq would damage Bosnia's standing in the Islamic world, the source of much development aid. The Serbs, whose fifty-nine senior officials, including the Parliament speaker of Republika Srpska, had just been fired by the international administrator for failing to cooperate with the war-crimes tribunal in the Hague, complained about the "hypocrisy" of involvement in Iraq while Bosnia itself was still governed, de facto, by foreigners. In a Friday sermon at Sarajevo's Begova Džamija, the second most senior cleric in the country, Ismet Spahić, decried American actions in Iraq as "genocide."

Near the mosque, I bought a glossy-covered magazine, *Saff*, the favorite publication of Bosnian Islamists. Inside were the lengthy discourses of Islamist ideologues such as Salman al Awda, the Saudi cleric I had visited behind Jeddah's Chuck E. Cheese, and articles describing the heroic feats of the Iraqi resistance against American occupation. The magazine was dead-set against involvement in the war. Wanting to hear more, I set up a meeting with *Saff*'s editor in chief, Kemal Baković.

Baković was immediately recognizable by his long beard and short pants. An Arabic speaker, he had studied in Zarqa, in Jordan—the hometown, he smiled, of the man described by the United States as Qaeda's chieftain in Iraq, Abu Musab al Zarqawi. At the university, Baković said, he felt an immediate bond with Palestinian refugees—the majority of Jordan's population. "They were the closest to us here. Of all the Arabs, they are the ones in the same situation as we were, and things that are normal to them are also normal to us," he said.

On Iraq, his sympathies were equally obvious. "The Iraqis are fighting for their freedom. . . . They were attacked. Their children are dying." So, I wondered aloud, why was the Bosnian government, on the urging of the main Muslim party, rushing to join the American military effort there? "They just want to score some brownie points with the Americans, that's it," Baković scoffed. "It's so wrong. We are all sick of wars here in Bosnia. These guys, if they get killed in Iraq, they'll be killed for a foreign idea, not for their own country. Nobody will take care of their kids."

Some other Bosnians, he added quickly, had already joined the war in Iraq, on the rebel side. Baković told me he recently met, in Sarajevo, a young Bosnian Islamist who had just returned from Fallujah, where he participated in attacks on American soldiers. "I asked him whether he had a *fatwa* from religious scholars to fight there," Baković said. "He answered that he didn't need any *fatwa* because it was a clear duty for him." Baković wouldn't tell me how to find the man, but he showed me the transcript of his interview with him.

In the interview, Baković had asked the jihadi what he would do if he encountered fellow Bosnian Muslims serving alongside Americans in Iraq.

"The Iraqi fighters won't give preferences, won't look at what flag patch you carry on the shoulder, or ask what's your name. They will shoot at anyone who's on the enemy side," the man answered coolly. "And so will I."

The trickle of Bosnian Islamists into Iraq shouldn't have been surprising. After all, other Bosnians, following their wartime mujahedeen comrades in arms, had battled the Russians in Chechnya; in fact, at least two died there in 2000. After meeting Baković, I strolled through Sarajevo's main street, stopping again by the Islamist bookstalls. In addition to videos about Bosnia's own war and the Palestinian intifada, the stalls all seemed to hold the same collection of DVDs about Chechnya.

I bought a couple and settled down to watch them in my room at the Holiday Inn. Although graced with a Bosniak-language cover, the DVDs were actually in Arabic. *Good vs. Evil: The Final Battle* promised one title. The footage began with tedious scenes of mujahedeen—mostly Saudis, according to their noms de guerre—training in the Chechen mountains and then ambushing Russian patrols. On the sound track, chants of the Quran alternated with guerrilla songs and rousing sermons delivered by unidentified speakers. At one point, the video became especially graphic, first showing Chechen children blown to pieces by Russian bombing, and then a couple of frightened Russian soldiers captured by the insurgents.

Presumably the intention of this montage was to make viewers enjoy the following several minutes of torture inflicted on the helpless Russian captives. When the close-ups of gore had concluded, it was back to exploding Russian trucks and barracks. The voiceover intoned: "Jihad is a duty of all Muslims, a duty that cannot be neglected until we liberate Palestine, and then until we liberate Chechnya, and Tashkent, and Bukhara, and then Andalusia and then the coast of France and then all other Islamic lands taken from us by unbelievers." I was intrigued by this ever-expanding jihadi geography, which presumably included my Roman home, in an area where an Arab army once camped, among the usurped lands of Islam. Such jihadi porn made many an emotional youth in the Arab world and beyond run away to glory in Afghanistan or Chechnya. I wondered how many Bosnians would do the same.

Switching off the DVD, I flipped on the TV for current jihad news on CNN. Two Russian passenger planes had just gone down, blown up by the Chechens, and the bloody massacre of Russian children in the town of Beslan was, unbeknownst to the world, in the final stages of preparation. An Italian journalist, Enzo Baldoni, had been kidnapped by militants in Iraq. The hostage takers looked only at Baldoni's passport before killing him, because Italy's government participated in an American-run occupation, even if Baldoni himself had opposed it. Two French journalist friends were also taken hostage, including Georges Malbrunot, the colleague with whom I had ducked Hezbollah Katyushas in an Israeli bomb shelter. I saw Georges, too, on CNN that day. He and his friend turned out to be lucky; unlike so many hostages in Iraq, they were released, alive, following four months of captivity.

The last time I visited Sarajevo, Danny Pearl lost his life. Since then, the world has become an even bloodier place, and the killing of innocents like him no longer seemed exceptional. I was beginning to feel guilty for enjoying Holiday Inn's relative luxury—and, it seemed, for bringing bad luck to my friends every time I stepped on Bosnia's soil.

✦ ✦ ✦

Depressed, I figured I could get my spirits raised by Mustafa Ceric, the *reis ul ulema,* or supreme religious leader of the Bosnian Muslims.

Cerić's reputation, which extends well beyond Bosnia, is that of a rare voice of sober, European Islam, a man who favors dialogue and scorns the shrill rhetoric that's so common among his fellow clerics. Here, I hoped, was a prominent Muslim who could offer some consolation that the deepening spiral of violence might still be stopped. A well-traveled scholar and former ambassador, with a PhD from the University of Chicago, Cerić spoke fluent English. He greeted me in his large reception room at a Sarajevo mosque; a black-and-white portrait of Izetbegović kneeling in Muslim prayer held place of pride on the wall.

We started by talking about Bosnia, and Cerić hastened to establish his moderate credentials. He assured me that he cherished the country's multiethnic character—a result, he reminded me, of the tolerance displayed by the Balkans' Muslim Ottoman rulers. "I enjoy living in Sarajevo as it is." Cerić stretched his arms. "I meet a Catholic, a Jew here on the streets every day. I have a dialogue every day. . . . I don't know if I would be a happier person living in a pure environment where there are only Muslims."

As our conversation drifted to the crisis in the wider Muslim world after September 11, Cerić abandoned the detached professorial tone with which he had greeted me. His voice suddenly brimmed with vigor. "Muslims are now in the focus. Muslims are surrounded by an environment where they don't have support from the rest of the world, even if their cause is legitimate," he lamented. "Muslim life is very cheap. You can see now, in Najaf."

All over the world, wherever there was a war, Muslims were involved. "We have to find out: is it that the world is wrong and we are right? And if that's the case, then all the Muslims should fight for their rights," he said.

Was this indeed the case? I interrupted him.

Cerić smiled bitterly.

In reply, he told me a joke about a Belgrade cabbie who drove into oncoming traffic on a highway. Zooming past honking cars, the cabbie kept complaining that everyone was driving on the wrong side of the road. "I don't want us to be the same way, like this driver in Belgrade. I would like to invite Muslims to think seriously how to save the friends that we have in this world," Cerić said. "We now risk losing those who are our real friends in the West."

This was a two-way warning. The West, he went on to say, was also quickly losing potential Muslim allies.

"Muslims all over the world are now in a very deep cultural shock. They have difficulty to think rationally after the events in Iraq. If you see every day the scenes of your relatives being killed, and no one is doing anything about it . . . Why Abu Ghraib could happen? Why Srebrenica could happen? Your mind is getting stretched. The Muslims feel that they are threatened, that the West is trying to enslave them, literally."

Impressed by this outpouring of raw emotion, I asked the cleric whether he shared his deputy's description of American actions in Iraq as genocide—a heavy word for Bosnia, which itself had experienced genocide so recently. Cerić wouldn't endorse or disavow the imam, nor would he condemn those Bosnians who were heading off to join the Iraqi insurgents.

In early 2003, he said by way of explanation, Bosnia's Islamic hierarchy issued a statement against America's looming Iraqi invasion, while at the same time cautioning the believers not to mistake the Iraqi war for a religious clash between Christian and Muslim civilizations. "But now . . . now people are beginning to change their views," Cerić said, looking at me. "People are questioning the [Western] motivations— and, of course, including the factor of Islam, of religion, of culture." He clasped his hands before getting up and abruptly ending our meeting. "Everyone sees. I don't think we have a safer world now than before. This is now out of our control."

Glossary of Religious and Political Terms

✦ ✦ ✦

Words in *italics* refer to terms defined elsewhere in the glossary.

abaya. A black, long-sleeve, floor-length outer garment that all women in Saudi Arabia must wear in public. In this book, the term is also used to describe similar clothing in other Muslim countries.

Arab. A person whose native language and culture are Arabic. While most Arabs are Muslim, and the *Quran* was revealed in Arabic, Arabs account for only a minority of the world's Muslim population. At the same time, countries such as Lebanon, Egypt, Syria, and Iraq have large communities of Christian Arabs.

Ayatollah. In the *Shiite* hierarchy, the highest-ranking scholar of Islam.

burka. A dress that covers a woman's entire body, allowing her to see and breathe through a grille that renders her face invisible. Formerly mandatory in Afghanistan, the garment is still widely used there and in parts of Pakistan.

caliph. Leader of the Muslim *ummah*. For centuries until its abolition in 1924, the title was held by the sultans of the Ottoman Empire.

fatwa. Binding decision made by an Islamic authority.

gris-gris. A West African term for animist amulets.

Hadith. The record of *Prophet Mohammed*'s sayings or of the examples he set. The Hadith comes second after the *Quran* as the source of Muslim law.

hajj. Annual pilgrimage to Mecca, conducted on certain days of the Hajj month of the *Islamic* calendar. The hajj, one of the five traditional pillars of Islam, is an obligation during the lifetime of every Muslim who can afford the trip.

hajji. Someone who has performed the *hajj*. Among American soldiers in Iraq and Afghanistan, the term was used as a derogatory reference to the natives.

hijab. A head covering that a Muslim woman is mandated by religious law to wear. More generally, the term refers to a belief in properly modest attire.

imam. A Muslim prayer leader.

Islamic. Following the religion of Islam. In this book, the adjective is used interchangeably with the term "Muslim."

Islamist. In this book, a reference to people who subscribe to the ideas of *political Islam*. Islamists may be *Sunni* or *Shiite*.

jambiya. The curved dagger worn by Yemeni males.

jihad. Literally, "striving." In modern political discourse, the term most often refers to Muslim holy war against unbelievers. *Islamists,* who usually consider jihad to be the sixth pillar of Islam, maintain that participation in jihad whenever Muslims are oppressed is mandatory for every believer.

keffiyeh. Checkered headdress, usually red or black. Although, in various countries in the Muslim world, different words are used to refer to this item of clothing, this book uses the most familiar term.

maddhab. A recognized school of *Islamic* jurisprudence. *Sunni* Islam is divided into four principal maddhabs—Hanbali, Hanafi, Shafii, and Maliki.

madrassa. A school that primarily teaches *Islamic* subjects.

Mahdi. The messiah who would restore the glory of Islam.

mufti. The supreme *Islamic* religious authority for a given territory.

mujahed (plural **mujahedeen**). Someone who is fighting a *jihad*. The term was widely used to refer to Afghan *Islamic* fighters against

Soviet occupation, in the 1980s, and foreign volunteers fighting on the Muslim side in the Bosnian civil war, in the early 1990s. Groups like Qaeda also use the term to identify their members.

mullah. *Islamic* cleric.

political Islam. A stream of thought, formulated in the 1920s and 1930s by Hassan al Banna, the founder of Egypt's Muslim Brotherhood, and Abu Ala Mawdudi, leader of Pakistan's Jamaat-e-Islami, that seeks to reunite Muslim lands in a single *Islamic* state and that wants Muslims to be governed strictly according to Islamic religious law.

Prophet Mohammed (570–632). According to Islam, Mohammed is the "seal of the prophets" who received God's final revelation, the *Quran,* and who founded the *Islamic* state.

Qaeda. Literally, the "base." The term is used in the book to refer to Osama Bin Laden's organization and an affiliated web of militant *salafi* groups around the world.

Quran. The holy book of Islam that, Muslims believe, is the literal word of God as revealed to *Prophet Mohammed.* Only the Quran's original Arabic text is considered perfect. The Quran is divided into suras (chapters), which, in turn, are made up of ayas (verses).

Ramadan. The Muslim month of fasting, when, during daylight, believers must abstain from food, drink, smoking, and sex.

salafi. From Salaf al Salih, literally, "righteous predecessors." The term refers to *Prophet Mohammed*'s companions. According to salafism, both as a modern religious ideology and as a form of *political Islam,* only that early generation of Muslims was pure; innovation should be rejected; and the ways of Mohammed and his early companions should be emulated, in everything from political organization to hairstyle and attire. Many *Sunni* salafis consider both *Shiites* and *Sufis* to be heretics.

Sharia. Literally, "the *Islamic* way." The term refers to the entire body of *Islamic* law.

sheikh. A term of respect, used for tribal leaders, prominent clerics, and other notables, not necessarily religious.

Shiite. The smaller of the two main sects of Islam. The term comes from Shiat Ali, or Party of Ali, the supporters of *Prophet Mohammed*'s son-in-law, who believed that he was wrongly bypassed as Mohammed's immediate successor as *caliph* of the Muslim *ummah*. Shiites are a majority in Iran, Iraq, Azerbaijan, and Bahrain, and a plurality in Lebanon.

Sufism. A current in Islam that focuses on the religion's esoteric aspects and often ascribes mystical powers to certain people or objects.

Sunna. *Prophet Mohammed*'s way, the totality of his sayings, practices, and actions, and the example for Muslims to emulate.

Sunni. The larger of the two main sects of Islam and the one followed by the vast majority of Muslims. Unlike the *Shiites,* the Sunnis do not believe that only *Prophet Mohammed*'s blood relatives could be *caliphs*. The two sects also differ in religious practices and in organization.

Taliban. Literally, "students." The name was used by Afghan religious students led by Mullah Omar, who established a theocratic regime in the 1990s and gave shelter to Osama Bin Laden and Qaeda until the U.S. intervention in late 2001.

ulema. *Islamic* scholars.

ummah. The global *Islamic* community, which includes every Muslim.

Wahhabi. Followers of Mohammed bin Abdel Wahhab, the ultrapurist eighteenth-century cleric who lived in what is now Saudi Arabia. Wahhabis themselves prefer the name *Muwahiddun,* or Unitarians. In political discourse, the label Wahhabi is often applied to anyone following *salafi* Islam.

Acknowledgments

✦ ✦ ✦

This book would not have been possible without the endurance of my wife, Susi, my son, Jonathan, and my daughter, Nicole Tamar—who, in response to her teacher's question about daddy's job, replied: "To go away for a long time." All this time that I spent on the road since September 2001, my family dreaded watching the news on TV and had to cope on their own. That's a debt I can never repay.

Almost every day from late 2001 to 2005, I spoke on the phone with my *Wall Street Journal* editor, Bill Spindle. Regardless of the hour back in New York, his guidance and support in times of trouble were unstinting. I thank him for this, and for the freedom that I had to explore the Muslim world.

My friend and one-time bureau chief at the *Journal,* Ian Johnson, encouraged me to think as a book writer, provided a valuable tutorial in crafting proposals, and then read through the entire manuscript. His observations made it a much better book. Any errors are, of course, all mine.

Also at the *Journal* I'd like to thank Fred Kempe, who hired me, first to write articles that required wearing a pin-striped suit rather than combat boots. His interest and experience in the Middle East were always a help. My thanks also go to Paul Steiger, Dan Hertzberg, Mike Miller, Amy Stevens, Marcus Brauchli, John Bussey, Lora Western, Steve Adler, and other *Journal* editors who have had to deal with me and my stories.

While the bulk of material in this book is original, and the first-person narrative differs, by its very nature, from the dispassionate *Journal* style, most of the journeys described here have been made while reporting for the newspaper. Inevitably, some of the quotes used here have appeared in my articles for the *Journal* over the years. The opinions in this book are all mine, and should in no way be construed as representing the *Journal*'s.

Special gratitude is due to a friend and a colleague who is no longer with us—Danny Pearl. In the months before his cruel death, he shared with me scores of contacts in the Arab world—an act of generosity that is not all that common in the competitive reporting profession. I still don't have the courage to delete his number from my cell phone's memory.

I also owe thanks to all those *Journal* colleagues who provided company and friendship in Iraq, Kuwait, and beyond, making it all much more fun than it would have been otherwise: Chip Cummins, Farnaz Fassihi, Yochi Dreazen, Michael Phillips, Helene Cooper, Nick Kulish, David Luhnow, Neil King, David Cloud, Alan Cullison. To Hugh Pope go particular thanks for his historical insights, frequent conversation, and for sharing with me his experiences in the world of books.

My traveling companions in Iraq—Marc Epstein and then Philippe Gelie—endured much closer proximity to me, day and night, in a land then without showers, than would otherwise be recommended. Their war-correspondent instincts made us all safer when bombs and bullets were flying. Philippe, a longtime friend, also read the entire manuscript and made very helpful observations. So did another old friend, Christophe Boltanski, of *Liberation*. For their friendship and advice, I am thankful.

Other colleagues and friends whose company made travels in the Islamic world more pleasant are too numerous to list. But I'd like to thank Bill Glauber, Rod Nordland, Ilene Prusher, Saad al Enezi, Laurie

Goering, Simon Robinson, Mariane Pearl, Anthony Shadid, Dan Murphy, Sophie Shihab, Khaled Owais, Stephanie Sinclair, Luigi Offeddu, Ivan Watson, and Georges Malbrunot. Ambassador Vincenzo Prati was a genial host in Kuwait, as was Robert Silverman at Saddam's palace in Tikrit. I would also like to express my appreciation to Lieutenant Colonel Hector Mirabile, Captain Mike Berdy, Major Beverly Beavers, Sergeant Matt Fearing, and all those other American soldiers who made me safe and shared with me their tents and MREs (and, sometimes, lobster tails) while I traveled with them in Iraq and Afghanistan.

The research and reporting for this book would have been impossible without interpreters and fixers—often a correspondent's eyes and ears in an unfamiliar country. I was blessed with some of the most intelligent, courageous assistants, and many of them are mentioned in the book. Among those unnamed in the text, special thanks go to Jehona Gjurgjeala in Kosovo and Jasenko Žigić in Bosnia. Some, especially those in Iraq, I cannot name in full because of concern for their safety at a time when any interaction with a Westerner can be a death sentence. One day, I hope, such caution will no longer be necessary. In the meantime, thank you Samira, Jaffar, Haaqi, Munaf, and Jabbar.

I thank my good New York friends, Debra Lau Whelan and John Whelan, and Chrystyna and Roman Czajkowsky, for providing hospitality and company in Manhattan while I was immersing myself in the intricacies of the publishing world. Chrystyna worked her usual magic for the author photograph on the jacket.

My razor-sharp agent, Jay Mandel, recognized the book's potential on the basis of a then half-baked proposal and half a chapter; he matched me with a first-class publisher on the first try. His assistant, Liza Gennatiempo, was always a pleasure to work with, too. Last but not least: Vanessa Mobley at Henry Holt was a great editor, seeking perfection and improving the manuscript with a smart touch that any author might dream of. Her assistant, Daniel Reid, was also immensely helpful. We spent long hours making it a better work. I have been told that book editors no longer edit. I can vouch for one who does, burning the midnight oil when she has to.

Index

✦ ✦ ✦

About the Author

✦ ✦ ✦

YAROSLAV TROFIMOV, who reported from the Middle East for a variety of publications through the 1990s, joined *The Wall Street Journal* in 1999 and became the newspaper's roving foreign correspondent for the Middle East, Africa, Central Asia, and the Balkans in 2001. He lives with his family in Rome.